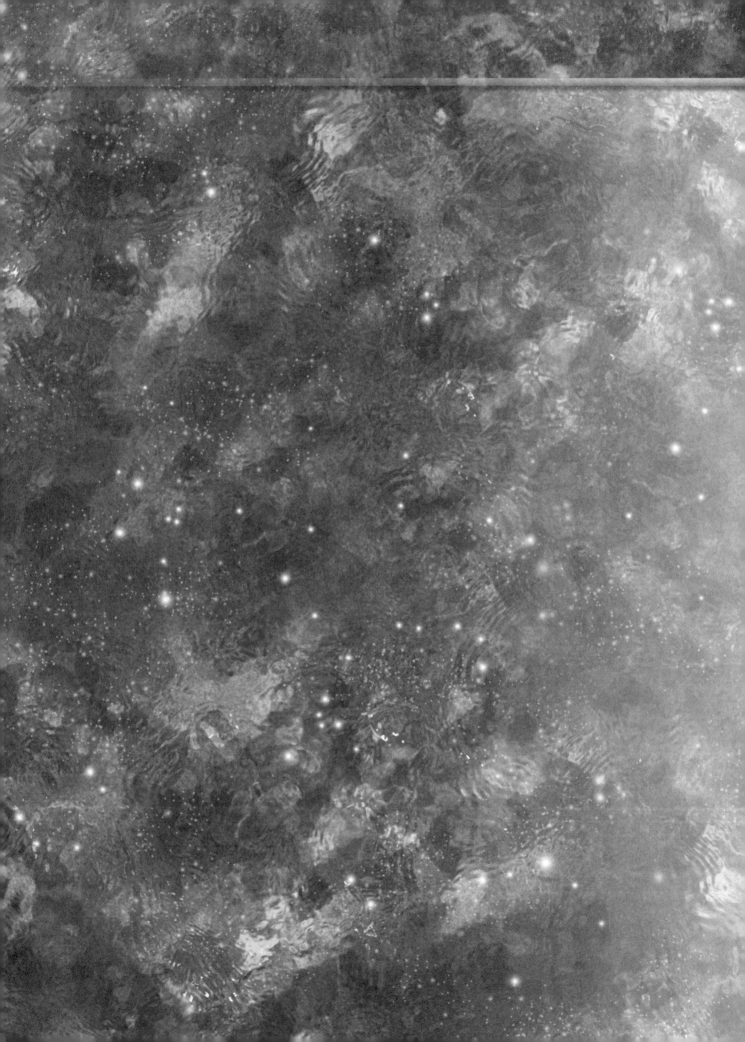

HOUGHTON MIFFLIN HARCOURT

Tennessee Science

HOUGHTON MIFFLIN HARCOURT

Printed in the U.S.A.

ISBN: 978-0-547-08461-9

1 2 3 4 5 6 7 8 9-KDL-17 16 15 14 13 12 11 10 09 08

Program Authors

William Badders
Director of the Cleveland Mathematics
    and Science Partnership
Cleveland Municipal School District,
Cleveland, Ohio

Douglas Carnine, Ph.D.
Professor of Education
University of Oregon,
Eugene, Oregon

James Feliciani
Supervisor of Instructional Media and Technology
Land O' Lakes, Florida

Bobby Jeanpierre, Ph.D.
Assistant Professor, Science Education
University of Central Florida,
Orlando, Florida

Carolyn Sumners, Ph.D.
Director of Astronomy and Physical Sciences
Houston Museum of Natural Science,
Houston, Texas

Catherine Valentino
Author-in-Residence
Houghton Mifflin,
West Kingston, Rhode Island

Contributing Author

Michael A. DiSpezio
Writer and Global Educator
JASON Project
Cape Cod, Massachusetts

Tennessee Teacher Reviewers

Melinda Carr
West View School
Limestone, Tennessee

Peggy Greene
Gray Elementary School
Gray, Tennessee

Loretta Harper
Goodlettsville Elementary
Goodlettsville, Tennessee

Donna Lachman
Boones Creek Middle School
Johnson City, Tennessee

Gloria R. Ramsey
Science Specialist
Memphis City Schools
Memphis, Tennessee

Richard Sherman
Warner Enhanced Option School
Nashville, Tennessee

Contents

UNIT A
Life Science

Passion flower, *Passiflora incarnata*, the Tennessee state wildflower

Eastern newt on forest floor,
Scenic River, Tennessee

Contents

UNIT B
Earth Science

**Downtown skyline,
Cumberland River,
Nashville, Tennessee**

Cascade near Grotto Falls,
Great Smoky Mountains
National Park, Tennessee

Contents

UNIT C
Physical Science

The Chattanooga Choo Choo

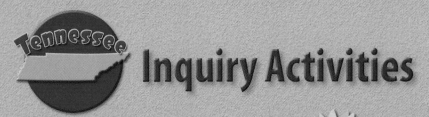

Inquiry Activities

LIFE A SCIENCE

Technology and Engineering: Build a Better Glass

EARTH B SCIENCE

Technology and Engineering: Build a Water Barrier

PHYSICAL **C** SCIENCE

Technology and Engineering: Build a Brake

Grade 4 Embedded Inquiry

GLE 0407.Inq.1 Explore different scientific phenomena by asking questions, making logical predictions, planning investigations, and recording data.

GLE 0407.Inq.2 Select and use appropriate tools and simple equipment to conduct an investigation.

GLE 0407.Inq.3 Organize data into appropriate tables, graphs, drawings, or diagrams.

GLE 0407.Inq.4 Identify and interpret simple patterns of evidence to communicate the findings of multiple investigations.

GLE 0407.Inq.5 Recognize that people may interpret the same results in different ways.

GLE 0407.Inq.6 Compare the result of an investigation with what scientists already accept about this question.

Coverage of these standards occurs in Directed Inquiry, Guided Inquiry, and other features.

Grade 4 Embedded Technology & Engineering

GLE 0407.T/E.1 Describe how tools, technology, and inventions help to answer questions and solve problems.

GLE 0407.T/E.2 Recognize that new tools, technology, and inventions are always being developed.

GLE 0407.T/E.3 Identify appropriate materials, tools, and machines that can extend or enhance the ability to solve a specified problem.

GLE 0407.T/E.4 Recognize the connection between scientific advances, new knowledge, and the availability of new tools and technologies.

GLE 0407.T/E.5 Apply a creative design strategy to solve a particular problem generated by societal needs and wants.

Coverage of these standards occurs in Directed Inquiry, Guided Inquiry, Focus On, Technology and Engineering Projects, and other features.

Tennessee, Great Smoky Mountains National Park, Foothills Parkway overlook

Grade 4 Life Science

Standard 1 - Cells

GLE 0407.1.1 Recognize that cells are the building blocks of all living things.

Chapter 1: Life Processes

Standard 2 – Interdependence

GLE 0407.2.1 Analyze the effects of changes in the environment on the stability of an ecosystem.

Chapter 3: Energy in Ecosystems

Standard 3 - Flow of Matter and Energy

GLE 0407.3.1 Demonstrate that plants require light energy to grow and survive.

GLE 0407.3.2 Investigate different ways that organisms meet their energy needs.

Chapter 1: Life Processes
Chapter 3: Energy in Ecosystems

Standard 4 – Heredity

GLE 0407.4.1 Recognize the relationship between reproduction and the continuation of a species.

GLE 0407.4.2 Differentiate between complete and incomplete metamorphosis.

Chapter 1: Life Processes

Standard 5 - Biodiversity and Change

GLE 0407.5.1 Analyze physical and behavioral adaptations that enable organisms to survive in their environment.

GLE 0407.5.2 Describe how environmental changes caused the extinction of various plant and animal species.

Chapter 2: Adaptation and Extinction
Chapter 3: Energy in Ecosystems

Grade 4 Earth and Space Science

Standard 6 -The Universe

GLE 0407.6.1 Analyze patterns, relative movements, and relationships among the sun, moon, and earth.

Chapter 4: Cycles and Patterns in Space

Standard 7 – The Earth

GLE 0407.7.1 Investigate how the Earth's geological features change as a result of erosion (weathering and transportation) and deposition.

GLE 0407.7.2 Evaluate how some earth materials can be used to solve human problems and enhance the quality of life.

Chapter 5: Slow Changes on Earth

Standard 8 -The Atmosphere

GLE 0407.8.1 Recognize the major components of the water cycle.

GLE 0407.8.2 Differentiate between weather and climate.

Chapter 6: Using Weather Data

Womens' Basketball Hall of Fame, Knoxville, Tennessee

Grade 4 Physical Science

Standard 9 - Matter

GLE 0407.9.1 Collect data to illustrate that the physical properties of matter can be described with tools that measure weight, mass, length, and volume.

GLE 0407.9.2 Explore different types of physical changes in matter.

Chapter 7: Properties of Matter

Standard 10 – Energy

GLE 0407.10.1 Distinguish among heat, radiant, and chemical forms of energy.

GLE 0407.10.2 Investigate how light travels and is influenced by different types of materials and surfaces.

Chapter 9: Light

Watts Barr Dam, Tennessee River, midway between Knoxville and Chattanooga

Standard 11 – Motion

GLE 0407.11.1 Recognize that the position of an object can be described relative to other objects or a background.

GLE 0407.11.2 Design a simple investigation to demonstrate how friction affects the movement of an object.

GLE 0407.11.3 Investigate the relationship between the speed of an object and the distance traveled during a certain time period.

Chapter 10: Motion and Machines

Standard 12 - Forces in Nature

GLE 0407.12.1 Explore the interactions between magnets.

GLE 0407.12.2 Observe that electrically charged objects exert a pull on other materials.

GLE 0407.12.3 Explain how electricity in a simple circuit requires a complete loop through which current can pass.

Chapter 8: Electricity and Magnetism

The Nature of Science

Do What Scientists Do

Meet Dr. Kenneth Sulak. He works for the United States Geological Survey. He studies fish and other animals that live deep in the ocean. Dr. Sulak wants to find out what kinds of animals live far below the surface. He wants to know how many of them there are and how they live. He also wants to know how deep-sea animals interact with animals in the shallower water above them.

Dr. Sulak's research depends on submersibles. A ship with a crane lowers a sub into the Gulf of Mexico. In it, Dr. Sulak can travel far below the surface to observe and collect deep-sea life.

HARBOR BRANCH
OCEANOGRAPHIC

Scientists investigate in different ways.

The ways scientists investigate depend on the questions they ask. Dr. Sulak observes animals in their natural habitats. Often, he measures water temperatures. Often scientists ask questions that can be answered by doing a fair test called an experiment.

Ocean fishing, exploring for oil, and other human activities are moving into deeper and deeper water. Dr. Sulak helps keep track of how these activities affect deep-sea life. He shares what he learns by speaking to and answering the questions of other scientists. He also writes about it in science magazines.

Dr. Kenneth Sulak uses a microscope to learn more about deep-sea life. He has been surprised to discover how many animals live very deep in the ocean and that many deep-sea animals are bright red.

S3

You Can...

Think Like a Scientist

The ways scientists ask and answer questions about the world around them is called **scientific inquiry.** Scientific inquiry requires certain attitudes, or ways of thinking. To think like a scientist you have to be:

- curious and ask a lot of questions.

- creative and think up new ways to do things.

- able to keep an open mind. That means you listen to the ideas of others.

- open to changing what you think when your investigation results surprise you.

- willing to question what other people tell you.

Tides are changes in the level of the ocean that occur each day. What causes tides?

Use Critical Thinking

When you think critically you make decisions about what others tell you or what you read. Is what you heard or read fact or opinion? A *fact* can be checked to make sure it is true. An *opinion* is what you think about the facts.

Did anyone ever tell you how something works that you found hard to believe? When you ask, "What facts back up your idea?" you are thinking critically. Critical thinkers question scientific statements.

Tides seem to rise and fall at about the same time each day. I wonder what causes tides to keep changing that way?

I read that tides are caused by the pull of the Moon's gravity on Earth's oceans. The level of the oceans keeps rising and falling as the Moon and Earth move into different positions.

Science Inquiry

Using scientific inquiry helps you understand the world around you. For example, suppose you collect a sample of water from the ocean and put it in the freezer over night.

Observe The next day, you notice that the ocean water is not completely frozen. You also notice that ice cubes in the freezer are frozen solid.

Ask a Question When you think about what you saw, heard, or read, you may have questions.

Hypothesis Think about facts you already know. Do you have an idea about the answer? Write it down. That is your hypothesis.

Experiment Plan a test that will tell if the hypothesis is true or not. List the materials and tools you will need. Write the steps you will follow. Make sure that you keep all conditions the same except the one you are testing. That condition is called the *variable*.

Conclusion What do your results tell you? Do they support your hypothesis or show it to be false?

Describe your experiment with enough detail that others can repeat it. Communicate your results and conclusion.

My Salt Water Experiment

Observe It seems that ocean water does not freeze at the same temperature as plain water. Ocean water is salty.

Ask a question How does salt affect the freezing point of water?

Hypothesis Plain water will freeze before salt water because it has a higher freezing point than salt water.

Experiment I will put labeled containers of the same amount of salt water and plain water in a freezer. I will check on the containers every 3 minutes. I will record in which container the water freezes first.

Conclusion Plain water turns to ice before salt water. The results support my hypothesis. Plain water has a higher freezing point than salt water.

Inquiry Process

Here is a process that some scientists follow to answer questions and make new discoveries.

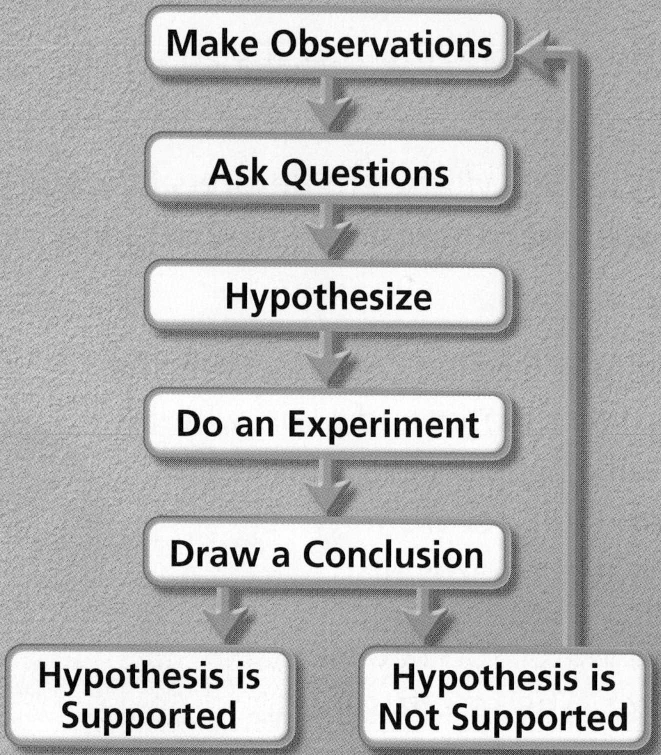

```
Make Observations
        ↓
   Ask Questions
        ↓
    Hypothesize
        ↓
  Do an Experiment
        ↓
  Draw a Conclusion
     ↓          ↓
Hypothesis is   Hypothesis is
Supported       Not Supported
```

Science Inquiry Skills

You'll use many of these inquiry skills when you investigate and experiment.

- Ask Questions
- Observe
- Compare
- Classify
- Predict
- Measure

- Hypothesize
- Use Variables
- Experiment
- Use Models
- Communicate
- Use Numbers

- Record Data
- Analyze Data
- Infer
- Collaborate
- Research

Try It Yourself!

Experiment With an Energy Sphere

When you touch both metal strips of the Energy Sphere, the sphere lights. This works with two people—as long as they are in contact with one another.

1 What questions do you have about the Energy Sphere?

2 How would you find out the answers?

3 Write your experiment plan and predict what will happen.

You Can...

Be an Inventor

Alberto Behar's interest in space led him to a career in space engineering. Dr. Behar helped to invent a new kind of Martian rover. Called the tumbleweed, it looks more like a giant beach ball than a vehicle. It moves when the wind blows it.

The idea for the tumbleweed came about by accident. During a test of a rover with large inflatable wheels, one of the wheels fell off. The wind blew the wheel several kilometers before someone caught it. The idea of a wind-blown rover was born.

The tumbleweed has performed very well in tests on Earth. Dr. Behar thinks it may soon be used to explore the surface of Mars.

"When I was about seven or eight, I wanted to be an astronaut. I checked out all of the books on space I could at the library..."

What Is Technology?

The tools people make and the things they build with tools are all technology. A toy car is technology. So is a race car.

Scientists use technology, too. For example, a laser beam can be used to make very precise measurements. Scientists also use microscopes to see things they cannot see with just their eyes.

Many technologies make the world a better place to live. But sometimes a technology that solves one problem can cause other problems. For example, farmers use fertilizer to increase the yields of their crops. But fertilizer can be carried by rain water into lakes and streams where it can harm fish and other living things.

A Better Idea

"I wish I had a better way to _____." How would you fill in the blank? Everyone wishes they could find a way to do their jobs more easily or have more fun. Inventors try to make those wishes come true. Inventing or improving an invention requires time and patience.

George Hansburg patented the pogo stick in 1919. It was a Y-shaped metal stick with two foot rests and a spring. Today's pogo sticks are not much different.

Pogo Stick

spring

foot rest

How to Be a Good Inventor

1. **Identify the problem.** It may be a problem at school, at home, or in your community.

2. **Think of a solution.** Sometimes the solution is a new tool. Other times it may be a new way of doing an old job or activity. Decide which idea you predict will work best. Think about which one you can carry out.

3. **Plan and build.** A sample, called a *prototype,* is the first try. Your idea may need many materials or none at all. Choose measuring tools that will help your design work better.

4. **Test and improve.** Use your prototype, or ask someone else to try it. Keep a record of how it works and what problems you find. The more times you try it, the more information you will have. Improve your invention. Use what you learned to make your design work better. Draw or write about the changes you make and why you made them.

5. **Communicate.** Show your invention to others. Explain how it works. Tell how it makes an activity easier or more fun. If it did not work as well as you wanted, tell why.

You Can...

Make Decisions

Trouble for the Everglades

For many years, the water of the Florida Everglades has had too much phosphorus. The phosphorus comes from nearby farms and cities. Phosphorus in fertilizers washes into streams and rivers. Phosphorus in laundry detergents washes down drains. Much of the phosphorus ends up in the water of the Everglades.

Some types of plants and animals have not been able to stand the high phosphorus levels. They have decreased in numbers or even gone extinct. Scientists are trying to reduce the amount of phosphorus entering the Everglades. They are also looking for ways to remove the phosphorus that is already there.

Deciding What to Do

What methods are best to help lower phosphorus levels in the water of the Everglades?

Here's how to make your decision about the phosphorus problem. You can use the same steps to help solve problems in your home, in your school, and in your community.

Learn ➡ Learn about the problem. Take the time needed to get the facts. You could talk to an expert, read a science book, or explore a web site.

List ➡ Make a list of actions you could take. Add actions other people could take.

Decide ➡ Think about each action on your list. Decide which choice is the best one for you or your community.

Share ➡ Communicate your decision to others.

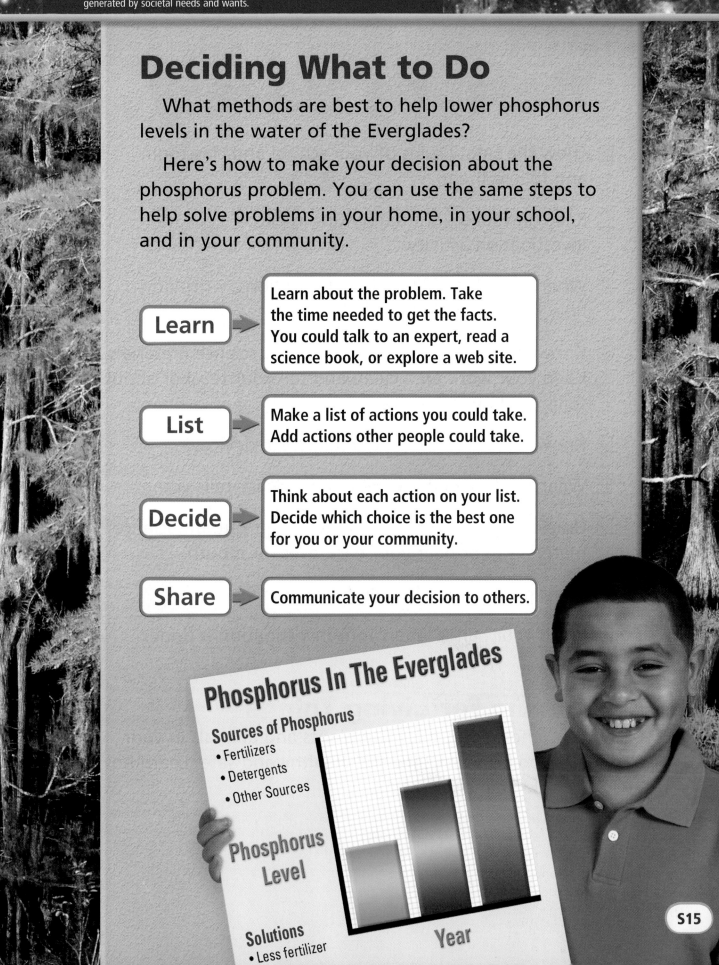

Phosphorus In The Everglades

Sources of Phosphorus
- Fertilizers
- Detergents
- Other Sources

Phosphorus Level

Year

Solutions
- Less fertilizer

Science Safety

☑ Know the safety rules of your school and classroom and follow them.

☑ Read and follow the safety tips in each Investigation activity.

☑ When you plan your own investigations, write down how to keep safe.

☑ Know how to clean up and put away science materials. Keep your work area clean and tell your teacher about spills right away.

☑ Know how to safely plug in electrical devices.

☑ Wear safety goggles when your teacher tells you.

☑ Unless your teacher tells you to, never put any science materials in or near your ears, eyes, or mouth.

☑ Wear gloves when handling live animals.

☑ Wash your hands when your investigation is done.

Caring for Living Things

☑ Learn how to care for the plants and animals in your classroom so that they stay healthy and safe. Learn how to hold animals carefully.

LIFE UNIT A SCIENCE

TENNESSEE

The Elephant SANCTUARY

Elephants use their long trunks in many ways.

You probably wouldn't believe someone who tells you that elephants are roaming through fields in Tennessee. However, the Elephant Sanctuary in Hohenwald is home to dozens of elephants.

Goals of the Sanctuary

The Elephant Sanctuary has two important goals. The first is to provide a home for elephants that have spent much of their lives in a zoo or a circus. Living in large, open areas, the elephants can behave like elephants in the wild. The sanctuary's second goal is to educate people about elephants.

Elephant Adaptations

Adaptations are body parts or behaviors that help a living thing survive in its environment. It's not easy for elephants to bend down to reach the ground. Their long trunks are adaptations that help them reach their food—grasses near the ground and leaves high in trees.

At the Elephant Sanctuary, elephants can roam over large areas of land.

Elephants eat only plants. Like other animals that eat plants, elephants must grind up their food. Their teeth are adaptations that help them do this. Their teeth are flat like grinding stones instead of sharp like knives.

In the wild, elephants live in the warmer parts of Africa and Asia. Adaptations, such as their large ears, help them keep cool.

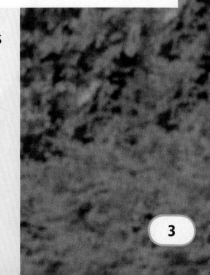

Barns provide elephants at the sanctuary with a warm place to stay.

Think and Write

1 Scientific Thinking Do you think elephants have many of the same adaptations as polar bears? Explain.

2 Science and Technology In Africa, researchers place collars with microphones on some elephants. These help researchers locate elephants. What is one question researchers may be trying to answer?

Mussels in Tennessee

When you think about the animals that live in Tennessee, do you think of mussels? Many people don't even know what mussels look like. Mussels are small animals that live inside two hard shells. You probably guessed that mussels are related to clams.

Tennessee is home to more than 100 kinds of mussels. The Hatchie River has 37 kinds. Most mussels need clean waterways with sand and gravel on the bottom. Because many waterways have changed over time, there are not many good places left for mussels to live. As a result, many kinds of mussels are endangered. That means that very few remain. These remaining mussels must reproduce or they may become extinct.

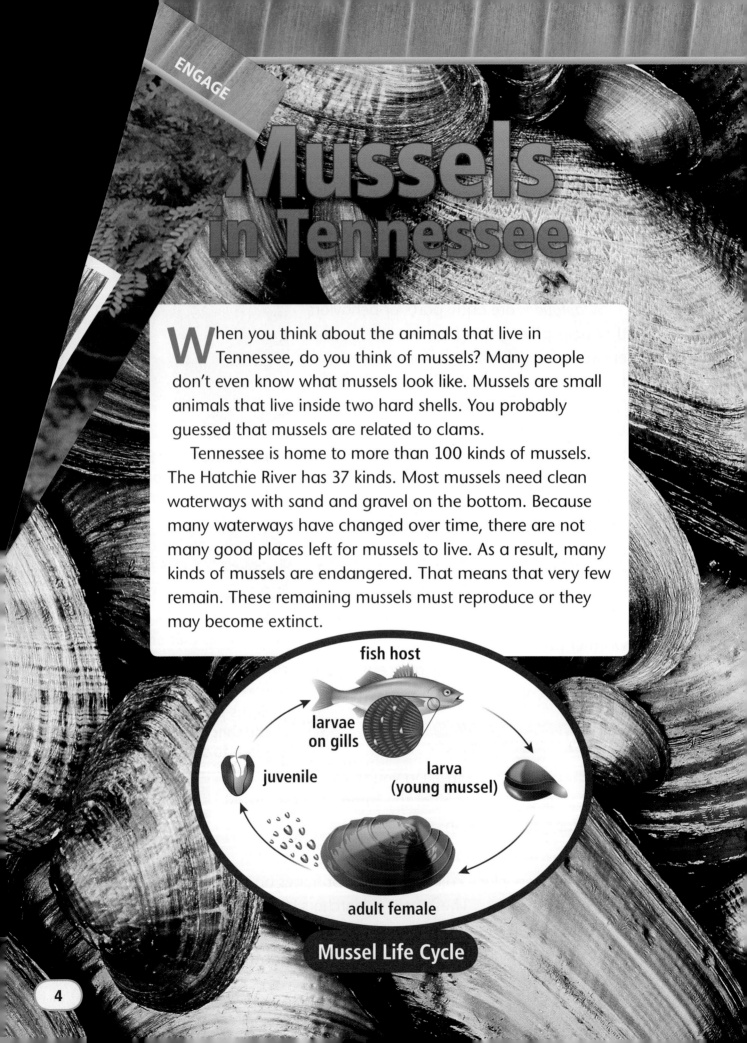

fish host

larvae on gills

larva (young mussel)

juvenile

adult female

Mussel Life Cycle

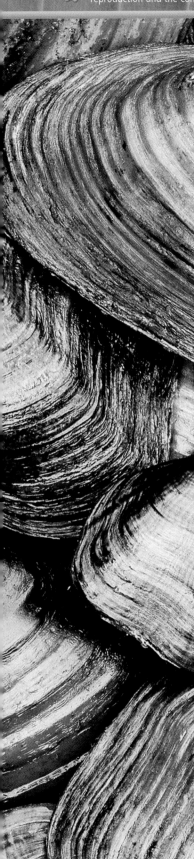

Mussel Adaptations

Mussels have physical adaptations that help th[ey] survive. Their hard shells help protect them. A part[of the] body called the foot can extend out of the shell.

Behaviors can also be adaptations. The mussel us[es] its foot to burrow into the sand. This helps protect it f[rom] predators.

A Strange Life Cycle

To reproduce, a female mussel releases thousands of immature mussels into the water. These mussels are calle[d] larvae. They are very small and do not have shells. The larvae attach to the gills of fish and ride to a new location, which may be upstream. After a few days, they fall off the gills and begin to grow where they land. It takes a few years for young mussels to become adults and be able to reproduce.

Think and Write

❶ **Scientific Thinking** Why is it important that young mussels attach to the gills of fish?

❷ **Science and Technology** Mussels are important to Tennessee. How might knowledge of their life cycle help people design mussel farms?

Tennessee mussels are adapted to life in moving water.

em
of their
es
rom

The Return of the Elk

The landscape of Tennessee has changed a great deal over time. Many settlers cleared land for farms in the 1800s. When coal and other mineral resources were discovered, the land was mined. These changes harmed many native plants and animals of Tennessee.

Elk are one kind of animal that completely vanished from the area. An elk is a large kind of deer. The white-tailed deer is another species of deer in Tennessee. Compared to white-tailed deer, elk are much larger and have hair that is thicker and redder.

Young elk look like their parents.

Elk Survival

Elk are well-adapted to live in forests and grasslands. Their stomach has four chambers, which helps them digest the plants they eat. In winter, elk grow thicker coats of fur that help keep them warm.

Returning Elk to Tennessee

Wildlife managers are reintroducing elk to parts of the Appalachian Mountains in which they used to live. One of these locations is in the Great Smoky Mountains National Park. Elk were released in North Carolina, but they have been seen in Tennessee. Elk have also been reintroduced to the Land Between the Lakes National Recreation Area in northern Tennessee. Scientists hope the elk will reproduce and form larger herds.

This elk has been fitted with a radio collar. It enables scientists to track the elk's movements.

Think and Write

❶ **Scientific Thinking** Why is it important that the herds of elk reintroduced to Tennessee reproduce?

❷ **Science and Technology** When elk are released into a new location, a radio collar is often placed around their necks. Scientists can locate the elk using the collar. Why might it be important for scientists to be able to locate the animals?

...ter Glass

...he Problem Sometimes ...nother has difficulty picking up ...g glass.

...of a Solution You can design ...s that is easier to hold or a cover ...she can use to get a better grip. List ...aracteristics that your solution must have ...o be useful. For example, someone must be able to hold and lift a glass easily.

Plan and Build Using your list, sketch and label the parts of your design. Think of the materials you could use. Then build your solution.

Test and Improve Test your solution. Then improve it, if necessary. Provide sketches and explanations of what you did.

Communicate

1. Was your design successful? Explain.

2. How did the device that you made solve this problem?

3. Explain one improvement you made to your design. Tell why you did this.

Possible Materials

- masking tape
- cardboard tubes
- scissors
- rubber bands
- glue
- scrap cardboard
- paper clips
- string
- clay
- foam
- rubber gloves
- plastic cups

 GLE 0407.T/E.5 Apply a creative design strategy to solve a particular problem generated by societal needs and wants.

TENNESSEE SCIENCE

UNIT A

Life Science

Tennessee

Guiding Question

How do living things survive and interact with their environment?

Chapter 1

Life Processes

LESSON 1

From a blade of grass to the human body—what basic unit makes up all living things?

LESSON 2

Roots, stems, leaves, and flowers—how do these parts help plants survive?

LESSON 3

From tiny seeds to blooming flowers—how do plants grow and reproduce?

LESSON 4

A bird hatches from an egg and a worm-like animal becomes a beetle—how do the life cycles of animals differ?

Fun Facts

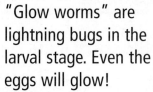

"Glow worms" are lightning bugs in the larval stage. Even the eggs will glow!

Vocabulary Preview

adult   nymph

★ cell   organ

chlorophyll   organism

egg   photosynthesis

embryo   reproduce

germinate   root

larva   seed

leaf   stem

life cycle   tissue

life process

life span

metamorphosis

★ = Tennessee Academic Vocabulary

 Vocabulary Strategies

Have you ever seen any of these terms before? Do you know what they mean?

State a description, explanation, or example of the vocabulary in your own words.

Draw a picture, symbol, example, or other image that describes the term.

Glossary p. H16

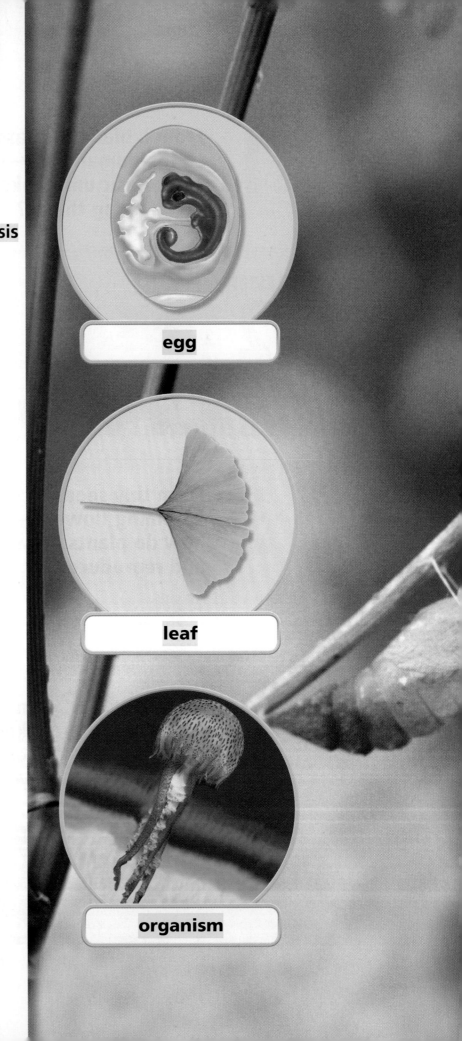

egg

leaf

organism

metamorphosis

Start with Your Standards

Inquiry

GLE 0407.Inq.1 Explore different scientific phenomena by asking questions, making logical predictions, planning investigations, and recording data.

GLE 0407.Inq.4 Identify and interpret simple patterns of evidence to communicate the findings of multiple investigations.

GLE 0407.Inq.5 Recognize that people may interpret the same results in different ways.

Life Science

Standard 1 Cells

GLE 0407.1.1 Recognize that cells are the building blocks of all living things.

Standard 3 Flow of Matter and Energy

GLE 0407.3.1 Demonstrate that plants require light energy to grow and survive.

GLE 0407.3.2 Investigate different ways that organisms meet their energy needs.

Standard 4 Heredity

GLE 0407.4.1 Recognize the relationship between reproduction and the continuation of a species.

GLE 0407.4.2 Differentiate between complete and incomplete metamorphosis.

Interact with this chapter.

 www.eduplace.com/tnscp

Lesson 1

 **TENNESSEE STANDARDS**

GLE 0407.1.1 Recognize that cells are the building blocks of all living things.

GLE 0407.Inq.1 Explore different scientific phenomena by asking questions, making logical predictions, planning investigations, and recording data.

 Guiding Question

How Are Living Things Organized?

Why It Matters...

Meerkats pop up from their underground homes. They sniff out tasty centipedes for themselves and their playful young. They stand on their hind legs to watch for enemies. Meerkats and all living things grow and develop and react to their surroundings.

PREPARE TO INVESTIGATE

Inquiry Skill

Ask Questions You ask questions to find out how or why something happens. Some of these questions can be answered through scientific investigations.

Materials

- slide
- cover slip
- microscope
- iodine solution
- prepared slide (human cheek cells)
- dropper
- onion
- paper towel
- disposable gloves
- goggles

Directed Inquiry

Close Up!

Procedure

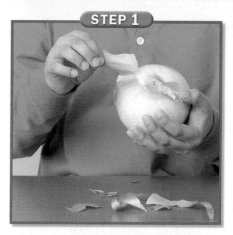
STEP 1

1. **Collaborate** Work with a partner. Peel an onion until you find one of the thin, filmy layers of onion skin between the thick layers.

2. Work on a paper towel. Put a piece of the filmy layer on a slide and put a cover slip over it. Put a small drop of iodine solution at the edge of the cover slip. **Safety:** Put on gloves and goggles. Iodine solution is poisonous and can stain.

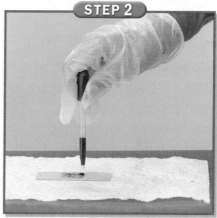
STEP 2

3. **Compare** Take off your goggles and gloves. Under the microscope, examine the slide you prepared. Then examine the slide of human cheek cells that your teacher gives you.

4. **Record Data** In your Science Notebook draw one tiny unit (a cell) from the onion skin slide. Label your drawing plant cell. Repeat for one tiny cell from the cheek cell slide. Label this drawing animal cell. **Safety:** Be careful. Microscopes have delicate parts.

STEP 3

Think and Write

1. **Compare** How was the plant cell different from the animal cell? How were the cells alike?

2. **Ask Questions** Write a question about how the cells function in a living thing.

Guided Inquiry

Ask Questions What questions do you have about what you observed in this Investigate activity? Compare your questions with those of your classmates.

0407.1.1

Characteristics of Living Things

Living Things

What is the difference between a bronze duck and a live duck? The live duck can carry out life processes. The bronze duck cannot. A **life process** is a function that a living thing performs to stay alive and produce more of its own kind.

All living things carry out life processes. One of these processes is to take in nutrients (NOO tree uhntz), materials used by living things to grow and develop. Living things also **reproduce** (ree pruh DOOS), or make more living things of their own kind.

The yellow duck has more in common with grass and leaves than with the bronze duck. ▼

Life Processes

Life Process	Plants	Animals
Take in materials such as nutrients and gases	Take in carbon dioxide, water, and minerals	Take in oxygen from the air and nutrients from food
Grow and develop		
Release energy	Release energy from the food they make	Release energy from the food they eat
React to surroundings		
Give off wastes	Give off oxygen as a waste product of making food. Other processes give off water and carbon dioxide.	Give off carbon dioxide and other waste
Reproduce		

FOCUS CHECK How do plants and animals release energy?

Plant and Animal Cells

A **cell** (sehl) is the basic unit that makes up all living things. Cells are so small that you can see them only with a microscope. They carry out life processes. All cells have parts. Some parts are the same in both plant cells and animal cells. One part that all cells have in common is a membrane (MEHM brayn), a thin surface that holds the cell together.

Plant Cell

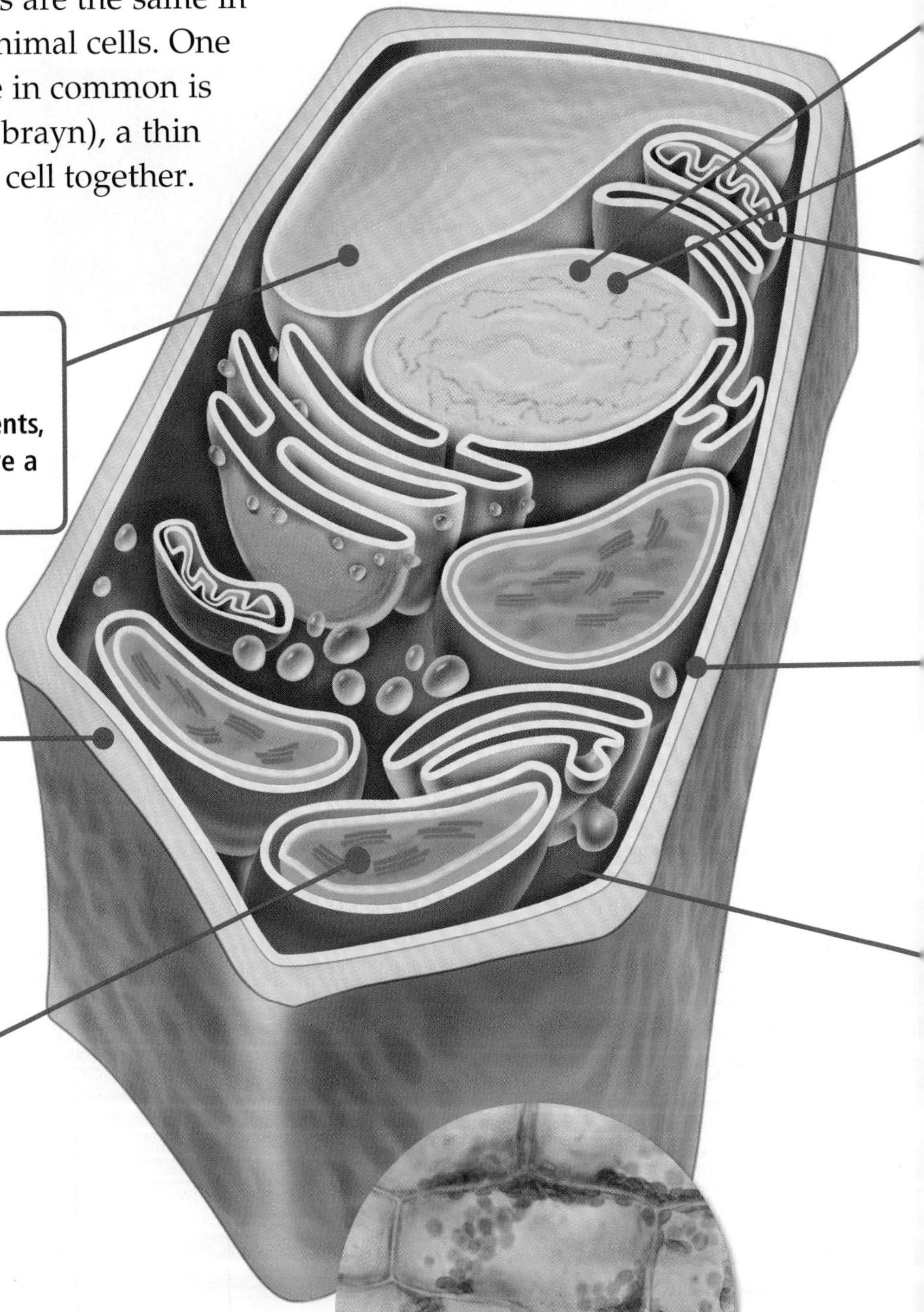

Vacuole
The vacuole is a storage container for food, nutrients, or wastes. Plant cells have a few large vacuoles.

Cell Wall
Plant cells have rigid walls around them. These walls help give plants their shape.

Chloroplast
The chloroplast is where the plant makes food. It contains a green material called chlorophyll.

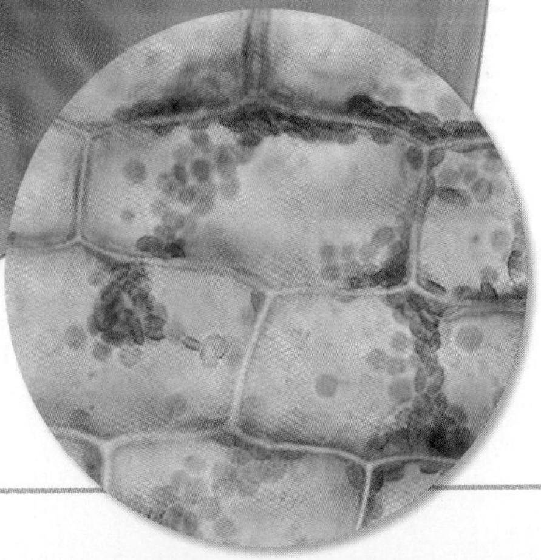

Plant cells ▶

Animal Cell

Nucleus
The nucleus is the control center of the cell.

Chromosomes
Chromosomes are like tiny blueprints for that particular plant or animal.

Mitochondria
The mitochondria are the power sources of a cell. They break down food to release energy.

Cell Membrane
The cell membrane acts like a skin that holds the cell together. It is the outer layer of an animal cell and is inside the cell wall in plant cells.

Cytoplasm
Cytoplasm is a jellylike material that fills the cell. The other parts of the cell float in the cytoplasm.

Vacuole
The vacuole is a storage container for food, nutrients, or wastes. Animal cells have many small vacuoles.

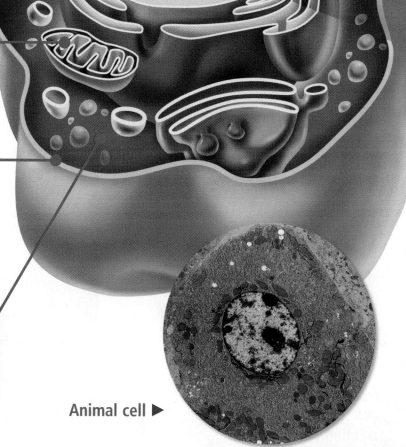

Animal cell ▶

FOCUS CHECK What parts do plant and animal cells have in common? What parts do they not have in common?

Express Lab

Activity Card
Model a Cell

Simple Organisms

An **organism** (AWR guh nihz-uhm) is any living thing that can carry out life processes on its own. Some organisms are simple and some are complex.

Single Cells Some simple organisms consist of single cells. These single cells can carry out all of the same life processes as a plant or animal made of many cells.

Algae (AL jee) are single-celled organisms that have chloroplasts and can make their own food. Algae and green plants give off oxygen as a waste product of making food. Oxygen (AHK sih-juhn) is a gas found in air and water. Algae produce much of the oxygen on Earth.

Instead of making their own food, some single-celled organisms, such as bacteria, rely on other living things for food. Bacteria (back TIHR ee uh) are tiny single-celled organisms found in all living things—including you!

Most bacteria are helpful. Some help break down dead plant and animal material. Some help turn milk into cheese or yogurt. Some even kill other bacteria that are harmful to animals. Some of the bacteria found in your body help you break down the food you eat.

Although most bacteria are helpful, some bacteria can cause people to become sick.

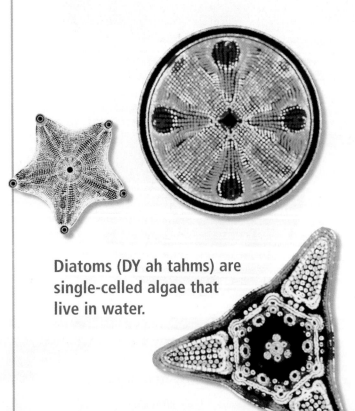

Diatoms (DY ah tahms) are single-celled algae that live in water.

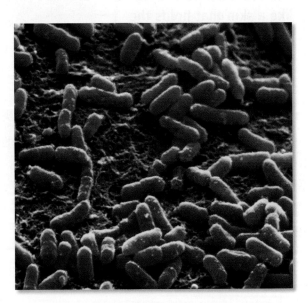

▲ Some *E. coli* bacteria help you get nutrients from food. Others can cause diseases.

Volvox is a globe-shaped colony of similar cells. The cells are connected by thin strands of cytoplasm.

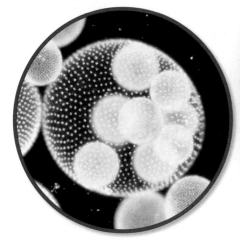

Many Cells Most of the organisms you are familiar with have more than one cell. Your own body consists of billions and billions of cells. You have many different kinds of cells, which perform different jobs. But some many-celled organisms are much simpler. The volvox (VAHL vahks) is one of the simplest many-celled organisms. It is found in most pond water. All of its cells are nearly identical.

Jellies are larger many-celled organisms, but they have very simple bodies. They do not have distinct organs (AWR guhnz). An **organ** is a special part of an organism that performs a specific function. Your heart is one of your organs. So is your brain. Jellies have no hearts, brains, or other organs.

🎯 **FOCUS CHECK** How are jellies like algae? How are they different?

▲ Jellies range in size from 1 cm to 2.5 m (about 7 ft).

pancreas

pancreas tissue

The cells of this lizard are organized into tissues that make up organs, such as the pancreas. Organs form organ systems, such as the digestive system.

Complex Organisms

Cells are the basic building blocks of all organisms. In complex organisms, there are many different kinds of cells. In your body, for example, you have skin cells, blood cells, stomach cells, and many other kinds of cells. In plants, different kinds of cells make up different parts, such as the roots or the leaves.

In complex organisms, cells that are similar form one kind of tissue (TIHSH oo). A **tissue** is a group of similar cells that work together. Some examples are muscle tissue, nerve tissue, and stomach tissue. Different kinds of tissue are organized into organs, such as the stomach, the lungs, and the eyes.

Complex organisms also have organ systems. An **organ system** is a group of organs that work together to carry out life processes. Your stomach is one of the organs in your digestive system, which takes in nutrients and eliminates wastes. Your nervous system receives information from your surroundings and other parts of your body. It helps control how you react to that information.

FOCUS CHECK How are organs and tissue alike? How are they different?

Lesson Wrap-Up

Visual Summary

A living thing is made of cells and can carry out life processes.

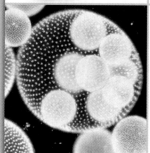

Some simple organisms are made of a single cell. Others are made of many cells that are similar.

In complex organisms, cells are organized into tissues, which make up organs. Organs form organ systems.

✔ Check for Understanding

MODERN MICROSCOPES

Scientists use microscopes to view cells. Many microscopes are large and costly. Research how scientists store microscopes. How could you make a better case to store a microscope? Design a case to protect a microscope.

✔ **0407.T/E.4**

Review

❶ **MAIN IDEA** How are all living things alike?

❷ **VOCABULARY** Use the term *tissue* in a sentence about the bodies of animals.

❸ **READING SKILL: Compare and Contrast** How are a person and a wax model of that person alike? How are they different?

❹ **CRITICAL THINKING: Evaluate** Someone says that something as small as a single cell could not really be alive. How would you respond to this statement?

❺ **INQUIRY SKILL: Ask Questions** Pose a question about simple and complex organisms. Use the Internet or library resources to find the answer.

TCAP TCAP Prep

The part of a cell that directs all the cell's activities is the ____.

A vacuole
B cell wall
C nucleus
D cytoplasm

SPI 0407.1.1

Go Digital Technology

Visit **www.eduplace.com/tnscp** to find out more about life processes.

TENNESSEE STANDARDS

GLE 0407.Inq.3 Organize data into appropriate tables, graphs, drawings, or diagrams.

GLE 0407.3.2 Investigate different ways that organisms meet their energy needs.

Guiding Question

How Do Plants Carry Out Life Processes?

Why It Matters...

In the springtime, the new stems and leaves of a fern unroll. These parts help the plant carry out its life processes. Your life and the lives of almost all of the animals on Earth depend on plants carrying out their life processes.

PREPARE TO INVESTIGATE

Inquiry Skill

Use Numbers You use numbers when you measure, estimate, and record data.

Materials

- four bean seedlings in plastic cups, labeled *All, No Air, No Water,* and *No Light*
- resealable plastic bag
- cardboard box
- water
- metric ruler
- markers

Science and Math Toolbox

For step 1, review **Making a Chart to Organize Data** on page H10.

Directed Inquiry

What's Needed

Procedure

1. **Collaborate** Work with a partner. In your *Science Notebook,* make a chart like the one shown. Measure the height of each of the four bean seedlings. Record the heights in the correct rows under *Day 1.*

2. **Experiment** Water the *All* and *No Air* seedlings. Put the *No Air* seedling inside a resealable bag. Close the bag. Put the *All, No Air,* and *No Water* seedlings in a sunny window.

3. **Use Variables** Water the *No Light* seedling and put it inside a cardboard box. Close the box and put it where no light will reach the seedling.

4. Check your seedlings every other day. Except for the *No Water* seedling, add water when the soil is dry.

5. **Use Numbers** When you check your seedlings, measure and record the height of each in your chart.

Think and Write

1. **Predict** For each seedling, make a line graph of your results. Predict how your graphs would change if you continued the experiment for another week.

2. **Infer** What are three needs of plants? What happens to plants when their needs are not met?

STEP 1

Seedlings	Day 1	Day 3	Day 5	Day 7	Day 9
All					
No Air					
No Water					
No Light					

STEP 2

STEP 3

Guided Inquiry

Design an Experiment Sketch several kinds of leaves and cut out each picture. Group the leaves by their similarities. Name each group and label the differences you observe within each group.

0407.3.3

Life Processes of Plants

VOCABULARY

chlorophyll
leaf
photosynthesis
root
seed
stem

GRAPHIC ORGANIZER

Classify As you read, compare different plant parts. Classify plants according to their different kinds of parts.

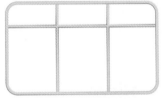

GLE 0407.3.1 Demonstrate that plants require light energy to grow and survive.

GLE 0407.3.2 Investigate different ways that organisms meet their energy needs.

Plant Parts

Plants are living things. They are made of cells, and they carry out all of the same life processes that you do. The one thing that makes most plants different from animals is that plants make their own food. Plants have special parts that allow them to make food, take in nutrients, reproduce, and perform other life processes.

The main parts of a plant are the roots, the stems, and the leaves. The **root** takes in water and nutrients from the ground. The **stem** carries food, water, and nutrients to and from the roots and leaves. A **leaf** (leef) uses sunlight and air to help the plant make food.

All of a plant's parts work together. A plant absorbs water and nutrients through its roots. Water and nutrients move to the plant's leaves through stems. In most plants, food is made in the plant's leaves. A plant needs roots, stems, and leaves to carry out its life processes.

FOCUS CHECK Name three parts of a plant.

There are many different types of plants. Most use similar parts to carry out life processes.

Parts of a plant

Flower
A flower is the plant part where seeds are produced. A seed is an undeveloped plant sealed in a protective coating.

Leaf
The leaves are the food factories of a plant.

Stem
Stems move water and nutrients from the roots to the leaves and carry food from the leaves to all parts of the plant.

Root
Most roots have tiny root hairs that soak up moisture. Some roots, such as carrots, also store food for the plant.

Express Lab

Activity Card
Make a Terrarium

Succulent leaves

Broadleaf

Comparing Plant Parts

Plants can be classified by their parts. Succulents (SUHK yuh luhnts) have thick leaves that help the plant store water. Succulents usually grow in dry areas.

Broadleaf plants often grow in moist areas. Broad leaves help the plant trap energy from sunlight.

Plants with needle-like leaves, such as those on pine trees, can withstand both dry and cold climates. Such plants do not shed all their leaves in the fall, like broadleaf plants do.

Plants can also be classified by the different kinds of roots they have. Some plants have one large, main root. This kind of root is called a taproot. Parsnips and carrots are examples of taproots. Some taproots grow deep into the ground.

Other plants have roots that branch out in a netlike pattern. No one root is much larger or more important than the others. These kinds of roots are called fibrous roots. Fibrous roots gather water from a wide area. Many plants have fibrous roots.

Needle-like leaves

Taproot system

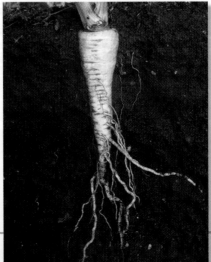

Fibrous root system

Barrel cactuses have thick stems.

Plants have different kinds of stems. Some stems, such as tree trunks, are woody. Woody stems are stiff. They have an outer layer of bark that protects them. Woody stems can survive cold temperatures. So woody plants live for many years.

Other plants have soft stems. These stems are held up by water in their tubes. Plants with soft stems usually cannot survive freezing temperatures. Soft-stemmed plants tend to be smaller and live for a shorter time than woody plants.

Many cactuses have very thick stems that store water. So cactuses can survive long periods without rain.

Another way to classify plants is by how they reproduce. Some plants, such as pine trees, produce seeds inside stiff cones. Others, such as peach trees, produce seeds inside fruit. Fruits are formed only by flowers. Plants can be grouped according to whether they are flowering or non-flowering.

FOCUS CHECK **What are two types of roots?**

Woody stems of an azalea

Soft stems of carnations

Photosynthesis

Energy from sunlight strikes leaves

Carbon dioxide from the air enters plant

Oxygen is released into air

Water moves from roots through stems to leaves

How Plants Make Food

The process plants use to make food is called **photosynthesis** (foh-toh SIHN thih sihs). Photosynthesis usually takes place in a plant's leaves. Most leaf cells have special parts called chloroplasts (KLAWR-uh plasts) that contain chlorophyll. **Chlorophyll** (KLAWR uh fihl) is a green material that can trap energy from sunlight. It also gives leaves their green color.

Leaves take in carbon dioxide from the air through tiny holes. Water that is absorbed through the plant's roots reaches the leaves through tubes in the stem.

In the chloroplasts, the process of photosynthesis changes carbon dioxide and water into food. The food that is produced is sugar.

Tubes in the stem carry the sugar made in the leaves to other parts of the plant. In the process of photosynthesis, oxygen is also produced. The oxygen is a waste product that is released into the air.

⊙FOCUS CHECK Compare the materials taken in with the materials produced during photosynthesis.

Lesson Wrap-Up

Visual Summary

 Most plants have roots, stems, and leaves. These parts help plants carry out life processes.

 Basic plant parts—roots, stems, and leaves—differ in different types of plants.

 Plants use the energy of sunlight to make food in a process called photosynthesis.

Check for Understanding

DESIGNING A PLANT

Scientists alter plants to meet different needs. What if we could grow grapes the size of basketballs? Design a modified plant of your own, starting from a plant you are familiar with. Write an explanation of the advantages of your modified plant. Describe the life process that the plant goes through.

✔ 0407.T/E.2

Review

1 MAIN IDEA How do roots help plants meet their needs?

2 VOCABULARY What is chlorophyll?

3 READING SKILL: Classify Two bushes each have woody stems. What other features could you use to classify the bushes?

4 CRITICAL THINKING: Analyze If a plant does not get any sunlight, which life process can it no longer carry out?

5 INQUIRY SKILL: Use Numbers The data shows the height of bean plants given different amounts of light and water: Plant A, extra light, 10 cm; Plant B, extra water, 7 cm; Plant C, normal light and water, 6 cm. Which factor affected plant growth the most?

TCAP Prep

What gas do plants need for photosynthesis?

A carbon dioxide
B carbon monoxide
C oxygen
D nitrogen

GLE 0407.3.1

Technology

Go Digital

Visit **www.eduplace.com/tnscp** to learn more about photosynthesis.

TENNESSEE STANDARDS

GLE 0407.4.1 Recognize the relationship between reproduction and the continuation of a species.
GLE 0407.Inq.3 Organize data into appropriate tables, graphs, drawings, or diagrams.

Guiding Question

How Do Plant Life Cycles Vary?

Why It Matters...

Some plants live for only a few months, while others live for many years. It's hard to believe, but this Bristlecone pine tree has been alive for over 4,700 years. Scientists can learn what the environment was like thousands of years ago by studying long-living trees.

PREPARE TO INVESTIGATE

Inquiry Skill

Compare When you compare two things, you observe how they are alike and how they are different.

Materials

- paper plate
- 4 different kinds of fruit
- plastic knife
- hand lens

Science and Math Toolbox

For step 3, review **Using a Hand Lens** on page H2.

Directed Inquiry

Seed Search

Procedure

1 **Research** In your *Science Notebook*, make a chart like the one shown.

2 **Collaborate** Work with a partner. Place one piece of fruit on a plate. Open it so that you can see the seeds inside. You may break the fruit open with your hands or cut the fruit open with a plastic knife. **Safety:** Be careful when using the knife.

3 **Observe** Look closely at the seeds with a hand lens. Count the number of seeds. Note the color, size, and shape of the seeds. Observe how the seeds look in the fruit that surrounds them. Record your observations and draw a sketch of the seeds.

4 **Compare** Repeat steps 2 and 3 with three kinds of other fruit. Compare the seeds from the four different fruits.

Think and Write

1. **Compare** In what ways are the four types of seeds similar? In what ways are they different?

2. **Infer** What do you think seeds do? Why do you think seeds are found inside fruit?

STEP 1

Type of Fruit	Sketch of Seed	Observations

STEP 2

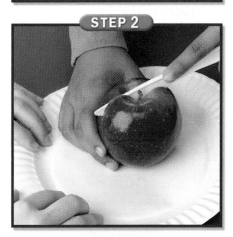

STEP 3

Guided Inquiry

Design an Experiment
Use a damp paper towel, radish seeds, and a resealable plastic bag. Plan an experiment to show what happens when a seed sprouts. Test your plan.

✔ 0407.Inq.3

Plant Life Cycles

VOCABULARY

embryo
germinate
life cycle
life span

GRAPHIC ORGANIZER

Sequence Use the chart to show how a flowering plant grows from producing a seed to making a new plant to dying.

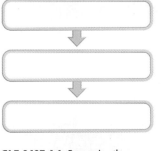

GLE 0407.4.1 Recognize the relationship between reproduction and the continuation of a species.

Life Cycle of a Flowering Plant

A small seed is planted in the soil. The seed sprouts and grows into a tall tree. In time the tree flowers and then begins releasing its own seeds. One day the tree dies.

You just read about the life cycle of a tree. A **life cycle** (lyf SY kuhl) is a series of stages that occur during the lifetime of all living things. The changes that can occur during any life cycle include birth, development into an adult, reproduction, and death. Flowering plants, including trees and grasses, produce flowers during their life cycles. Flowers produce seeds that will grow into new plants. If a plant species did not reproduce, it would eventually die out.

Parts of a Flower

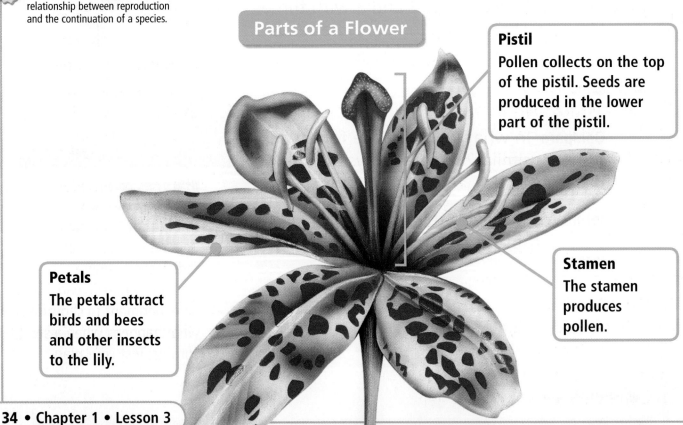

Pistil
Pollen collects on the top of the pistil. Seeds are produced in the lower part of the pistil.

Stamen
The stamen produces pollen.

Petals
The petals attract birds and bees and other insects to the lily.

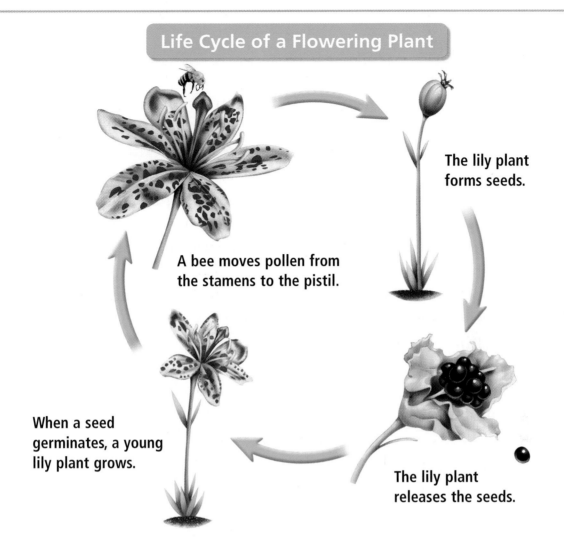

Life Cycle of a Flowering Plant

The lily plant forms seeds.

A bee moves pollen from the stamens to the pistil.

When a seed germinates, a young lily plant grows.

The lily plant releases the seeds.

The stamen (STAY muhn) of a flower makes pollen, which is needed to form seeds. Plants can form seeds when the pollen is moved from the stamens to the pistil (PIHS tuhl).

Wind, water, or animals move pollen from the stamens to the pistil. Brightly colored petals attract birds, bees, or other insects to a flower. When pollen moves from the stamens to the pistil, a plant will produce seeds.

Each seed contains an embryo in a protective coat. An **embryo** (EHM-bree oh) is a plant or animal in the earliest stages of development.

Some seeds will land in places where they can **germinate** (JUHR-muh nayt), or begin growing a new plant. The new plant grows and forms flowers, and the cycle begins again.

FOCUS CHECK What step in the plant life cycle comes after pollination?

Express Lab

Activity Card
Model a Plant Life Cycle

Life Spans of Plants

A **life span** is the length of time it takes for an individual organism to complete its life cycle. The length of a life span may vary from plant to plant. If you plant bean seeds, the plants will grow, produce seeds, and die all in one summer. If you plant a maple tree seed, the new tree may live for hundreds of years!

For flowering plants, the life span begins when a seed germinates. It ends with the death of the plant. The life spans of bean plants are a few months. Redwood trees have life spans of thousands of years.

In organisms that are similar, such as trees, the smaller kinds usually have shorter life spans than the larger kinds. This is not always true, however. For example, both the Ponderosa pine and the Pacific yew have a life span of about 300 years. Ponderosa pines grow almost 40 m (131 ft) high, while Pacific yews do not even reach 20 m (66 ft).

FOCUS CHECK When does the life span of a flowering plant begin?

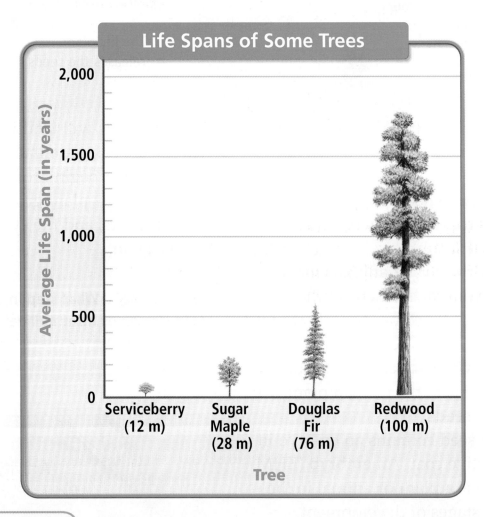

Life Spans of Some Trees

Average Life Span (in years)

2,000

1,500

1,000

500

0

| Serviceberry (12 m) | Sugar Maple (28 m) | Douglas Fir (76 m) | Redwood (100 m) |

Tree

Lesson Wrap-Up

Visual Summary

The parts of a flower include the petals, stamen, and pistil.

The life cycle of an organism includes birth, growth, reproduction, and death.

Plants have different life spans. A life span is the time it takes to complete one life cycle.

Check for Understanding

PLANT TROPISMS

Write and illustrate a pamphlet to explain what plant trophisms are. Your audience is a second grade class. Include phototropism and gravitropism plus others you find in research sources.

✔ 0407.5.3

Review

❶ **MAIN IDEA** What are the main stages in the life cycle of a flowering plant?

❷ **VOCABULARY** Use the terms *embryo* and *germinate* in a paragraph that describes the life cycle of plants.

❸ **READING SKILL: Sequence** What happens in the life cycle of a flowering plant after it produces seeds?

❹ **CRITICAL THINKING: Evaluate** You know that a tree near your school produces flowers. Someone tells you that the tree does not produce seeds. What would you say to that person?

❺ **INQUIRY SKILL: Compare** How is wind pollinating a flower similar to an insect pollinating a flower? How is it different?

TCAP Prep

The stamen of a flower___.

A protects the seed.
B holds the embryo.
C is part of the pistil.
D produces pollen.

SPI 0407.4.1

Technology

Visit **www.eduplace.com/tnscp** to investigate plant life cycles.

EXTREME Science

What's the BiG Stink?

Whoa! That smells!

Phew! What's that smell?
It's titan arum, one of the biggest, stinkiest flowers in the world. The titan arum is huge. It can measure 3 or 4 feet across and stand 10 feet high. And it smells like rotten meat!

This giant flower's smell is part of a trick. Carrion beetles, which eat dead animals, follow their antennas to the titan arum blossoms. As the beetles poke around, looking for dinner, pollen sticks to their legs. When the beetles go from plant to plant, the pollen drops off, and the huge flowers get pollinated. Without its stink, the titan arum wouldn't be able to reproduce and survive.

To make it smell more attractive to carrion beetles, the titan arum heats up. The heat helps spreads its scent as far as a half mile away.

GLE 0407.4.1 Recognize the relationship between reproduction and the continuation of a species.

EXTEND

How **TALL** is it?

10 feet tall

6 feet tall

The titan arum grows wild only in the rainforests of Sumatra, Indonesia.

TENNESSEE STANDARDS

GLE 0407.4.2 Differentiate between complete and incomplete metamorphosis.
GLE 0407.Inq.5 Recognize that people may interpret the same results in different ways.

How Do Animal Life Cycles Vary?

Why It Matters...

This sandhill crane has a young chick. How was the chick born? What will it look like when it becomes an adult? How will it produce young? You can learn the answers to these questions by studying the life cycle of a sandhill crane. Life cycles can teach us many things about animals.

PREPARE TO INVESTIGATE

Inquiry Skill

Record Data You can keep a record of your observations in writing or with devices such as audio and tape recorders and cameras.

Materials

- clear plastic container with lid
- pushpin
- plastic spoon
- mealworms
- oatmeal
- hand lens

Science and Math Toolbox

For step 3, review **Using a Hand Lens** on page H2.

Directed Inquiry

Monitor Mealworms

Procedure

STEP 1

1 **Collaborate** Work with a partner. Carefully use a pushpin to make air holes in the lid of a plastic container. Place a thin layer of oatmeal in the container. **Safety:** Be careful. Pushpins are sharp.

2 Use a plastic spoon to put mealworms gently in the container. Close the lid. **Safety:** Do not touch the mealworms.

STEP 2

3 **Record Data** Look closely at the mealworms with a hand lens. Draw a sketch of the mealworms and record your observations in your *Science Notebook.*

4 Add oatmeal as necessary. Repeat step 3 once a week for two months. Record all your observations.

STEP 3

Think and Write

1. **Analyze Data** A mealworm is actually one of the stages in the life cycle of a darkling beetle. What different stages of the life cycle have you observed? What stage do you think comes next?

2. **Communicate** Exchange observations with another team. Do your team's sketches and observations differ from the other team's sketches and observations? Discuss why this might be so.

Guided Inquiry

Research Use the library or Internet to learn more about the life cycle of mealworms. Find out where they live and what they eat. Make a poster to display your findings.

0407.4.2

Animal Life Cycles

Metamorphosis

What do alligators, robins, and mealworms have in common? They may not look alike, but they are all animals. They also all lay eggs during their life cycle. An **egg** is the first stage in the life cycle of most animals. All birds and most fish lay eggs. So do most reptiles, such as snakes, and amphibians, such as frogs. Even insects lay eggs.

Different types of adult female animals lay different numbers of eggs. An eagle may lay 2 or 3 eggs at a time. Some frogs lay thousands of eggs. An ocean sunfish can lay around 300 million eggs at one time.

When eggs hatch, offspring emerge. An offspring is a new living thing born when parents reproduce. An offspring develops into an **adult**, or a fully grown, mature organism.

GRAPHIC ORGANIZER

Compare and Contrast
Use the chart to compare and contrast the life cycle of an alligator, an insect, and a bird.

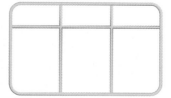

GLE 0407.4.1 Recognize the relationship between reproduction and the continuation of a species.

GLE 0407.4.2 Differentiate between complete and incomplete metamorphosis.

Life Cycle of an Alligator

egg white — embryo — yolk — shell

Egg

Alligator hatching

Young alligator

Adult

Life Cycle of a Mexican Bean Beetle

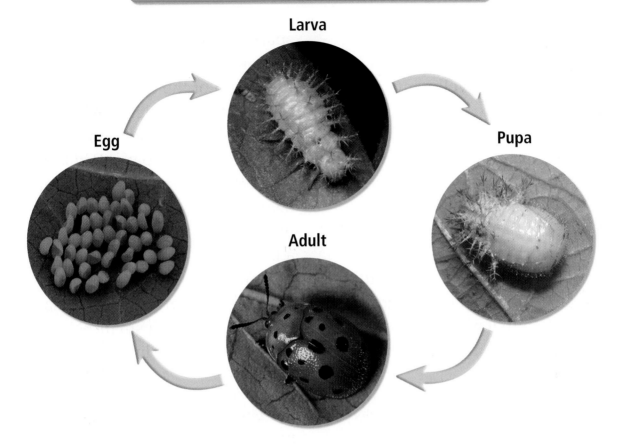

Larva

Egg

Pupa

Adult

The process in which some organisms change form in different stages of their life cycles is known as **metamorphosis** (meht uh MAWR-fuh sihs). Many insects change form four times, which is called complete metamorphosis.

The egg, the first stage, hatches into a wormlike form called a **larva** (LAHR vuh). The larva eats and grows larger. The mealworm is the larva stage of a darkling beetle.

Eventually the larva forms a hard casing around itself. This stage is the pupa (PYOO puh). The adult insect emerges from the pupa. The insect looks very different at each stage.

Some insects go through a three-stage life cycle known as incomplete metamorphosis. Eggs are the first stage. The second stage is called the **nymph** (nihmf). The nymph looks like the adult, but usually has no wings. As it matures, it sheds its outer casing several times, grows wings, and becomes an adult.

FOCUS CHECK How are complete and incomplete metamorphosis alike and different?

Express Lab

Activity Card
Experience Life Processes

Life Cycles and Life Spans

Many animals lay eggs as one stage of their life cycles. For example, baby birds hatch from eggs. The babies develop into adults. Birds reproduce when an adult female lays eggs. In time, the adult birds die.

Mammals, such as rabbits, bears, and humans, do not lay eggs. Instead, their young are born live. Like baby birds, these young grow and develop into adults. The adults reproduce and in time die. Each species of animal must reproduce or it will eventually die out.

The life spans given below are for the oldest known animal. Which animal lives the longest?

Just as life cycle stages vary, life spans of different kinds of animals vary. Remember, a life span is the length of the time it takes an organism to complete a life cycle.

In general, smaller animals have shorter life spans than larger animals of the same kind. A small lizard may live only two years, but its relative, the alligator, has a life span of 60 years. There are exceptions, however. Humans and elephants are both mammals. Humans are much smaller than elephants but can live longer.

⊙ FOCUS CHECK How do mammals and birds differ in the way they produce young?

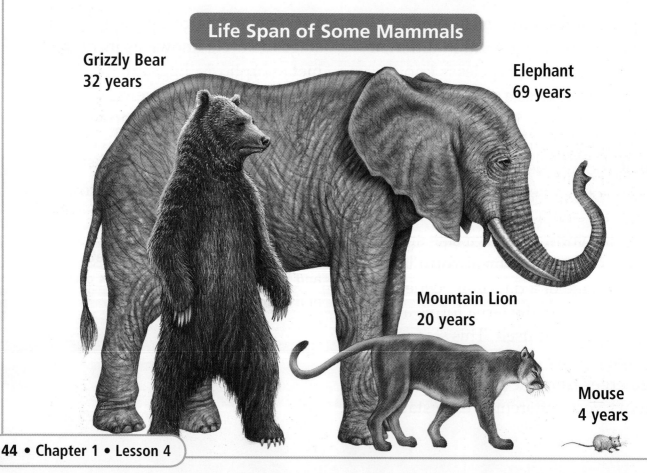

Life Span of Some Mammals

Grizzly Bear
32 years

Elephant
69 years

Mountain Lion
20 years

Mouse
4 years

Visual Summary

Stages in animal life cycles include birth, growing into an adult, reproduction, and death.

The life cycle of insects involves complete or incomplete metamorphosis.

Life spans for different kinds of animals vary. The size of an animal is often related to its life span.

Check for Understanding

METAMORPHOSIS

Study the metamorphosis of an animal such as a frog. Compare the cycle it goes through to the metamorphosis of the mealworm from the Investigate on p. 41. How are they similar? How are they different?

✔️ 0407.4.2

Review

❶ **MAIN IDEA** How does the life cycle of a rabbit differ from the life cycle of a bird?

❷ **VOCABULARY** Use the term *larva* in a sentence.

❸ **READING SKILL: Compare and Contrast** How are the life cycles of an alligator and a Mexican Bean beetle alike? How are they different?

❹ **CRITICAL THINKING: Apply** What questions would you ask in an interview of a scientist who studies fruit flies?

❺ **INQUIRY SKILL: Record Data** Make a bar graph to record the following data. Title your bar graph *The Life Spans of Different Snakes*. Garter snake, 8 years; Indigo snake, 17 years; Boa constrictor, 23 years; Anaconda, 30 years. Research how big each snake is.

TCAP TCAP Prep

The second stage of incomplete metamorphosis is the ___.

A nymph

B adult

C pupa

D egg

SPI 0407.4.2

Go Digital Technology

Visit **www.eduplace.com/tnscp** to investigate animal life cycles.

Long ago, people told myths, or made-up stories, about things in nature. One Greek myth is about how spiders came to be. Read the myth below. Then read *The Secret World of Spiders.* How are the two pieces alike and different?

THE ORCHARD BOOK OF GREEK MYTHS

by Geraldine McCaughrean
Illustrated by Emma Chichester Clark

Arachne boasted that she could weave better than any goddess. This made the goddess Athene angry. Athene decided to make an example of Arachne.

She took the shuttle out of Arachne's hands and pushed it into her mouth.
Then, ... she transformed Arachne.

Arachne's arms stuck to her sides, and left only her long, clever fingers.... Her body shrank down to a black blob ... an end of thread still curled out of its mouth. Athene used the thread to hang Arachne upon a tree, and left her dangling there.

"Weave your tapestries forever!" said the goddess. " ... people will only shudder at the sight of them and pull them to shreds."

It all came true. For Arachne had been turned into the first spider, doomed forever to spin webs in the corners of rooms, in bushes, in dark, unswept places. And though cobwebs are as lovely a piece of weaving as you'll ever see, just look how people hurry to sweep them away.

Arachne is the Greek word for spider. Spiders belong to a class called *arthropods*.

GLE 0407.4.1 Recognize the relationship between reproduction and the continuation of a species.

EXTEND

THE SECRET WORLD OF
Spiders

by Theresa Greenaway

Scientists have learned that all spiders are born from eggs, and they all produce silk.

Before laying her eggs, a female spider spins a small sheet of silk. This may be flat or cup-shaped. When it is ready, she lays her ... eggs on a silk sheet. The eggs and the sheet on which they were laid are now enclosed in more silk to make an egg sac. A long-legged cellar spider makes a flimsy egg sac that she holds in her jaws until the spiderlings hatch.

Wolf spiders and many other kinds make a much tougher egg sac. Wolf spider mothers carry theirs around by holding them with their spinnerets. Sheet-web and lynx spiders are among those that stand guard over their egg sac until the eggs hatch.

Inside each egg, a spider starts to develop, nourished by egg yolk. When it is ready to hatch, it tears the eggshell with a tiny egg tooth on its head.

The spider is standing over the egg sac.

Sharing Ideas

Note Book

1. **READING CHECK** In the myth of Arachne, how did the first spider come to be on Earth?

2. **WRITE ABOUT IT** Write a paragraph describing the relationship between spider eggs and the survival of spiders.

3. **TALK ABOUT IT** What facts did you learn about spiders from the second selection?

GLE 0407.5.1 Analyze physical and behavioral adaptations that enable organisms to survive in their environment. **Math GLE 0406.5.1** Collect, record, arrange, present, and interpret data using tables and various representations. **ELA GLE 0401.4.2** Collect, organize, and determine the reliability of researched information.

Math Digestive Tracts

The bar graph shows the body length and the length of the digestive tract for four animals. The data apply to typical animals, not all animals of the species.

1. Which is the longest of the four animals? Which has the longest digestive tract?

2. The human digestive tract is about 3 times as long as the body. Estimate to compare the lengths for each of the other animals.

3. What advantage do you think a long digestive tract provides? Use data from the table and facts you know to support your answer.

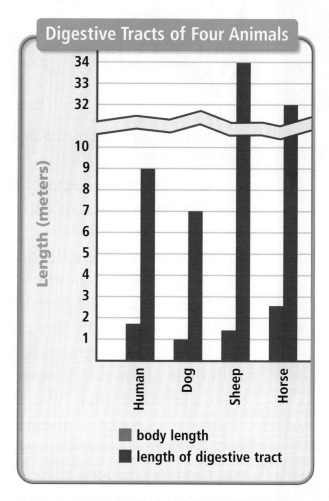

Digestive Tracts of Four Animals

Length (meters)

Human Dog Sheep Horse

- body length
- length of digestive tract

Writing Response to Literature

Read a book about an animal of your choice. The book may be fiction or nonfiction. Write a brief report about the book. Tell whether or not you found the book useful.

Pathologist

Pathologists are medical "detectives." They are doctors who solve medical mysteries using "clues," such as microscopic samples of tissues and cells. A pathologist helps find the causes and treatments for different diseases.

Most pathologists work in a laboratory. However, some work in operating rooms as part of a surgical team. Others work at state and county Medical Examiner's Offices and help solve crimes.

What It Takes!
- A medical degree
- Training in pathology

Licensed Practical Nurse

Licensed practical nurses give care and comfort to people who need medical attention. Their duties include taking temperatures, monitoring blood pressure, drawing blood, giving injections, and bandaging wounds. Licensed practical nurses work in hospitals, nursing homes, doctor's offices, and private homes.

What It Takes!
- A high-school diploma
- One or more years of training and earning a license

49

Vocabulary

Complete each sentence with a term from the list.

1. The process in which some organisms change form during different stages of life is called _____.

2. The basic building block of all living things is a/an _____.

3. In a plant or animal, a part that carries out a particular job is a/an _____.

4. Plants make food in a process called _____.

5. In most plants, the part where food is made is a/an _____.

6. The part of a plant that takes in water and nutrients from the ground is called a/an _____.

7. An organism that is fully grown is called a/an_____.

8. The second stage in complete metamorphosis is a/an _____.

9. Living things make more living things of their own kind when they _____.

10. A green material that helps plants make food is called _____.

adult
★ cell
chlorophyll
larva
leaf
life process
metamorphosis
organ
organism
photosynthesis
reproduce
root
stem

TCAP Inquiry Skills

11. **Use Numbers** Three bean plants were each given a different kind of fertilizer for a month. At the start, all plants were 5 cm tall. At the end of the month, the height of each plant was as follows: Plant A, 7 cm; Plant B, 5 cm; Plant C, 10 cm. Which fertilizer worked best? Which did not work at all?

    GLE 0407.Inq.4

12. **Analyze** How does the stem of a cactus help it survive in a dry environment? **GLE 0407.5.1**

Map the Concept

Use the following terms to fill in the concept map:

Photosynthesis

energy from sunlight
oxygen
carbon dioxide
food
water

Plant Takes In
_____ _____

↓

Plant Produces
_____ _____

GLE 0407.3.1

Critical Thinking

13. Analyze When dragonflies are born, they do not have wings. But adult dragonflies do have wings. Explain why this is so. **GLE 0407.4.2**

14. Apply At a museum, you see a statue of a horse. How is the statue different from a living horse? Discuss three life processes in your answer. **GLE 0407.4.1**

15. Ask Questions Write a question about an organism that could be answered by looking at part of the organism through a microscope. What would you need to view to answer your question? **GLE 0407.1.1**

16. Evaluate Animals give off carbon dioxide as waste. Plants give off oxygen as waste. Explain why these materials are not really being wasted. Explain your answer. **GLE 0407.3.1**

Check for Understanding

Cell Parts Poster

Make a three-dimensional model of a plant or animal cell by gluing household items, such as pasta, foam peanuts, and yarn, to a piece of poster board. Choose either a plant or animal cell. Be sure to include all the parts of the cell and label them. ✓ **0407.1.1**

TCAP TCAP Prep

Write the letter of the best answer choice.

17 Female adult birds, fish, reptiles and insects _____.

A germinate

B lay eggs

C have the same life span

D give birth to live young **SPI 0407.4.1**

18 Growing is a/an _____.

F organ system

G energy

H nutrient

J life process **SPI 0407.4.1**

19 The second stage of incomplete metamorphosis is called a/an_____.

A nymph

B egg

C adult

D pupa **SPI 0407.4.2**

20 When plants use sunlight to make food, they release _____.

F carbon dioxide

G oxygen

H chlorophyll

J chloroplast **SPI 0407.3.1**

Chapter 2

Adaptation and Extinction

LESSON 1

Jackrabbits have very large ears. How does this trait help them survive in the desert?

LESSON 2

Overhunting and the building of a dam— how might each threaten the survival of plants and animals?

Fun Facts

Fleas can jump 130 times higher than their own height.

Vocabulary Preview

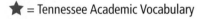

★ **adaptation**
camouflage
extinct
habitat
hibernate
migrate
mimicry
niche
species

★ = Tennessee Academic Vocabulary

Vocabulary Strategies

Have you ever seen any of these terms before? Do you know what they mean?

State a description, explanation, or example of the vocabulary in your own words.

Draw a picture, symbol, example, or other image that describes the term.

Glossary p. H16

extinct

camouflage

adaptation

habitat

Start with Your Standards

Inquiry

GLE 0407.Inq.1 Explore different scientific phenomena by asking questions, making logical predictions, planning investigations, and recording data.

GLE 0407.Inq.4 Identify and interpret simple patterns of evidence to communicate the findings of multiple investigations.

Life Science

Standard 5 Biodiversity and Change

GLE 0407.5.1 Analyze physical and behavioral adaptations that enable organisms to survive in their environment.

GLE 0407.5.2 Describe how environmental changes caused the extinction of various plant and animal species.

Interact with this chapter.

 www.eduplace.com/tnscp

 **TENNESSEE STANDARDS**

GLE 0407.5.1 Analyze physical and behavioral adaptations that enable organisms to survive in their environment.
GLE 0407.Inq.1 Explore different scientific phenomena by asking questions, making logical predictions, planning investigations, and recording data.

Guiding Question

How Are Organisms Adapted to Survive?

Why It Matters...

You may think the picture on this page shows a plant. In fact, you are looking at an animal. The lettuce sea slug hides from enemies by blending in with its surroundings. Many animals have colors or shapes that help them survive.

PREPARE TO INVESTIGATE

Inquiry Skill

Observe When you observe, you gather information about the environment using your five senses: seeing, hearing, smelling, touching, and tasting.

Materials

- black construction paper
- plastic jars
- scissors
- masking tape
- small index card
- mealworms
- clock or watch

Science and Math Toolbox

For step 5, review **Measuring Elapsed Time** on page H12.

Directed Inquiry

A Mealworm Home

Procedure

1. **Collaborate** Work with a partner. Use black construction paper to cover the outside of a plastic jar as shown.

2. Cut a square of black paper that is slightly larger than the opening of the jar. Position the square over the opening of the jar. Leaving a space, tape the square in place as shown.

3. Use an index card to lift a mealworm and place it in an uncovered plastic jar. **Safety:** Handle the mealworms gently.

4. **Observe** With your partner, use masking tape to join together the openings of the two jars. Place the joined jars on their side in a well-lit area.

5. **Record Data** Every 10 minutes for the next half hour, observe and record the location of the mealworm. When you are finished, have your teacher return the mealworm to a suitable environment.

STEP 1

STEP 2

STEP 3

Think and Write

1. **Predict** Suppose in step 4 you put the mealworm home in a dark place. How do you think this would affect the mealworm's movements?

2. **Infer** Based on your observations, what can you conclude about the type of environment a mealworm prefers?

Guided Inquiry

Design an Experiment
Choose an organism that lives near you. Observe it from a safe distance for a few minutes. Use a camera or other recording device, if available. Compare its appearance and actions to others of its kind.

0407.Inq.1

VOCABULARY

★ adaptation
  camouflage
  habitat
  hibernate
  mimicry
  niche

GRAPHIC ORGANIZER

Problem-Solution Use
a chart to show how an
organism's adaptation
solves a problem.

Problem	Solution

GLE 0407.5.1 Analyze physical
and behavioral adaptations that
enable organisms to survive in their
environment.

Adaptations For Survival

Plant and Animal Adaptations

Sharks live in water, and cactuses grow in dry deserts. It's clear that different plants and animals survive in different environments. The place where a plant or animal lives is called its **habitat** (HAB ih tat). The ocean is a dolphin's habitat. The habitat of a toucan is the rainforest.

Plants and animals have adaptations (ad-ap TAY shuhnz) that help them survive. An **adaptation** can be a physical feature or a behavior that helps a plant or animal survive.

The role a plant or animal plays in its environment is called its **niche** (nihch). A niche includes the kind of food an organism uses for energy. It also includes the conditions the organism needs to survive. Part of an opossum's niche is to eat berries. Many organisms can share a habitat, but each organism has its own niche.

⊙FOCUS CHECK Give an example of an adaptation and how it helps an animal survive.

A wood duck's feet have sharp claws that help it perch on branches. Its feet are also webbed, which helps it swim.

Adaptations to Habitat

Forest
The aye aye has large eyes that help it see at night. The aye aye's third finger is very long and thin. It uses it for digging food out of trees.

Rainforest
Water that stays on leaves can cause disease. The leaves of many rainforest plants have pointed ends that allow rainwater to drip off.

Desert
Light-colored fur helps the jackrabbit blend into its surroundings. Its large ears help it keep cool in the desert by giving off heat.

Tundra
The musk ox's habitat is cold and snowy much of the year. How does the musk ox's thick fur help it survive?

Camouflage

Have you ever seen an animal that looked like its surroundings--so much so that you almost didn't notice it? Such an animal has an adaptation called **camouflage** (KAM uh flahzh). Camouflage is the coloring, marking, or other physical appearance of an animal that helps it blend in with its surroundings.

Animals use camouflage to hide from both predators and prey. The camouflage of the lettuce sea slug on page 56 helps it hide from ocean predators. The color and pattern of the young deer's fur helps it blend into its forest habitat. The young deer is protected because predators have a hard time seeing it.

A Bengal tiger is a predator that uses camouflage. Its stripes help the tiger blend with the tall grass where it hunts at dawn and dusk. Its prey do not see the tiger approach.

Some animals change color as their environment changes. The coat of an arctic fox is gray in the summer, so the fox blends into the rocky ground. In winter, its coat turns white. This helps the fox blend into the snow. In both seasons, the fox can hunt without being seen.

▲ The white fur of the arctic fox helps camouflage it in snow.

◀ A young deer's light-brown fur and white spots look like patches of sunlight and shade.

Express Lab

Activity Card

Test Camouflage

Color and Mimicry

Some animals have bright colors that let other animals see them easily. This adaptation is called warning coloration. The bright colors of a bumble bee can warn of painful stings. The blue poison dart frog stands out in its habitat. The bright color warns predators that this frog is poisonous.

Some animals protect themselves by using mimicry (MIHM ih kree). **Mimicry** is an adaptaton in which an animal protects itself by looking like another kind of animal or like a plant. Many insects use mimicry. The South American owl butterfly has large spots on its wings that look like the eyes of an owl. These spots scare away birds that might want to eat the butterfly.

Mimicry is also useful to animals that hunt. By looking like an animal that is not a threat, a predator can fool its prey. For example, a leafy sea dragon looks like a floating clump of seaweed. Small sea animals are not afraid to get close. Yet when they do, the leafy sea dragon catches them with its tube-shaped mouth.

FOCUS CHECK **How does mimicry help an animal survive.**

◄ The South American owl butterfly uses mimicry to scare away birds.

The bright color of the blue poison dart frog makes the frog easy to see and warns predators to stay away. ▶

Behavior

Behavior, as well as appearance, can help a predator as it hunts its prey. Humpback whales blow circles of bubbles around schools of fish. The fish cannot escape from the circle and become easy prey for the whales. Wolves and other animals hunt in groups. The group surrounds the prey so it cannot easily escape.

Behavior also helps prey survive. Rabbits run in a zig-zag pattern, which helps them dodge predators. Zebras use their hooves and teeth to defend themselves.

In some places, winter brings freezing temperatures and snow. Animals such as bats, frogs, chipmunks have an adaptation that helps them survive such weather.

These animals **hibernate** (HY bur nayt). They go into a deep sleep, during which they use very little energy and usually do not need to eat. In this deep sleep, the animal's heartbeat and breathing rate slow down greatly.

FOCUS CHECK **What are two examples of behaviors that help animals hunt?**

▲ The kangaroo rat survives in the desert by staying in its burrow during the heat of the day.

◄ This archer fish catches insects by shooting them down with a strong jet of water.

Lesson Wrap-Up

Visual Summary

Some animals have adaptations to survive winter cold.

Behaviors can help a predator hunt for prey.

Camouflage helps animals blend into their surroundings.

Check for Understanding

ADAPTATION DISPLAY

Choose three animals. Research the adaptations and behaviors that help them survive. Look for unique or interesting examples, such as the venom of spiders or snakes, the camouflage of chameleons, or the hibernation of chipmunks. Create a poster or display that shows how each adaptation or behavior helps the animal survive

✔ 0407.5.1

Review

❶ **MAIN IDEA** Explain why it is important for plants and animals to be adapted to their environment.

❷ **VOCABULARY** What is camouflage?

❸ **READING SKILL: Problem-Solution** How does hibernation help frogs survive the winter?

❹ **CRITICAL THINKING: Apply** Some katydids (KAY tee dihds) look like the leaves they live on. What might happen to a katydid in the fall when the leaves change color?

❺ **INQUIRY SKILL: Observe** What features of an insect would you observe to determine its adaptations? Give examples

TCAP Prep

A hawk is a bird that hunts small animals. Its adaptations include its

A clawed feet only.
B sharp beak only.
C strong wings only.
D feet, beak, wings, and other body parts.

SPI 0407.5.1

Technology

Visit **www.eduplace.com/tnscp** to find out more about adaptations for survival.

Master of Disguise

Can a blob of seaweed grin? No, you're looking at a goosefish. This flat, shaggy fish has the perfect camouflage for its ocean-floor habitat. By blending into the background, it can hide from both its predators and prey.

Fortunately for the goosefish, other fish rarely notice its spooky face. They're too interested in one of its other remarkable features.

Attached to a spike on its head is a structure that looks like a worm. When prey approach this wiggling bait, the goosefish opens its big mouth. It gulps them down in an instant!

GLE 0407.5.1 Analyze physical and behavioral adaptations that enable organisms to survive in their environment.

EXTEND

Can You Find Me?

Bugs, beware! The goldenrod spider can camouflage itself by turning yellow or white to match its flowery hunting ground.

Hey! Some of those leaves have legs! The camouflage often fools prey and predators of the praying mantis.

Pink disguise! The body of a pygmy seahorse blends into the gorgonian coral it resembles.

TENNESSEE STANDARDS

GLE 0407.5.1 Analyze physical and behavioral adaptations that enable organisms to survive in their environment.

GLE 0407.Inq.4 Identify and interpret simple patterns of evidence to communicate the findings of multiple investigations.

Guiding Question

What Threatens the Survival of Species?

Why It Matters . . .

The giant panda eats only bamboo. To survive, it needs to eat large amounts. Yet people have cut down bamboo to use the land for other purposes. Because pandas have less bamboo to eat, they may not survive in the wild.

PREPARE TO INVESTIGATE

Inquiry Skill

Compare When you compare two things, you observe how they are alike and how they are different.

Materials

- 3 plastic containers of pond water, labeled A, B, and C
- flashlight

Science and Math Toolbox

For step 1, review **Making a Chart to Organize Data** on page H10.

Directed Inquiry

Algae Growth

Procedure

1 **Collaborate** Work with a partner. In your *Science Notebook*, make a chart like the one shown.

2 **Observe** Shine a flashlight through the side of each of three containers of pond water. Record your observations in the chart.

3 **Infer** Two of the containers have different amounts of plant food mixed with the pond water. One contains no plant food. Infer which jar contains a small amount of plant food, which contains a large amount of plant food, and which contains no plant food. Based on your observations in step 2, make an inference about which container has the most plant food.

4 **Observe** Put the containers in a sunny window for four days. Then repeat steps 2 and 3.

5 **Communicate** Write a brief paragraph in your *Science* Notebook explaining how you made your inferences.

Think and Write

1. **Predict** What effect do you think adding plant food would have on algae growth in a small pond?

2. **Hypothesize** In what way could adding plant food to a small pond be a threat to the survival of other organisms in the pond?

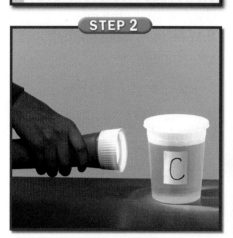

STEP 1

Container	A	B	C
Observations at start			
Inferences			
Observations after 4 days			
Inferences			

STEP 2

STEP 3

Guided Inquiry

Solve a Problem You notice that the water in a pond has begun to look cloudy. Working as a team, make a plan to find out what caused this change and what you might do to restore the pond.

Threats to Survival

VOCABULARY

extinct

migrate

species

GRAPHIC ORGANIZER

Cause and Effect Use a chart to show the effect that animals have on their environment.

GLE 0407.5.2 Describe how environmental changes caused the extinction of various plant and animal species.

How Organisms Change Environments

Swarms of South American leaf-cutter ants march to a tree. Each ant cuts a large piece of a leaf and carries it back to the nest. The leaves are used by the insects to grow fungi—their food source. In the process, an entire tree may lose all of its leaves and be destroyed. Organisms living in or on the tree have lost their home.

Whether it is an ant, a plant, or a human, every living thing causes changes in its environment. And these changes affect other living things.

Sometimes a change that is harmful to one organism is helpful to another. Although leaf-cutter ants destroy trees and other plants, they help fungi. In addition, new plants should grow where the old ones stood. Events and changes like these are common in any ecosystem.

Leaf-cutter ants can kill a tree, one leaf at a time.

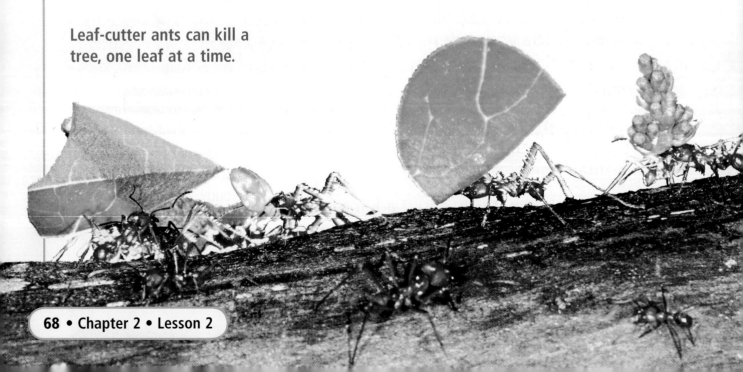

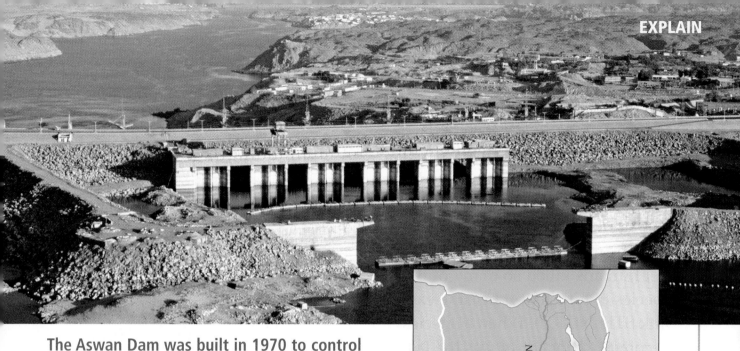

The Aswan Dam was built in 1970 to control floods that caused damage.

Nile River

EGYPT

Aswan Dam
Lake Nasser

Area that used to flood

For another example, think about a maple tree growing near a garden. As it grows, the tree provides a home for squirrels, birds, and other animals. Yet it also blocks the sunlight. Over time, only plants that require little light will survive beneath the tree.

Do you think humans change environments? Indeed, to meet their own needs, people have changed forests into cities, rivers into lakes, and hillsides into rubble. These changes have good and bad effects.

For example, the Aswan Dam in Egypt has helped people in many ways. The dam holds back the flood waters of the Nile River. By making water flow evenly, it improved river travel. It also provides electricity.

But the dam has done harm as well as good. Before the dam, flooding deposited silt along the river's banks, silt that enriched the soil. Today, farmers need to use more chemical fertilizers than ever before. Fish populations also have suffered.

The dam has disrupted the habitat of many plants and animals. Those that adapt best to the change have the best chance for survival.

FOCUS CHECK **What are some effects of the Aswan Dam?**

Express Lab

Activity Card
Protect Wildlife

Natural and Human Threats

Humans can be one of the biggest threats to the survival of a species (SPEE sheez). A **species** is a group of living things that produces living things of the same kind.

Once in America, passenger pigeons numbered in the millions. Yet humans killed so many of this species of bird that it became extinct (ihk STIHNGKT). When a species becomes **extinct**, it means the last member of that species has died.

Sometimes a species can be saved before it becomes extinct. Huge herds of American bison (BY suhn) once roamed the plains. They, too, were hunted so much that they were endangered, meaning almost extinct. The remaining bison were put into parks and reserves.

Some animals **migrate** (MY-grayt), or move to another region, when seasons change and food becomes scarce. Migrating animals face natural and human barriers. Natural barriers include mountain ranges. Some migrating birds will not cross mountains. Human barriers include highways. Migrating caribou usually will not cross highways.

FOCUS CHECK Name one threat to an organism's survival.

The Carolina northern flying squirrel is native to Tennessee. It is endangered because humans are clearing the trees in its habitat. ▼

▲ Martha was the last known passenger pigeon. She died in 1914.

Lesson Wrap-Up

Visual Summary

All living things cause changes in their environment.

Changes in a habitat, including changes made by humans, can have both good and bad effects.

There are human and natural threats to the survival of living things.

✔ Check for Understanding

EXTINCTION

Some organisms became extinct thousands and even millions of years ago. Compare some of these organisms to animals living today. How can fossils of extinct animals help protect endangered species?

✔ 0407.5.4

Review

1 MAIN IDEA Describe some things that can threaten the survival of a species.

2 VOCABULARY Use the term extinct in a sentence.

3 READING SKILL: Cause and Effect What positive and negative effects would building a new power plant have for different organisms?

4 CRITICAL THINKING: Analyze Do animals adapt better to a change than plants do? Give reasons to support your answer.

5 INQUIRY SKILL: Compare Use an example to explain how a threat to a species from natural causes differs from a threat that is caused by humans.

TCAP TCAP Prep

No members are left of a species that is

A endangered.
B extinct.
C protected.
D threatened.

SPI 0407.5.2

Go Digital Technology

Visit **www.eduplace.com/tnscp** to learn more about threats to survival.

DINOSAUR EXTINCTION

Scientists have found fossil bones from many kinds of dinosaurs. Some were the size of *Apatosaurus*, the dinosaur shown here. Others were small and birdlike. Still others were huge, ferocious predators, such as *Tyrannosaurus rex*.

Yet all dinosaurs share one thing in common: All died out at least 65 million years ago. Most scientists think that an asteroid struck Earth at that time. Others argue that volcanoes began erupting all at once. Either way, Earth's climate changed very quickly. The dinosaurs went extinct because their environment no longer supported their lives.

Matching mineral deposits from all over Earth are evidence of an asteroid strike, as argued by Walter Alvarez (right) and his father Luis (left). ▼

➤ **GLE 0407.5.2** Describe how environmental changes caused the extinction of various plant and animal species.

EXTEND

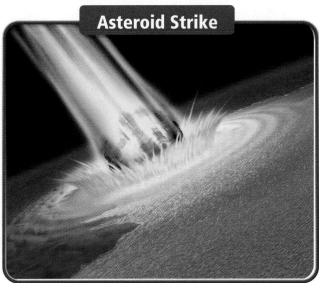

Asteroid Strike

How could an asteroid strike have changed Earth's climate? According to a theory, the strike raised a huge cloud of dust that blocked sunlight for years. Plants died, and dinosaurs soon followed.

Sharing Ideas

1. **READING CHECK** Describe one theory that explains how dinosaurs went extinct.

2. **WRITE ABOUT IT** Why is climate important for a species to survive? Include at least one example.

3. **TALK ABOUT IT** Do you think that studies of dinosaurs can apply to life on Earth today? Discuss.

GLE 0407.5.1 Analyze physical and behavorial adaptations that enable organisms to survive in their environment. **Math GLE 0406.2.4** Understand and use the connections between fractions and decimals. **ELA GLE 0401.4.1** Conduct research to access and present information.

Math Tennessee's Threatened and Endangered Species

The United States Fish and Wildlife Service has a list of Tennessee's threatened and endangered plants and animals. The list has 70 species of animals and 20 species of plants.

1. What fraction of the species on the list are plants?

2. Of the 70 animals on the list, 12 are threatened. Solve to find the decimal equal to the fraction 12/70. Round to the nearest hundredth.

$12 \div 70 =$ ☐

Writing Informational

Research a plant or an animal of your choice. Write an essay that describes the adaptations that help the animal survive in its environment. Be sure to cite the sources of your information.

Julia Kubanek

Your sense of smell is a response to certain chemicals in the air. First, your nose picks up such chemicals. Then your brain perceives them as an odor. Different odors may alert you to food, comfort, or danger.

Have you ever wondered if ocean animals have a sense of smell? As Professor Julia Kubanek would tell you, the answer often is yes. She studies how ocean animals use smell, or senses much like smell, to learn about their environment. She has shown that animals use chemical signals to find food, attract mates, or keep predators away.

This sponge releases a chemical that fish "smell." It tells the fish to keep away!

Vocabulary

Complete each sentence with a term from the list.

1. A group of living things that produces living things of the same kind is a/an _____.

2. The place where an organism lives is called its _____.

3. An adaptation in which an animal protects itself by looking like another kind of animal or a plant is _____.

4. An animal that goes into a deep sleep that helps it survive the winter is said to _____.

5. To help them hide, some animals have _____.

6. To move to another region when seasons change is to _____.

7. When the last member of a species dies, the species is _____.

8. The role of an organism in its environment is its _____.

9. Something that helps an organism survive is called a/an _____.

★ **adaptation**
camouflage
extinct
habitat
hibernate
migrate
mimicry
niche
species

TCAP Inquiry Skills

10. **Explain** Why are there so many endangered species in the world? List some of the ways humans can help bring these populations back.
    GLE 0407.5.2

11. **Compare** Compare camouflage and mimicry. How are they alike? How are they different? Give examples of each.
    GLE 0407.5.1

12. **Research** Research two endangered animals found in Tennessee. Describe the factors have made them in danger of extinction. **GLE 0407.5.2**

Map the Concept

Use the terms from the list to complete the concept map. You also may add other terms.

camouflage
pointed leaves
poison
talons
thick bark
thorns

Plants
_____
_____
_____

Adaptations

Animals
_____
_____
_____

GLE 0407.5.1

Critical Thinking

13. Synthesize Identify two adaptations that different organisms use to protect themselves from predators.

GLE 0407.5.1

14. Apply How might an ecosystem change if an animal that eats insects becomes extinct? GLE 0407.5.2

15. Evaluate Suppose a dam is built to stop flooding. In addition to flood control, what helpful effect might result? What harmful effect might also result? GLE 0407.5.2

16. Analyze How does hibernating help an animal when food is scarce?

GLE 0407.5.1

Check for Understanding

Tennesssee Plants and Animals

Research two or three plants or animals that are found in Tennessee. Find out how adaptations help them survive local weather conditions, as well as find food, shelter, and water. Make a poster to show your findings.

0407.5.1

TCAP Prep

Choose the letter of the best answer choice.

17 When does a chipmunk hibernate?

A over winter

B over summer

C during rainy weather

D when prey are scarce SPI 0407.5.1

18 A frog with which adaptation is most likely to be poisonous?

F camouflage

G slimy skin

H strong legs

J bright body color SPI 0407.5.1

19 In the 1800s, humans hunted huge numbers of American bison. The species almost became

A extinct

B exported

C endangered

D migrated SPI 0407.5.2

20 Camouflage may help an animal hide from

F predators only.

G prey only.

H predators and prey.

J small animals only. SPI 0407.5.1

Chapter 3

Energy in Ecosystems

LESSON

1

It moves from the Sun, to plants, to animals that eat plants, and to animals that eat other animals. What is it that goes from the Sun through this chain of living things?

LESSON

2

Every ecosystem is a complex web of relationships among different kinds of organisms. What animals might compete with each other to eat this grasshopper?

LESSON

3

A very small organism may help a large organism survive. What are some examples of this?

Fun Facts

Menu Menu

Snakes are true carnivores because they eat nothing but other animals.

Vocabulary Preview

carnivore
food chain
food web
herbivore
omnivore

 Vocabulary Strategies

Have you ever seen any of these terms before? Do you know what they mean?

State a description, explanation, or example of the vocabulary in your own words.

Draw a picture, symbol, example, or other image that describes the term.

Glossary p. H16

carnivore

omnivore

food web

herbivore

Start with Your Standards

Inquiry

GLE 0407.Inq.1 Explore different scientific phenomena by asking questions, making logical predictions, planning investigations, and recording data.

GLE 0407.Inq.3 Organize data into appropriate tables, graphs, drawings, or diagrams.

Life Science

Standard 2 Interdependence

GLE 0407.2.1 Analyze the effects of changes in the environment on the stability of an ecosystem.

Standard 3 Flow of Matter and Energy

GLE 0407.3.1 Demonstrate that plants require light energy to grow and survive.

GLE 0407.3.2 Investigate different ways that organisms meet their energy needs.

Standard 5 Biodiversity and Change

GLE 0407.5.1 Analyze physical and behavioral adaptations that enable organisms to survive in their environment.

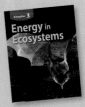

Interact with this chapter.

 www.eduplace.com/tnscp

TENNESSEE STANDARDS

GLE 0407.3.2 Investigate different ways that organisms meet their energy needs.
GLE 0407.Inq.3 Organize data into appropriate tables, graphs, drawings, or diagrams.

Guiding Question

What Are Food Chains?

Building Background...

Corn plants use the Sun's energy to grow. You eat corn for its taste and for the energy it contains. A salmon gets energy from the smaller fish it eats. You, or a hawk if it gets there first, get energy from the salmon. You or the hawk, the salmon, the small fish, and the corn are parts of food chains.

Science and Math Toolbox

For steps 1 and 3, review **Using a Hand Lens** on page H2.

PREPARE TO INVESTIGATE

Inquiry Skill

Ask Questions You ask questions to find out how or why something that you observe happens. Questions can lead to scientific investigations.

Materials

- goggles
- disposable gloves
- owl pellet
- paper towel
- tweezers
- toothpick
- hand lens

Directed Inquiry

What Owls Eat

Procedure

STEP 1

1. **Observe** Spread out a paper towel on your work surface. Use tweezers to place an owl pellet on the paper towel. An owl pellet is made up of the undigested food of an owl. Use a hand lens to observe it. **Safety:** Wear goggles and disposable gloves.

2. **Record Data** In your *Science Notebook*, make a chart like the one shown. Record what you observe using the hand lens.

STEP 2

Description of Item	Drawing

3. Use tweezers and a toothpick to gently pull apart the pellet into small pieces. Look at each piece through the hand lens. Record your observations in your chart.

4. **Classify** Group similar items when you find them. In your *Science Notebook*, list categories for the types of things you have found. **Safety:** Wash your hands thoroughly when you finish the activity.

STEP 3

Think and Write

1. **Classify** What items did you find? How did you group them? What observations support your way of grouping the items?

2. **Infer** Based on your observations, in what kind of ecosystem do you think an owl lives?

3. **Ask Questions** Write a list of questions you have about what other organisms live in an owl's ecosystem.

Guided Inquiry

Experiment Ask your teacher to help you find and use a microscope. **Observe** the objects that you found in the owl pellet. What did you learn about what owls can and cannot digest?

0407.3.3

Food Chains

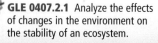
Energy from the Sun

All living things need energy to survive. They get that energy from food. Some animals eat plants. Some animals eat other animals that eat plants.

Plants do not eat food. Most plants make their own food through photosynthesis. Photosynthesis takes place in a plant's leaves. A material in the leaves traps light energy from the Sun. During photosynthesis, plants use carbon dioxide gas from the air and water in soil to make food in the form of sugar. The original source of energy for most living things is the Sun.

Sun

plant

Energy flows from the Sun to plants to prey to predators.

Predator and Prey

Recall that an animal that hunts other animals for food is called a predator. A fox is one kind of predator, and a rabbit is one of its prey. An animal can be both predator and prey. For example, a fox may be the prey of a bobcat.

The photographs show how energy flows from the Sun to plants and to animals. Recall that plants are producers and animals are consumers. When a consumer, such as a rabbit, eats a plant, it receives some of the plant's energy. When the rabbit becomes the prey of the fox, the fox receives some of the plant's energy.

In a pond ecosystem, tiny plants and plantlike organisms are the producers. They use the Sun's energy to make food. Tiny animals eat the plants. The tiny animals are prey to small fish. The small fish are eaten by larger fish.

In almost every ecosystem, energy flows from the Sun to producers, and then to consumers. Among the consumers, energy flows from prey to predator. When tiny animals in a pond eat the tiny plants, energy flows to the tiny animals. When predators eat the tiny animals, energy flows to the predators.

⊙FOCUS CHECK What is the relationship between a predator and its prey?

prey

predator

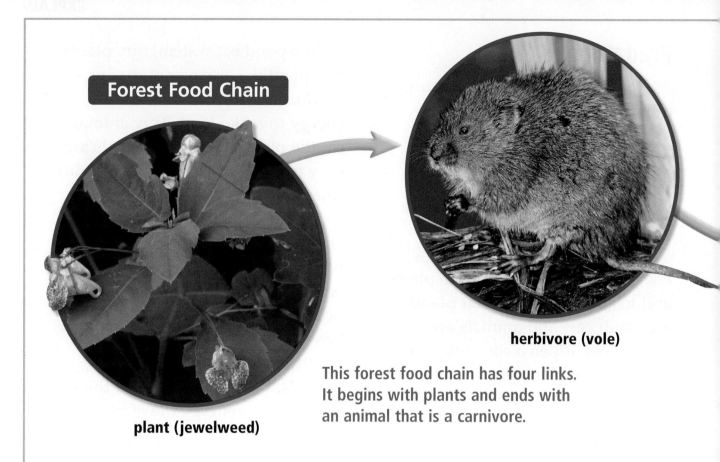

Forest Food Chain

plant (jewelweed)

herbivore (vole)

This forest food chain has four links. It begins with plants and ends with an animal that is a carnivore.

Food Chains

A **food chain** (chayn) shows the path of food energy in an ecosystem from plants to animals. In the food chain shown, a vole gets energy from eating a plant called jewelweed. A skunk gets energy from eating a vole. An owl gets energy from eating the skunk.

Food chains are different in different ecosystems. But the first link in any food chain is always a producer. In most ecosystems, the producers are green plants. Matter and energy enter the food chain through these plants. This happens when the plants, such as the jewelweed, use the energy in sunlight to make food through the process of photosynthesis.

The second link in the food chain shown is a vole. A vole is an herbivore (HUR buh vawr). An **herbivore** is an animal that eats only plants. The vole gets energy from the green plants it eats.

The third and fourth links in any food chain are either omnivores (AHM nuh vawrz) or carnivores (KAHR nuh vawrz). An **omnivore** is an animal that eats both plants and animals. A skunk is an omnivore. It eats insects, earthworms, mice, and voles. It also eats berries and nuts. A **carnivore** is an animal that eats only other animals. The great horned owl is a carnivore.

omnivore (skunk)

predator (owl)

In a pond ecosystem, tiny plants and plantlike organisms are the first link in the food chain. The tiny animals that eat these organisms are the second link in the chain. Recall that plant-eating organisms are herbivores. Other links in a pond food chain are the small and large fish that eat the herbivores.

A raccoon is an omnivore that is often a part of a pond ecosystem. A raccoon eats the small fish in the chain. Because it is an omnivore, it also eats plant parts such as berries and acorns.

Seaweed is the first link in some ocean food chains. Small animals called limpets eat the seaweed. Limpets are herbivores and the second link in the chain. Crabs eat limpets. Some crabs are omnivores, but most crabs are carnivores.

Seagulls eat crabs. They are omnivores and the last organisms in this food chain.

Organisms depend on each other for food, but they also compete with each other. Competition for resources can occur at several points in the same food chain. For example, seagulls eat both fish and crabs. But seals and other predators also eat fish and crabs. So seagulls, seals, and other predators compete for the fish and crabs in the ocean.

FOCUS CHECK What are the third and fourth links in a food chain?

Express Lab

Activity Card
Put Yourself in a Food Chain

87

The Energy Pyramid

As shown in the energy pyramid, at each link in a food chain some of the food energy is used. For example, plants do not store all the food that they make. Some of the energy from the food is used to develop flowers and seeds.

Only part of the energy that the plants captured from the Sun is available to jackrabbits that eat the plants. The jackrabbits use some of the energy to look for food, grow, and run from predators. So less energy is available to predators, such as bobcats, that eat jackrabbits.

In a food chain, the further a population of organisms is from producers (plants), the less energy is available to that population. For this reason, the population size of a predator is usually smaller than the population size of its prey. For the same reason, most food chains have only four or five links.

FOCUS CHECK What happens to available energy at each link in the food chain?

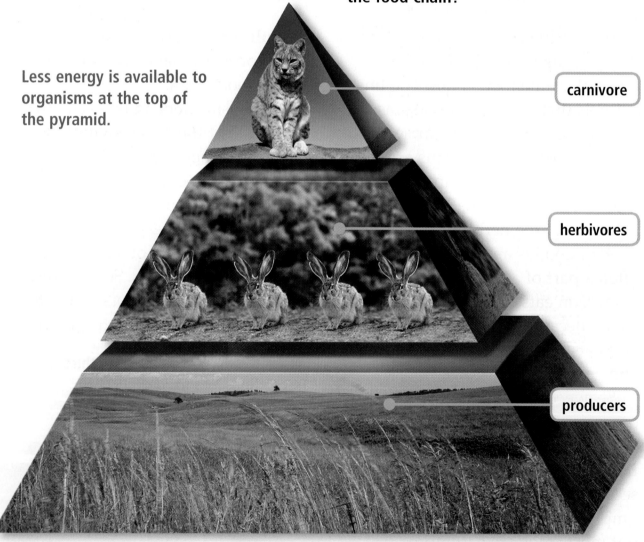

Less energy is available to organisms at the top of the pyramid.

carnivore

herbivores

producers

Lesson Wrap-Up

Visual Summary

Plants produce their own food using the Sun's energy. Animals eat plants and get some of that energy.

Many herbivores are prey for carnivores and omnivores. All animals are part of a food chain.

At each link in a food chain, some of the food energy is used. Less energy is available the further an organism is from the producers.

Check for Understanding

CLASSIFY ORGANISMS

Snakes, foxes, mice, and raccoons are all in the same ecosystem. Classify each of these animals as a carnivore, herbivore, or an omnivore.

✔ 0407.3.2

Review

❶ **MAIN IDEA** What is the primary source of energy in most ecosystems?

❷ **VOCABULARY** What does a food chain show?

❸ **READING SKILL:** Show the sequence of energy flow in an ecosystem.

❹ **CRITICAL THINKING:** Analyze How can an animal be both predator and prey? Explain.

❺ **INQUIRY SKILL:** Questions Write a list of questions you have about food chains in a fresh water ecosystem.

TCAP TCAP Prep

An herbivore cannot be a

A consumer.
B prey.
C plant eater.
D producer.

SPI 0407.3.1

 **Technology**

Visit **www.eduplace.com/tnscp** to find out more about food chains

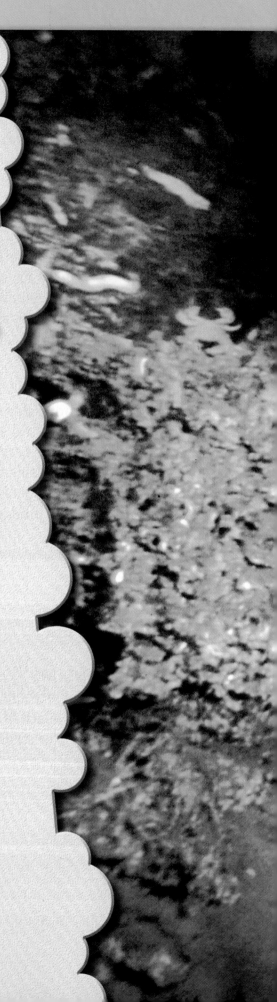

EXTREME Science

Dining in the Dark

Extreme pressure, extreme temperatures, no sunlight! What could possibly live near an undersea hydrothermal (hot water) vent? How about 2.4-meter-long tubeworms? Scientists were shocked to discover this new life form living in conditions that would kill most other creatures.

The tubeworm has no eyes, no mouth—and no inside structures! So, how does it eat? It doesn't! Tubeworms get the nutrients they need by absorbing food produced by bacteria that live inside them. The bacteria get their energy from chemicals coming out of the vents. They do not depend on the Sun, because there is no sunlight that deep in the ocean! The discovery that a food chain did not have to start with energy from the Sun was a big surprise to scientists.

GLE 0407.5.1 Analyze physical and behavioral adaptations that enable organisms to survive in their environment.

EXTEND

Almost all life on Earth depends on solar energy, but the giant tubeworms do just fine dining in the dark!

This hydrothermal vent, called a "black smoker," shoots out water that is more than 400°C—four times as hot as boiling water!

📕 **TENNESSEE STANDARDS**

GLE 0407.3.2 Investigate different ways that organisms meet their energy needs.

GLE 0407.Inq.3 Organize data into appropriate tables, graphs, drawings, or diagrams.

What Are Food Webs?

Building Background...

There are many different plants and animals in an African grassland ecosystem such as the one shown. Each plant and animal may be part of more than one food chain. All these food chains overlap to make a food web.

PREPARE TO INVESTIGATE

Inquiry Skill

Research When you do research, you learn more about a subject by looking in books, searching the Internet, or asking science experts.

Materials

- Food Web Support Master
- reference books
- 4 index cards
- construction paper
- markers or crayons
- scissors

Directed Inquiry

A Tangled Web

Procedure

STEP 2

1. **Research** Work with a partner. Use a reference book. From the Food Web Support Master provided, find a plant-eating animal. In your *Science Notebook,* record that animal and the plants it eats. Then research and record an animal from the list that eats the plant eater. Next, find a new animal that eats that one.

2. On separate index cards, draw and label each living thing from step 1.

STEP 3

3. **Use Models** Place the index cards in order on construction paper to show a food chain. Draw arrows to show how energy flows from one living thing to another.

4. **Experiment** Remove the index cards, and turn over your construction paper. Work with another team. Use cards from both teams to make a food web. A **food web** is two or more overlapping food chains. Draw arrows to show how energy flows.

STEP 4

Think and Write

1. **Infer** Does energy flow from plant eaters to animal eaters or from animal eaters to plant eaters? How do you know?

2. **Predict** What might happen if one kind of animal were removed from the web?

Guided Inquiry

Ask Questions What questions do you have about a food web in an ecosystem near your school?

Research answers for one or two questions by asking an expert.

✓ 0407.3.1

Food Webs

VOCABULARY

food web

GRAPHIC ORGANIZER

Classify Use the diagram below to list two food chains that overlap.

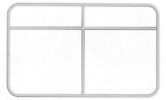

GLE 0407.2.1 Analyze the effects of changes in the environment on the stability of an ecosystem.

GLE 0407.3.2 Investigate different ways that organisms meet their energy needs.

Chains and Webs

Most ecosystems contain many different kinds of plants and animals. Each plant or animal is part of more than one food chain. When two or more food chains overlap, they form a **food web**. In a food web, at least one plant or animal from each food chain is part of another food chain.

For example, the creosote (KREE uh soht) bush, the grasshopper, the flicker, and the hawk form a food chain. They are also part of a food web. In the food web shown, the creosote bush is food not only for the grasshopper, but also for jackrabbits and kangaroo rats. The creosote bush is part of several food chains.

The hawk is also part of several food chains. The hawk may eat flickers, jackrabbits, and kangaroo rats. The arrows show some of the food chains that form this desert food web.

FOCUS CHECK What is the difference between a food chain and a food web?

The Mojave Desert is one type of land ecosystem where there are many overlapping food chains. ▶

Creosote bushes give off an odor like tar, but that doesn't stop animals from eating them.

Express Lab

Activity Card
Dissect a Food Web

A Desert Food Web

The red-tailed hawk can soar over the desert and spot prey from far away. In the Mojave Desert, it can find small mammals and birds to eat.

The creosote bush grasshopper feeds on only this type of bush. The grasshopper is food for birds in the desert.

A red-shafted flicker snatches insects with its long, barbed tongue.

Kangaroo rats eat the seeds of the creosote bush and burrow under it to avoid the desert Sun.

The jackrabbit moves quickly to escape predators such as the hawk. It may stop where it can hide and eat at the same time.

An Ocean Food Web

Seagulls are among many sea birds that dive to feed on fish.

algae

Krill, tiny shrimplike animals, eat algae. Krill are food for fish, sea birds, and marine mammals, such as whales.

Small fish such as Pacific herring are food for sea birds, larger fish, and some marine mammals such as whales.

Some kinds of whales eat krill. Others eat small fish.

salmon

An ocean food web is a huge network of relationships between organisms.

Sharks eat just about any fish they can find, including salmon.

Visual Summary

In every kind of ecosystem, energy enters food webs through plants and plantlike organisms.

Some plants and animals link together in many overlapping food chains to make a food web.

Many organisms, from tiny algae to giant whales, form overlapping food chains to make up an ocean food web.

Check for Understanding

PREDATOR BOOM

Look at the ocean food web. What would happen if the number of sharks doubled? What would happen if the algae dies out due to an oil spill in the area?

✔ 0407.2.1

Review

1 MAIN IDEA What is a food web?

2 VOCABULARY Describe one food web.

3 READING SKILL: Divide desert organisms into two categories, prey and predator. Are some organisms on both lists? Explain.

4 CRITICAL THINKING:
Synthesize What organisms would be affected if there were no algae in the ocean?

5 INQUIRY SKILL: Research List five words that you could use to search the Internet for more information on food webs.

TCAP Prep

Which of the following animals does not eat creosote bushes?

A grasshopper
B red-tailed hawk
C jackrabbit
D kangaroo rat

SPI 0407.2.1

Technology

Visit **www.eduplace.com/tnscp** to learn more about food webs.

Earth's ecosystems inspire writers of both fiction and science. Compare these two selections about the Everglades of Florida.

Some Rivers

by Frank Asch

Some rivers rush to the sea.
They push and tumble and fall.
But the Everglades is a river
with no hurry in her at all.
Soaking the cypress
that grows so tall;
nursing a frog,
so quiet and small;
she flows but a mile
in the course of a day,
with plenty of time
to think on the way.
But how can she cope
with the acres of corn
and sorrowful cities that drain her?
With hunters and tourists and levees
that chain and stain and pain her?
Does the half of her that's left
think only of the past?
Or does she think of her future
and how long it will last?
Some rivers rush to the sea.
They push and tumble and fall.
But the Everglades is a river
with no hurry in her at all.

GLE 0407.2.1 Analyze the effects of changes in the environment on the stability of an ecosystem.

EXTEND

The River of Grass

Prologue to Everglades: Buffalo Tiger and the River of Grass, **by Peter Lourie**

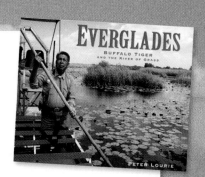

In the early sixteenth century the Spanish explorer Ponce de León searched the coast of Florida for the Fountain of Youth. He never discovered the mythical fountain, but if he had penetrated deeper into the peninsula that the Spaniards called "the land of flowers," he might have found something else: the Everglades, a slow-moving swamp that is in fact a huge, silent river.

The Everglades, called Pa-hay-okee, or "Grassy Water," by the Miccosukee Indians, is often only inches deep, yet it runs a hundred miles from Florida's Lake Okeechobee to the Gulf of Mexico and Florida Bay. In places it is seventy miles wide. It has been called a river of grass because of the dense waves of tawny sawgrass arcing gently to the south, pointing in the direction of the sluggish flow of the water.

The Miccosukee Indians have lived in the Everglades for more than a hundred years. When they first arrived they found the river of grass to be a kind of paradise. Even today, the Grassy Water dazzles the eye with its abundance of birds and other wildlife. Yet, unlike a hundred years ago, there is sadness in this bright spot on the planet. Great pressures from pollution and overdevelopment threaten to destroy the river of grass.

Sharing Ideas

1. **READING CHECK** According to both passages, what major problems threaten the stability of the Everglades?

2. **WRITE ABOUT IT** Why is the Everglades a special, unique place? Express your ideas.

3. **TALK ABOUT IT** What do you think should be done to protect the Everglades?

GLE 0407.2.1 Analyze the effects of changes in the environment on the stability of an ecosystem. **Math GLE 0406.1.4** Move flexibly between concrete and abstract representations of mathematical ideas in order to solve problems, model mathematical ideas, and communicate solution strategies. **ELA GLE 0401.3.1** Write for a variety of purposes and to a variety of audiences.

MATH How Many Limpets and Crabs?

Suppose that a huge wave uprooted a large amount of seaweed in an ocean ecosystem. Because they did not have enough seaweed to eat, half the limpets in the area died.

1. What additional information would you need to find out how many limpets were left?

2. Crabs eat limpets, as well as other organisms. Which of these statements is likely to be more accurate?

    a. The number of crabs in the area is likely to decrease slightly.

    b. The number of crabs in the area would decrease by half.

 ## Descriptive

Choose one plant or animal, such as a tree or an insect, that is part of the ecosystem you live in or one that you have visited. If possible, choose an organism that you have spent some time looking at. Write a description of the plant or animal. In your description include details that you would recognize by using your senses. For example, you would know that a rabbit had soft fur by using your sense of touch.

Pet-Store Owner

Squawk! Bark! Meow! If you like to spend your day with animals, you might want to work in a pet store.

A pet-store owner must provide for the needs of many kinds of animals. For example, fish need clean water, birds need perches, and large animals need space to move around. A pet store must provide healthy environments for all the animals it sells.

What It Takes!

- An interest in animals and people
- Skills in running a business

Ecologist

How will building new houses and roads change a nearby forest? Why are there fewer fish in a lake now than in the past? Ecologists look for answers to questions like these.

Ecologists study how living things interact with each other and with their environment. The ecologist's goal is to help people make wise decisions about things that may affect the natural world.

What It Takes!

- An interest in the natural world
- A college degree in life science

Vocabulary

Complete each sentence with a term from the list.

1. Two or more overlapping food chains form a _____.

2. An animal that only eats other animals is a/an _____.

3. A small fish eats algae. A big fish eats the small fish. This describes a/an _____.

4. A bear eats both berries and fish, so it is a/an _____.

5. An animal that eats only plants is a/an _____.

carnivore

food chain

food web

herbivore

omnivore

TCAP Inquiry Skills

6. **Ask Questions** Write a question about a food chain you might find in an ocean ecosystem. What research would you have to do to answer your question? **GLE 0407.Inq.1**

7. **Communicate** Look back at pages 82 and 83. Describe each part of the instructions for the investigation and tell why each is important.

GLE 0407.Inq.1

8. **Use Models** Draw a food web that includes at least six organisms. Label each organism to show its role.

GLE 0407.3.2

9. **Predict** A pond community is home to 40 turtles. A breeder adds 80 more turtles to the pond. What will happen to the pond community? **GLE 0407.2.1**

10. **Apply** Your friend tells you that she is a vegetarian and does not eat meat. What kind of consumer is your friend? Explain. **GLE 0407.3.2**

Map the Concept

Use the concept map to show a food chain. Write each term in the correct place on the map.

hawk

insect

grass

skunk

GLE 0407.3.2

1._____

2._____

3._____

4._____

Critical Thinking

11. Analyze How does an herbivore benefit from the Sun's energy?

GLE 0407.3.1

12. Evaluate Tell whether the following statement is accurate: Herbivores and carnivores are more important to a food web than are omnivores. Give reasons for your answer. Use examples in your explanation. **GLE 0407.3.2**

13. Synthesize What would be the likely effect on an ocean food web if one type of fish in the web were to die off?

GLE 0407.2.1

14. Apply Why are there usually only four or five links in a food chain?

GLE 0407.3.2

 **Check for Understanding**

Parts of a Food Chain

Design an experiment to show the effects of competition and interdependency on a food chain, such as a city park. Identify what tools you would use to conduct your experiment. ✔ **0407.2.2**

TCAP **TCAP Prep**

Write the letter of the best answer choice.

15 Plankton form the _____ of an ocean food chain.
- **A** middle
- **B** end
- **C** beginning
- **D** consumers   SPI 0407.3.1

16 An herbivore might eat _____.
- **F** grass.
- **G** worms.
- **H** omnivores.
- **J** insects.   SPI 0407.3.1

17 A food web may include _____.
- **A** carnivores.
- **B** herbivores.
- **C** producers.
- **D** all of the above.   SPI 0407.3.1

18 In a food chain, as an organism gets further from the producer, the amount of energy available _____.
- **F** increases.
- **G** decreases.
- **H** remains the same.
- **J** decreases then increases.   SPI 0407.3.1

5 Biodiversity and Change

Performance Indicator: **SPI 0407.5.1 Determine how a physical or behavioral adaptation can enhance the chances of survival.**

1 A butterfly has markings on its wings that resemble owl eyes. What are the markings an example of?

A camouflage
B hibernation
C mimicry
D migration

2 Which animal uses echolocation to locate objects?

F

G

H

J

1 Cells

Performance Indicator: **SPI 0407.1.1 Compare basic structures of plant and animal cells.**

3 Which part of a plant cell gives the cell shape?

A mitochondria
B nucleus
C vacuole
D cell wall

5 Biodiversity and Change

Performance Indicator: **SPI 0407.5.2 Infer the possible reasons why a species became endangered or extinct.**

4 Which of these changes would most harm the organisms of a pond community?

  A the death of the largest fish in the pond
  B several days of heavy rain
  C people draining much of the pond's water
  D the arrival of winter

5 What event could explain the graph data?

  F The species went extinct in 2002.
  G The animals migrated every spring.
  H The animals hibernated every winter.
  J The animals were overhunted and became endangered.

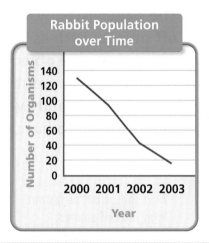

Rabbit Population over Time

3 Flow of Matter and Energy

Performance Indicator: **SPI 0407.3.1 Determine how different organisms function within an environment in terms of their location on an energy pyramid.**

6 Which of the following would likely be found at the top of an energy pyramid?

  A carnivore
  B scavenger
  C herbivore
  D omnivore

7 Which part of the plant uses sunlight and air to help the plant make food?

  F 1 only
  G 3 only
  H 2 and 3
  J 3 and 4

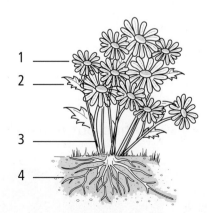

Discover More

Most bats sleep during the day and are active at night. An insect-eating bat uses echolocation to find food. To echolocate, the bat uses its ears and its ability to make high-pitched sounds.

The bat constantly sends out high-pitched sounds. The sounds bounce off objects, such as trees, houses, and flying insects. The sounds return from the objects as echoes. The bat uses its highly sensitive hearing to interpret the echoes. The bat can tell from the echo the exact location and even the size and speed of an object. That's a handy ability to have when hunting flying insects in the dark.

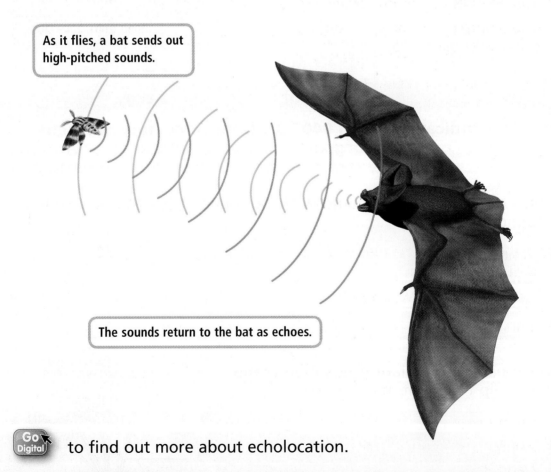

As it flies, a bat sends out high-pitched sounds.

The sounds return to the bat as echoes.

Go Digital ▸ to find out more about echolocation.

EARTH UNIT B SCIENCE

TENNESSEE

TENNESSEE EXCURSIONS AND ENGINEERING PROJECT

How's the Weather?

What is the climate of your area? How is the weather in your area? What is the difference? Weather is what is happening in the atmosphere right now. Weather is rain or snow or a thunderstorm or a cold front. Weather is the reason for a sunny day with no clouds. Climate tells us about average weather over a long period of time. When you want to know what the weather will be like in two months, you have to know your area's climate. If it is usually dry and mild in April, then it will most likely be that way every April. There will be days when the weather doesn't match that description, but overall the climate pretty much stays the same.

The National Weather Service monitors weather all over the country.

Tracking Climate and Weather

The National Weather Service, or NWS, was formed in 1870. President Grant wanted the military to take weather readings from the middle of the country. Because most weather moves from west to east, weather for the eastern and southern parts of the country could be predicted. This would help protect people and their property, including businesses and farms. Over many years of observations, the NWS was able to describe the climate for many areas of the country.

Nashville has an office of the NWS called a Weather Forecast Office. There are 122 of these offices around the country. They gather and interpret data related to weather. Using all of the data from all of the offices allows the NWS to predict weather for the entire country many days ahead of time. This helps people and businesses plan their activities. The information also helps the NWS make climate predictions. Scientists at the NWS combine recent weather data with what is known about the climate of the region. Using this data, they predict what the temperatures and precipitation will be like over the next several months or even years. The NWS can predict whether the climate will change or remain as it has in the past.

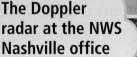

The Doppler radar at the NWS Nashville office

Think and Write

1 Scientific Thinking The climate data of your area shows that January is cold and snowy. If there are a few days that are sunny and warmer, will this affect the overall climate? Why or why not?

2 Science and Technology Research different instruments and technologies that have been used over the years to track weather. How have they changed? How have they stayed the same?

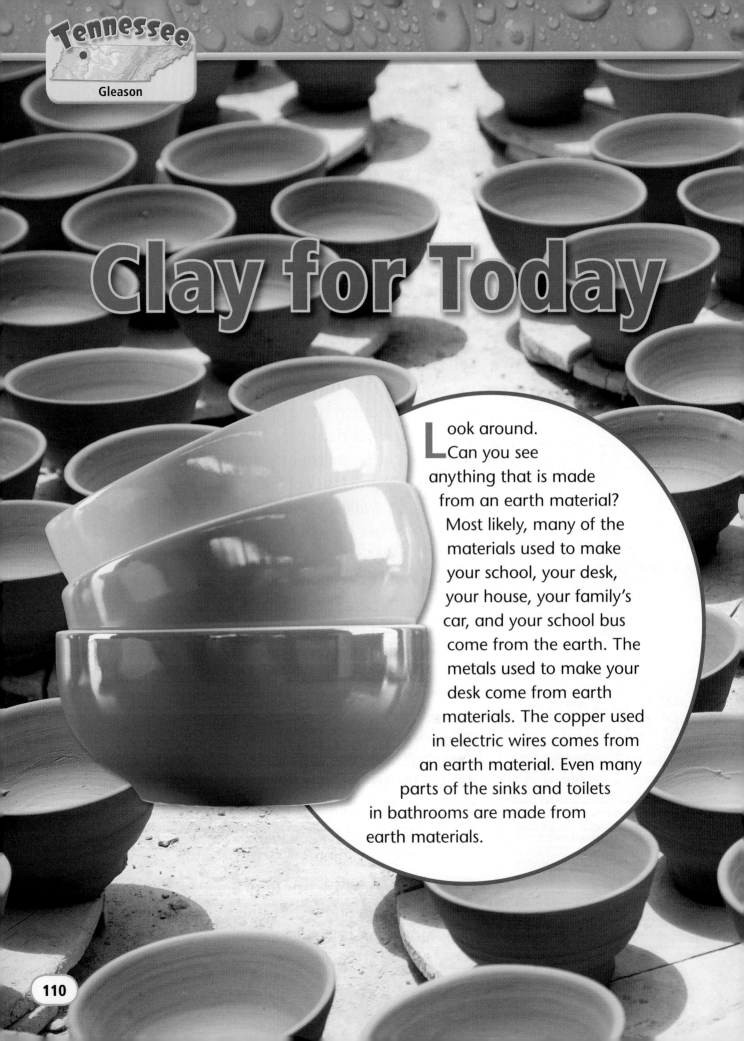

Clay for Today

Look around. Can you see anything that is made from an earth material? Most likely, many of the materials used to make your school, your desk, your house, your family's car, and your school bus come from the earth. The metals used to make your desk come from earth materials. The copper used in electric wires comes from an earth material. Even many parts of the sinks and toilets in bathrooms are made from earth materials.

GLE 0407.7.2 Evaluate how some earth materials can be used to solve human problems and enhance the quality of life.

ENGAGE

Tennessee Ball Clay

Ball clay is an earth material. It is used to make sinks, toilets, pottery, kitchen and bathroom tiles, dinner plates, bricks, and many other things. Ball clay is stronger and more flexible than other clays. When it is mixed with other clays, it adds strength and flexibility to the mixture. This makes ball clay perfect for use in items that need to be molded into a specific shape.

Near Gleason, Tennessee, mines produce almost 400 million kg (882 million lb) of ball clay each year. This clay is shipped all over the world and used in all kinds of different products. Ball clay gets its name from the old way people mined it. They cut it from the ground in cubes. After the cubes had been handled a little bit, the corners became smooth and rounded and the cubes became balls. The name is still used even though mining procedures and tools have changed. Ball clay is an earth material that helps improve people's lives in many different ways.

Modern ball clay mining

Ball clay is used to make many everyday items, such as these bowls.

Think and Write

1 Scientific Inquiry Research different types of clay. List factors that determine the appropriate use for each type of clay you researched.

2 Scientific Thinking If you had clays with different properties, how would you find out the best ways to use them?

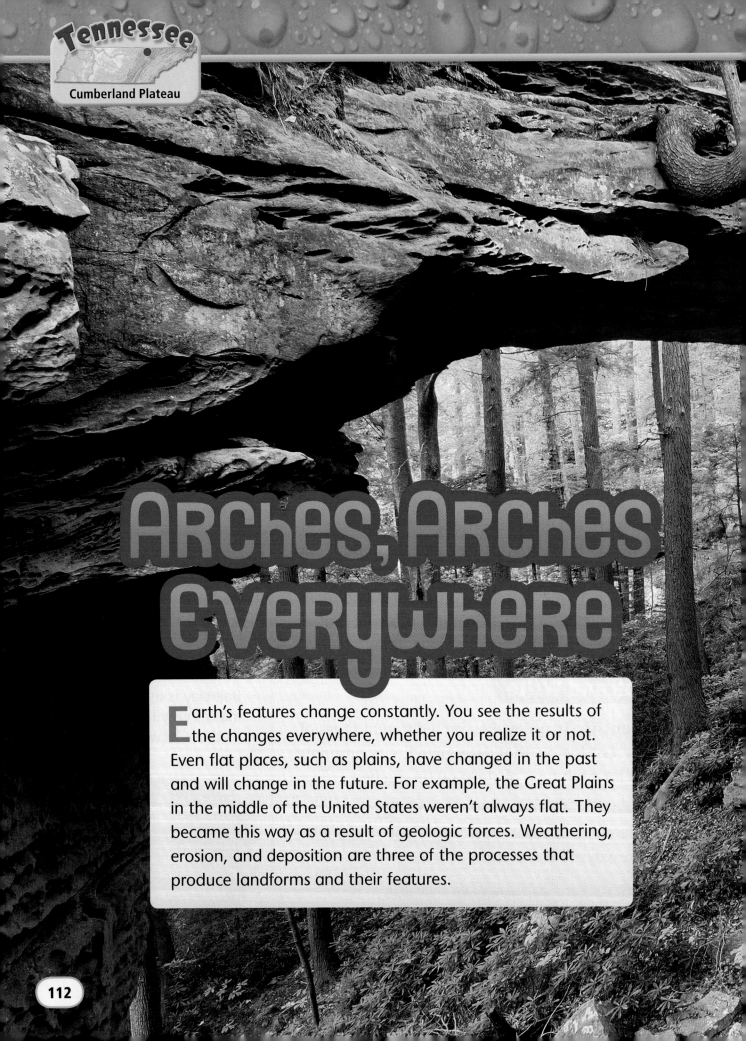

Arches, Arches Everywhere

Earth's features change constantly. You see the results of the changes everywhere, whether you realize it or not. Even flat places, such as plains, have changed in the past and will change in the future. For example, the Great Plains in the middle of the United States weren't always flat. They became this way as a result of geologic forces. Weathering, erosion, and deposition are three of the processes that produce landforms and their features.

GLE 0407.7.1 Investigate how Earth's geological features change as a result of erosion (weathering and transportation) and deposition.

ENGAGE

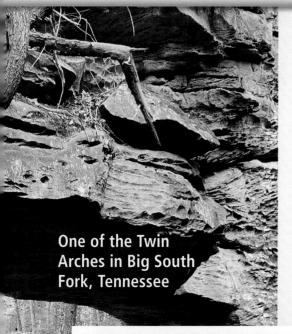

One of the Twin Arches in Big South Fork, Tennessee

Nature's Bridges

The Cumberland Plateau formed from materials that were weathered, eroded, and deposited from the Appalachian Mountains to the east. This process took millions of years. During and after the plateau's formation, weathering, erosion, and deposition have also shaped the plateau's features. That is why the Cumberland Plateau is full of cliffs, waterfalls, hills, valleys, and natural arches.

Some natural arches are formed by water as it cuts through rock during many, many years. The arches are made of strong earth material. Much of the surrounding material is not as strong. Water breaks up and washes away the weaker material, leaving the stronger material still standing.

Other arches are formed in a similar way, but cold weather and gravity are also involved. Cracks form in the weaker material and fill with water. During cold weather the water freezes and expands. This weakens the material even more. Gravity then goes to work, leaving only the stronger material standing. The arches that result show you how processes combine to shape Earth's features.

Weathering, erosion and deposition haven't stopped. The arches and other features of the Cumberland Plateau will continue to change as time passes.

Weathering, erosion, and deposition change many of Earth's features, including this river and the surrounding area.

Think and Write

❶ **Scientific Inquiry** Research the arches in the southwestern United States. How are they like and unlike the arches in Tennessee?

❷ **Scientific Thinking** How are natural bridges like bridges made by people?

Build a Water Barrier

Identify the Problem You have a favorite fishing spot next to a river, but the river's water has eroded the land. Now the river is getting close to the path that you take to the fishing spot.

Think of a Solution You can build a water barrier to keep the river away from its banks. Design a model barrier to slow down the erosion. List the characteristics your barrier must have in order to slow the erosion. For example, it must be tall enough to prevent the water from coming over it.

Plan and Build Using your list, sketch and label the parts of your water-barrier design. Think about the materials you could use. Then build your model.

Test and Improve Test your barrier and then work to improve it. Provide sketches and explanations of what you did.

Possible Materials

- clay
- potting soil
- scissors
- craft sticks
- mesh
- glue
- scrap cardboard
- string
- nylon hose
- funnel
- balloons

Communicate

1. What part of your model barrier worked well?

2. What part of your model barrier could have worked better?

3. Explain one improvement that you made to your design.

GLE 0407.T/E.5 Apply a creative design strategy to solve a particular problem generated by societal needs and wants.

Earth Science

Tennessee

Guiding Question

How is Earth affected by geological cycles and the influence of people?

Chapter 4

Cycles and Patterns in Space

Star paths in the night sky

LESSON

1

The Sun seems to rise in the east, travel across the sky, and set in the west. Where is the Sun at night?

LESSON

2

Temperatures can be scorching hot in summer and icy cold in winter. What causes the seasons to change?

LESSON

3

Within two weeks, the Moon seems to change from a thin sliver of light to a glowing circle. What causes this change?

Fun Facts

The moon is moving away from Earth at a rate of about 3 cm (about 1 in) per year.

Vocabulary Preview

axis
crescent moon
equator
full moon
new moon
★ phases of the Moon
quarter moon
revolve
rotate
season
waning moon
waxing moon

★ = Tennessee Academic Vocabulary

 Vocabulary Strategies

Have you ever seen any of these terms before? Do you know what they mean?

State a description, explanation, or example of the vocabulary in your own words.

Draw a picture, symbol, example, or other image that describes the term.

Glossary p. H16

full moon

rotate

waxing moon

season

Start with Your Standards

Inquiry

GLE 0407.Inq.1 Explore different scientific phenomena by asking questions, making logical predictions, planning investigations, and recording data.

GLE 0407.Inq.3 Organize data into appropriate tables, graphs, drawings, or diagrams.

GLE 0407.Inq.4 Identify and interpret simple patterns of evidence to communicate the findings of multiple investigations.

GLE 0407.Inq.6 Compare the results of an investigation with what scientists already accept about this question.

Earth Science

Standard 6 The Universe

GLE 0407.6.1 Analyze patterns, relative movements, and relationships among the sun, moon, and earth.

Interact with this chapter.

 www.eduplace.com/tnscp

TENNESSEE STANDARDS

GLE 0407.6.1 Analyze patterns, relative movements, and relationships among the sun, moon, and earth.

GLE 0407.Inq.3 Organize data into appropriate tables, graphs, drawings, or diagrams.

Guiding Question

What Causes Day and Night?

Why It Matters...

In early morning, the Sun comes up in the east. During the day, it travels across the sky, giving light and warming Earth. In the evening, it sets in the west. But the Sun doesn't actually move. The Sun appears to move because Earth is slowly spinning.

Science and Math Toolbox

For step 3, review **Using a Tape Measure or Ruler** on page H6.

PREPARE TO INVESTIGATE

Inquiry Skill

Measure When you measure, you use tools to find distance, mass, or other information about an object.

Materials

- large square sheet of paper
- 2 metric rulers
- modeling clay
- watch or clock

Directed Inquiry

Shadows in the Sun

Procedure

STEP 1

1. **Collaborate** Work with a partner. Place a square sheet of paper outdoors in a sunny area. Hold a ruler in the center of the paper while your partner molds the clay around the base, as shown. The clay should keep the ruler standing upright.

2. In your *Science Notebook*, make a two-column chart. Title one column *Time* and the other column *Shadow Length (cm)*.

STEP 2

3. **Measure** Trace the shadow made by the ruler on the paper. Use a metric ruler to measure the length of the shadow. Have your partner record the time of day and the shadow length in the chart.

4. **Observe** Repeat step 3 once each hour for the rest of the school day.

5. **Use Numbers** In your *Science Notebook*, make a bar graph to display the data you collected.

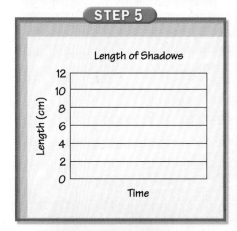

STEP 5

Length of Shadows

Think and Write

1. **Draw Conclusions** In what ways did the shadow change during the day?

2. **Analyze Data** Did the shadow's length change by the same amount each hour?

3. **Predict** What do you think the length of the shadow will be two hours after the last time you measured?

Guided Inquiry

Design an Experiment
Bring the ruler setup indoors. Use a flashlight to produce the same shadows as the Sun did. Observe the position of the model Sun for each shadow.

0407.Inq.3

Day and Night

VOCABULARY

axis

rotate

GRAPHIC ORGANIZER

Cause and Effect Use the chart below to explain what causes day and night.

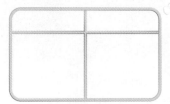

GLE 0407.6.1 Analyze patterns, relative movements, and relationships among the sun, moon, and earth.

Rotating Earth

While you are enjoying breakfast in Tennessee, night is falling in places half way around the world. How can this be so?

Hundreds of years ago, people believed that the Sun moved around Earth. They concluded this because the Sun appears to rise in the east, climb across the sky, then set to the west.

Knoxville, Tennessee

Athens, Greece

When one side of Earth is facing the Sun, the other side is in darkness. When it is afternoon in Knoxville, it is night in Athens, Greece.

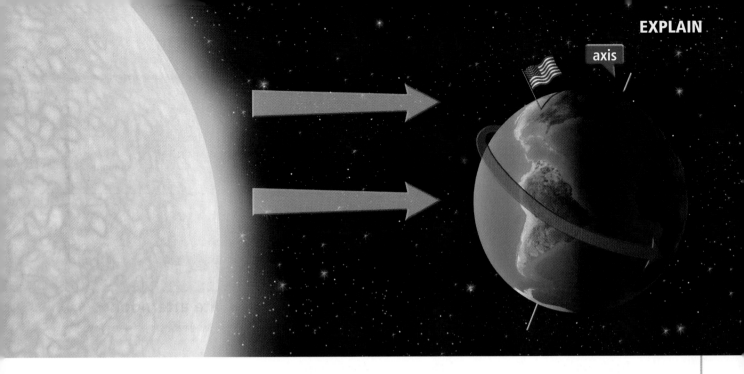

axis

In fact, the cycle of day and night occurs because Earth rotates. To **rotate** (ROH tayt) is to turn on an axis. An **axis** (AK sihs) is an imaginary line through the center of an object. Earth's axis passes through the North and South Poles.

Remember that Earth is a sphere. Only one half of it receives light and heat from the Sun at any given time. The other half is dark, and it is nighttime there. Because Earth rotates, the half that is light and the half that is dark keep shifting positions.

Imagine the Sun is just about to rise over Tennessee. As Earth rotates, the position of Tennessee gradually moves to face the Sun. The Sun appears to rise in the eastern part of the sky.

As the day goes on, the Sun appears to move across the sky. But the Sun is not truly moving. Instead, Earth is rotating, causing the Sun to look like it is moving.

As Earth continues to rotate, Tennessee turns away from the Sun's light. Eventually, the Sun appears to set in the west. It becomes dark, and night has arrived. Now it is daytime on the other side of Earth.

FOCUS CHECK What causes the Sun to appear to move across the sky?

▲ What time of day is it for the part of Earth marked by the flag? What will happen as the day continues?

Express Lab

Activity Card
Model Day and Night

123

Changing Shadow Length

early morning

noon

late afternoon

As the Sun appears to move across the sky from east to west, shadows grow shorter and then grow longer again.

Sunrise and Sunset

Which room of your home gets the most sunlight when you wake up in the morning? Which room gets the most when you come home from school? It is probably not the same room.

In the morning, the Sun appears to rise in the east. As Earth turns, the Sun seems to move west and rise higher in the sky. At noon, the Sun seems to be at its highest point. Earth continues to turn, and the Sun seems to move west until it sets in the west.

As Earth turns, the position of the Sun in the sky changes. This causes the angle at which sunlight strikes your part of Earth to change. The changing angle of sunlight causes shadows to change throughout the day. When the Sun is low in the sky, shadows are long. When the Sun is high in the sky, shadows are short.

In ancient times, people used the positions and lengths of shadows to tell the time of day. You can do this, too! Study the shadow made by a tall object, such as a tree or a flagpole. It will change in much the same way every day.

⊙**FOCUS CHECK** **What causes shadows to change in length during the day?**

Lesson Wrap-Up

Visual Summary

Earth rotates on its axis, causing the cycle of day and night.

As Earth rotates, the Sun appears to rise in the east, move across the sky, and set in the west.

Throughout the day, sunlight strikes Earth at different angles. This causes the length and angle of shadows to change.

Check for Understanding

TRACK THE SUN

Record the position of the Sun throughout the school day. Describe its position relative to things that do not move, such as buildings or roads. Use a model of Earth and the Sun to explain the changes you observe. Record your observations in your *Science Notebook*.

✔ 0407.Inq.3

Review

❶ **MAIN IDEA** What causes day and night?

❷ **VOCABULARY** Use the terms rotate and axis to describe how Earth moves.

❸ **READING SKILL Cause and Effect** What effect does the Sun have on the side of Earth where it is daytime?

❹ **CRITICAL THINKING: Apply** Suppose you called a friend in Athens, Greece, soon after you eat dinner. Is it likely that your friend just finished eating dinner also? Explain.

❺ **INQUIRY SKILL: Measure** What can you measure to tell whether it is morning or noon where you live? Explain.

TCAP Prep

The Sun appears to move from _____ across the sky.

A north to south
B east to west
C west to east
D south to north

GLE 0407.6.1

Technology

Visit **www.eduplace.com/tnscp** to find out more about day and night.

Catching Some Rays

For most people "catching some rays" means putting on some sunscreen and sunning themselves. To some scientists at NASA, catching some rays meant sending the spacecraft *Genesis* around the sun to collect and bring home tiny bits of solar dust from the solar winds. The solar wind is a high-speed stream of tiny particles that the sun gives off. Astronomers think that these samples will give them clues about how the solar system formed.

How did the craft collect its samples? Scientists signaled *Genesis* to flip its lid as it passed through the solar wind. Once the lid was open, five collector plates—the size of bicycle tires— swung out and acted like giant flytraps, collecting stray bits of solar dust.

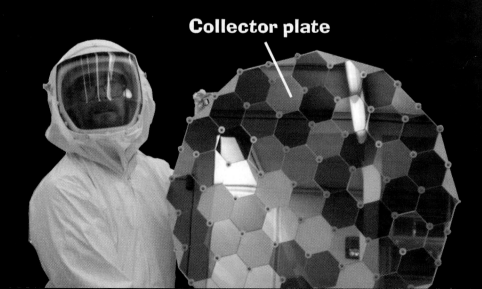

Collector plate

GLE 0407.6.1 Analyze patterns, relative movements, and relationships among the sun, moon, and earth.

EXTEND

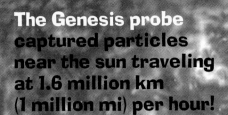

The Genesis probe captured particles near the sun traveling at 1.6 million km (1 million mi) per hour!

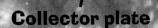

Collector plate

TENNESSEE STANDARDS

GLE 0407.6.1 Analyze patterns, relative movements, and relationships among the sun, moon, and earth.

GLE 0407.Inq.1 Explore different scientific phenomena by asking questions, making logical predictions, planning investigations, and recording data.

Guiding Question

What Causes the Seasons?

Why It Matters . . .

Why do the days grow shorter and cooler as summer changes to fall? Seasons change because Earth is tilted on its axis as it moves around the Sun.

When your part of Earth begins to tilt away from the Sun, sunlight strikes it less directly. Less daylight and less warmth mean that fall has arrived and winter will follow.

PREPARE TO INVESTIGATE

Inquiry Skill

Use Models You can use a model of an object, process, or idea to better understand or describe how it works.

Materials

- globe
- modeling clay
- toothpicks
- lamp

Directed Inquiry

Earth's Tilt

Procedure

STEP 1

1. Work with a partner. As shown, place a lump of clay with a toothpick on each pole of a globe. The toothpicks represent Earth's axis.

2. **Observe** Hold the globe so the North Pole points at a drawing of Polaris your teacher taped to a wall.

STEP 2

3. **Use Models** Use a lamp as a model of the Sun. As you hold the globe, have your partner place the lamp so that it shines on the globe. **Safety:** Do not touch the bulb. It will get hot.

4. **Record Data** Draw your Earth-Sun model. Mark *X* on the part of Earth that is getting the most direct light.

STEP 5

5. **Use Models** While holding the globe so the axis stays pointed at Polaris, walk around the lamp to the opposite side. Draw the model again. Mark *O* on the drawing to show the part of the globe that is now receiving the most direct light.

Think and Write

1. **Use Models** Describe how Earth's motion changes the amount of direct light received by different parts of Earth.

2. **Draw Conclusions** What season would it be for the place marked *X*? For the place marked *O*?

✔ 0407.Inq.1

Guided Inquiry

Design an Experiment
Rotate the globe as you hold it next to the lamp. Predict whether Tennessee gets more hours of sunlight on a summer day or on a winter day. Experiment to find out.

129

Seasons

VOCABULARY

equator
revolve
season

GRAPHIC ORGANIZER

Sequence Fill in the chart to relate Earth's motion to the changing seasons.

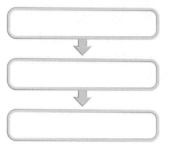

GLE 0407.6.1 Analyze patterns, relative movements, and relationships among the sun, moon, and earth.

Revolving Earth

As you learned, the cycle of day and night is caused by Earth's rotation on its axis. Yet what causes the cycle of the seasons? Seasons are explained by another way that Earth moves through space.

Earth moves through an orbit, or path around the Sun. To move in a path around another object is to **revolve** (rih VAHLV). It takes one year for Earth to revolve once around the Sun. The orbit is in the shape of an ellipse (ee LIHPS). An ellipse is a circle that is flattened and stretched out. The shape of Earth's orbit is close to being a circle. It is flattened only a little.

Seasons Because Earth's axis is tilted, parts of Earth have four different seasons. ▶

Summer When the Northern Hemisphere is tilted toward the Sun, it is summer here. ▶

Summer

As the diagram shows, Earth's axis is tilted compared to its orbital path. This means that the Sun's rays strike Earth's surface at a different angle at different times of the year. The tilt causes Earth's seasons to change. A **season** is one of the four parts of the year—spring, summer, fall, and winter.

The **equator** (ee KWAY tur) is an imaginary line that circles Earth halfway between the North and South Poles. It divides Earth into northern and southern halves, each called a hemisphere.

In June, Earth's Northern Hemisphere, where you live, is tilted toward the Sun. It receives strong, direct sunlight, so it is summer here. In December, the Northern Hemisphere is tilted away from the Sun. It receives weak, indirect sunlight. It is winter here. At the same time the Southern Hemisphere is tilted toward the Sun, so it is summer there.

FOCUS CHECK In December the Southern Hemisphere is tilted toward the Sun. What season is it there in March?

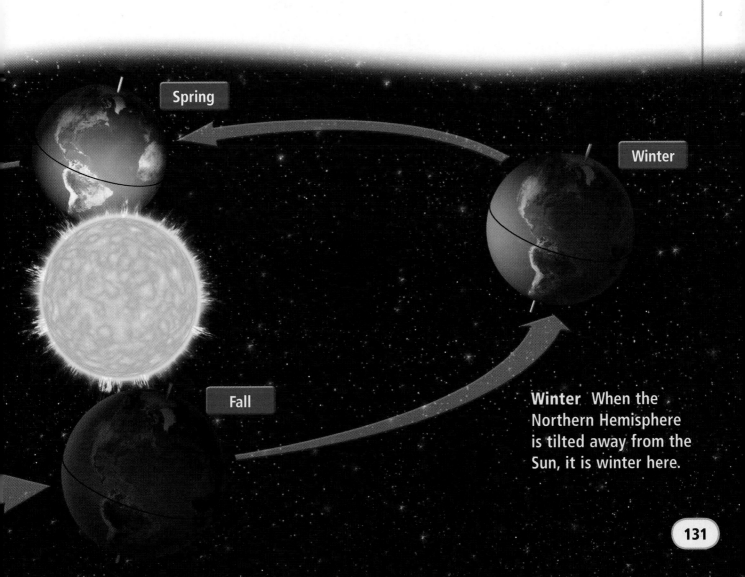

Spring

Winter

Fall

Winter When the Northern Hemisphere is tilted away from the Sun, it is winter here.

Changing Position of the Sun

As you learned earlier, the Sun changes position in the sky during the day. It appears to rise in the east and to set in the west. But have you noticed another way the position of the Sun changes? This change occurs gradually over the course of the year, and it causes the seasons.

Suppose that you are outside on a day in June. At noon, the Sun appears very high in the sky. It is very hot, and soon you are looking for some shade.

Now suppose that it is noon in December, and you are outside at recess. The Sun appears much lower in the sky. Even if you are sitting in the Sun, you might feel chilly. What causes this difference?

June 21

▲ **12:00 Noon, June 21, the Northern Hemisphere:**
The Sun appears high in the sky. Summer temperatures tend to be warm or hot.

December 21

◄ **12:00 Noon, December 21, the Northern Hemisphere:** The Sun appears lower in the sky than it did in June. Winter temperatures tend to be cool or cold.

In June, the Northern Hemisphere is tilted toward the Sun. This makes the Sun appear high in the sky. Sunlight shines more directly on the Northern Hemisphere. In addition, the Sun rises earlier and sets later than during other seasons. For these reasons, summers tend to be warm or hot.

In December, the Northern Hemisphere is tilted away from the Sun. The Sun appears lower in the sky, and days are shorter. The Sun's rays are less direct, so the land and water are heated less. Thus, winters tend to be cool or cold.

🎯**FOCUS CHECK** In the Northern Hemisphere, how does the Sun's position in the sky change with the seasons?

Express Lab

Activity Card
Model Earth's Tilt

Length of Day and Night Changes

Does the Sun appear to rise and set at the same time every day? No, it does not. The length of day and night changes throughout the year. This is caused by the tilt of Earth's axis.

As Earth revolves around the Sun, different parts of Earth are tilted toward the Sun. In June, the North Pole is tilted toward the Sun. So places north of the equator face the Sun for more hours than they face away from it. They have more hours of daylight and fewer hours of darkness.

In December, the Northern Hemisphere is tilted away from the Sun. This means that places north of the equator face away from the Sun for more hours than they face toward it. So, in these places, there are more hours of darkness than daylight. The shorter amounts of daylight also help make winter colder than summer.

FOCUS CHECK In what season do the days have the fewest hours of daylight?

7:00 P.M. in June in Lenoir City, Tennessee

7:00 P.M. in December in Lenoir City, Tennessee

Lesson Wrap-Up

Visual Summary

Earth revolves around the Sun once a year. Earth's axis is tilted, so each hemisphere leans toward the Sun in summer and away from the Sun in winter.

The Sun appears to rise higher in the sky in summer than in winter.

Daylight lasts longer in summer than in winter.

The changing amounts of sunlight throughout the year cause seasonal changes in the weather.

✓ Check for Understanding

SEASONAL CHANGES

Make a diorama, poster, or other model to explain Earth's seasonal changes. Show the Sun, Earth's orbit around the Sun, and Earth's tilted axis. Analyze your model and communciate how each component contributes to Earth's seasonal changes.

✓ 0407.Inq.4

Review

❶ **MAIN IDEA** Why is the Sun lower in the sky in winter?

❷ **VOCABULARY** Describe the location of the equator.

❸ **READING SKILL: Sequence** In the Southern Hemisphere, does the Sun appear lower in the sky in June or in December?

❹ **CRITICAL THINKING: Evaluate** Would seasons occur even if Earth were not tilted on its axis? Explain.

❺ **INQUIRY SKILL: Use Models** How would you place Earth and its axis in an Earth–Sun model for December?

TCAP Prep

Earth's tilted axis as it revolves around the Sun is the cause of Earth's

A cycle of day and night.
B cycle of seasons.
C elliptical orbit.
D spherical shape.

Technology

Visit **www.eduplace.com/tnscp** to find out more about Earth's motion.

TENNESSEE STANDARDS

GLE 0407.6.1 Analyze patterns, relative movements, and relationships among the sun, moon, and earth.

GLE 0407.Inq.4 Identify and interpret simple patterns of evidence to communicate the findings of multiple investigations.

What Are the Phases of the Moon?

Guiding Question

Why It Matters...

One evening, you notice that the Moon appears to be a thin sliver. Several nights later, the shape of the Moon is a half-circle. After another few days, a full moon is shining through your window.

Why does the Moon appear to change shape? For the answer, you must study how the Moon and Earth move through space.

PREPARE TO INVESTIGATE

Inquiry Skill

Communicate When you communicate, you share information using words, actions, sketches, graphs, charts, or diagrams.

Materials

- lamp
- plastic-foam ball with craft-stick handle

Directed Inquiry

Moon Motion

Procedure

STEP 2

1. Use a ball with a stick handle to stand for the Moon. Use a lamp or other light to stand for the Sun. You will be an observer on Earth. **Safety:** Do not touch the bulb. It will get hot.

2. **Use Models** Stand in front of the Sun model with your back to it. Hold the Moon model at arm's length in front of you and above your head. Look at the shape the light makes on the Moon.

STEP 3

3. **Observe** Slowly make a quarter turn in place and stop, keeping the Moon model in front of you.

4. **Record Data** In your *Science Notebook,* draw the shapes of light and dark that you observed on the Moon model in steps 2 and 3.

STEP 4

5. **Use Models** Repeat step 3 two more times. Face a different direction each time. Draw the shapes of light and dark you observe.

Think and Write

1. **Communicate** Write three sentences explaining why the shapes in your drawings are alike or different.

2. **Infer** If you look at the Moon on different nights, do you think it will look the same? Explain.

Guided Inquiry

Ask Questions Write a question about how the Moon appears to move each night. With an adult, observe the Moon. Record where you see it every hour for three hours.

✔ 0407.6.1

Moon Phases

GRAPHIC ORGANIZER

Compare and Contrast
Use the chart to compare a full moon and a new moon.

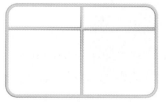

GLE 0407.6.1 Analyze patterns, relative movements, and relationships among the sun, moon, and earth.

Earth's Moon

The Moon is a sphere made of rock that revolves around Earth once every $27\frac{1}{3}$ Earth days. As it revolves, the Moon also rotates once on its axis in the same amount of time. As a result, the same side of the Moon, the near side, always faces Earth. The other side faces away from Earth, so you cannot see it from Earth.

The Moon does not make its own light. "Moonlight" is really sunlight reflecting from the Moon's surface. To reflect means to bounce off. The reflected sunlight makes the side of the Moon facing the Sun look bright.

When seen from Earth, the Moon appears to change shape in a regular cycle. The Moon's cycle lasts about four weeks, which gave rise to the word *month*. ▶

▲ The Moon's surface reflects light, but the Moon does not make its own light.

If the same side of the Moon always faces Earth, why does the Moon appear to change shape? As it revolves around Earth, the Moon's near side receives different amounts of sunlight. At one point during the Moon's revolution around Earth, the Moon's near side receives no sunlight. The near side of the Moon is dark, and you cannot see it. This is called a **new moon**.

As the Moon revolves around Earth, a small part of the near side becomes sunlit and can be seen from Earth. This thin shape is called the **crescent** (KREHS uhnt) **moon**.

When the Moon has revolved one quarter of its orbit around Earth, half the Moon's near side is sunlit. This is called a **quarter moon**, because you see one quarter of the entire Moon. When the Moon has revolved halfway around Earth, the Moon's entire near side is sunlit. This is the **full moon**.

Following a new moon, an increasing amount of the Moon's near side is sunlit. This is called a **waxing moon**. Following a full moon, a decreasing amount of the near side is sunlit. This is called a **waning moon**. After about a month, the Moon reaches the point in its orbit where none of its near side is sunlit. This is a new moon again.

FOCUS CHECK What are two different ways that the Moon moves?

The Moon in Motion

The different ways the Moon looks throughout the month are called the **phases of the Moon**. The diagram below shows the Moon's position at each phase. The photos on the next page show how each Moon phase looks as seen from Earth.

◎ FOCUS CHECK How is the way the moon looks from Earth different from the way it looks from space?

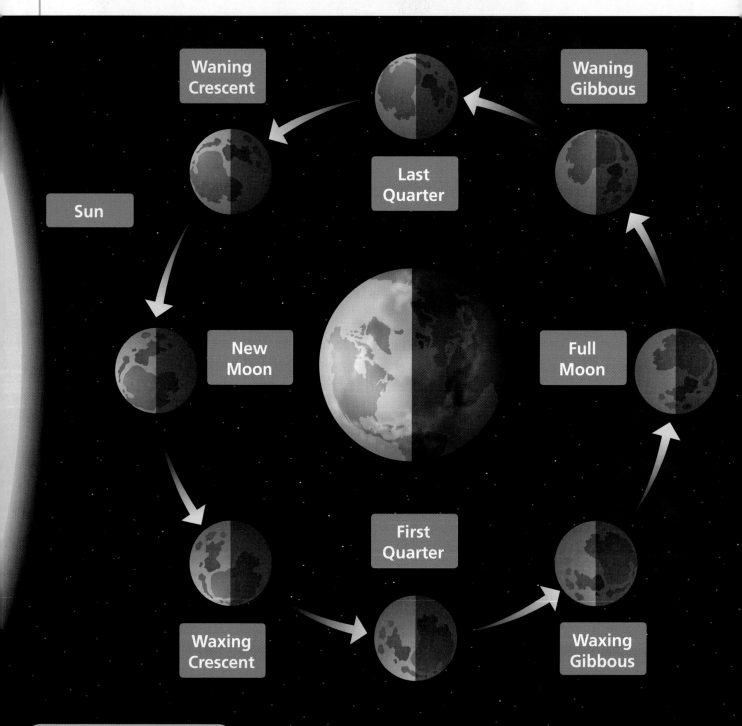

Waning Crescent

Last Quarter

Waning Gibbous

Sun

New Moon

Full Moon

Waxing Crescent

First Quarter

Waxing Gibbous

Last Quarter
Half of the Moon's near side is sunlit.

Waning Crescent
The Moon looks like a thin sliver.

Waning Gibbous
The Moon looks almost full.

New Moon
None of the Moon's near side is sunlit.

Full Moon
All of the Moon's near side is sunlit.

Waxing Crescent
The Moon looks like a thin sliver.

Waxing Gibbous
The Moon looks almost full.

First Quarter
Half of the Moon's near side is sunlit.

Eclipses

Objects in space block some of the sun's light, producing shadows. An eclipse occurs when one body in space blocks light from reaching another body in space.

Eclipses we see on Earth are solar eclipses and lunar eclipses. They are alike because both occur when Earth, the sun, and the moon line up. However, solar and lunar eclipses also differ.

A solar eclipse occurs when the moon—always a new moon—casts a shadow on Earth. In some places the moon seems to cover the sun, and the sky gets dark.

A lunar eclipse occurs when the moon—always a full moon—passes through the shadow of Earth. Earth blocks the sun's light from reaching the moon, and the moon appears to be red. This is because Earth's atmosphere scatters red light, which then reflects off the moon.

FOCUS CHECK How do solar and lunar eclipses differ?

Solar eclipse

Lunar eclipse

Express Lab

Activity Card
See Solar and Lunar Eclipses

Lesson Wrap-Up

Visual Summary

The Moon revolves around Earth once every $27\frac{1}{3}$ days. The Moon reflects light from the Sun.

As the Moon revolves around Earth, different amounts of its near side are sunlit. This causes the cycle of moon phases.

The shapes of the Moon's phases include a dark new moon, a thin crescent, a half-circle, and a full circle.

Check for Understanding

MOON PHASES

Observe the Moon this evening. Classify the phase of the Moon you observe. Draw a diagram to show the positions of Earth, the Moon, and the Sun during this phase.

✔ 0407.6.2

Review

❶ **MAIN IDEA** Why does the Moon's shape look different on different nights?

❷ **VOCABULARY** Make a sketch of a quarter moon.

❸ **READING SKILL: Compare and Contrast** How does a full moon compare with a quarter moon?

❹ **CRITICAL THINKING: Evaluate** Suppose you see a waxing gibbous moon. Your friend says that the new moon will be the next phase you can see. Is your friend correct? Explain why or why not.

❺ **INQUIRY SKILL: Communicate** Draw a diagram to show what causes moonlight.

TCAP Prep

If the near side of the Moon receives no sunlight, you see a _____ moon.

A crescent
B new
C waning
D waxing

SPI 0407.6.1

Technology

Visit **www.eduplace.com/tnscp** to find out more about the Moon.

Drawing the Moon

In ancient times, artists usually drew the Moon as a circle or a sliver in the sky. They drew the Moon's surface as if it were perfectly smooth because they thought it was.

The invention of the telescope allowed astronomers to see and draw the features of the Moon more accurately and in more detail. They saw that dark areas on the Moon were low plains and shadows in craters. Telescopes also helped them learn why the Moon seemed to change shape.

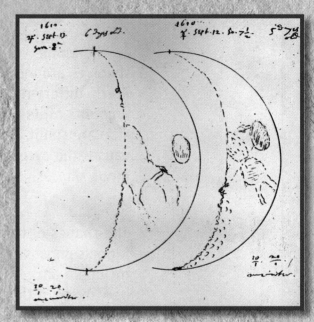

▲ Thomas Harriot was the first astronomer to draw the Moon while looking through a telescope. He made sketches over a period of weeks in 1609 and 1610 showing different Moon phases.

◄ Harriot also drew this "map" of the Moon that showed its surface features, including craters.

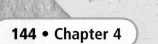

GLE 0407.Inq.6 Compare the results of an investigation with what scientists already accept about this question.

EXTEND

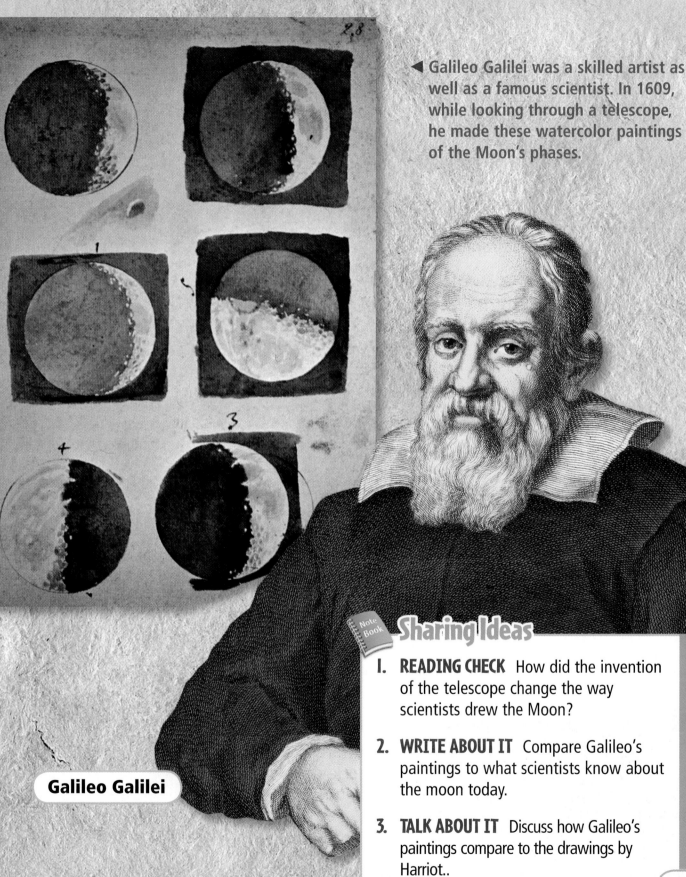

◄ Galileo Galilei was a skilled artist as well as a famous scientist. In 1609, while looking through a telescope, he made these watercolor paintings of the Moon's phases.

Galileo Galilei

Sharing Ideas

1. READING CHECK How did the invention of the telescope change the way scientists drew the Moon?

2. WRITE ABOUT IT Compare Galileo's paintings to what scientists know about the moon today.

3. TALK ABOUT IT Discuss how Galileo's paintings compare to the drawings by Harriot..

GLE **0407.8.2** Differentiate between weather and climate. **Math GLE 0406.5.1** Collect, record, arrange, present, and interpret data using tables and various representations. **ELA GLE 0401.4.1** Conduct research to access and present information.

Math Average Temperature

The graph shows the average temperature by month for two Tennessee cities: Memphis and Knoxville. Use the graph to answer the following questions.

1. Compare the data for the two cities. What trends do the data show?

2. Is the temperature always higher in Memphis than in Knoxville? Explain.

3. In what fraction of the months of the year is Memphis's average temperature below 50°F?

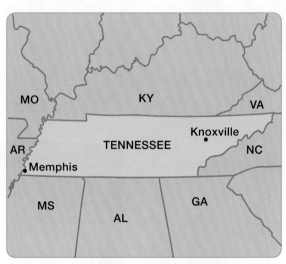

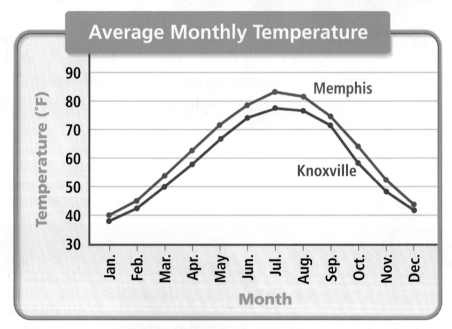

Average Monthly Temperature

 **Response to Literature**

Seasons bring different conditions to different places. Read a book that involves a season or change of seasons. Write a summary of the book. You may include pictures in your report.

Harry McSween

As a child, Harry McSween wanted to be either a scientist or an astronaut. His job as a professor of geological sciences at the University of Tennessee in Knoxville combines both of these interests.

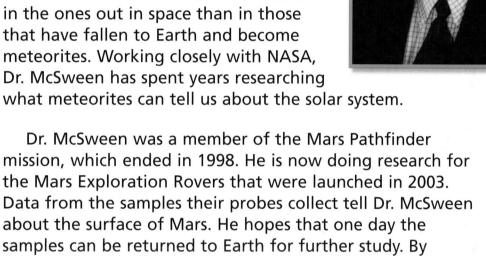

For the last 30 years, Dr. McSween has studied meteoroids. He is more interested in the ones out in space than in those that have fallen to Earth and become meteorites. Working closely with NASA, Dr. McSween has spent years researching what meteorites can tell us about the solar system.

Dr. McSween was a member of the Mars Pathfinder mission, which ended in 1998. He is now doing research for the Mars Exploration Rovers that were launched in 2003. Data from the samples their probes collect tell Dr. McSween about the surface of Mars. He hopes that one day the samples can be returned to Earth for further study. By comparing Martian rocks with meteorites found on Earth, Dr. McSween hopes to learn more about Earth and our solar system.

Vocabulary

Complete each sentence with a word from the list.

1. The ways the Moon looks when seen from Earth are the _____.

2. An imaginary line through the center of an object is called a/an _____.

3. When all of the Moon's near side is sunlit, it is a/an _____.

4. An imaginary line that circles Earth halfway between the North and South Poles is the _____.

5. When the Moon's near side receives no sunlight, it is a/an _____.

6. To move in a path around another object is to _____.

7. When the Moon becomes visible again and appears as a thin shape, the phase is called a/an _____.

8. When half of the Moon's near side is sunlit it is a/an _____.

9. Spring, summer, fall, and winter are each a/an _____.

10. To turn on an axis is to _____.

axis
crescent moon
equator
full moon
new moon
★ phases of the Moon
quarter moon
revolve
rotate
season
waning moon
waxing moon

TCAP Inquiry Skills

11. **Use Models** Suppose the Moon stopped rotating on its axis. Would you still see the phases of the Moon? How could you use a model to test your prediction? **GLE 0407.6.1**

12. **Predit** How does a drawing of the sky's appearance last night help you predict its appearance tonight? **GLE 0407.Inq.3**

13. **Use Models** The length of a day on Mercury is 59 Earth days. About how many months is this? **GLE 0407.6.1**

Map the Concept

Complete the concept map using these terms:

revolves   phases of the Moon
rotates   pattern of day and night

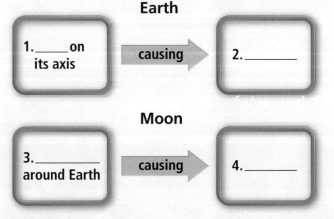

Earth

1. _____ on its axis → causing → 2. _____

Moon

3. _____ around Earth → causing → 4. _____

GLE 0407.6.1

Critical Thinking

14. Apply Your family calls a relative who lives in a different country. It is 1:00 in the afternoon in Georgia. Is it possible that your relative will be in bed for the night? Explain.　　**GLE 0407.6.1**

15. Synthesize The Moon is much smaller than the Sun. But they look about the same size when viewed from Earth. Explain why this is.

GLE 0407.6.1

16. Evalute You hear someone say that the Sun rises in the morning, moves across the sky, and sets at night. How would you evaluate this statement?

GLE 0407.6.1

Check for Understanding

Model the Seasons

Review the models you made earlier. Build a model or draw a diagram that shows Earth's orbit around the Sun. Use it to explain why weather changes with the seasons. Discuss your model in either a written or oral presentation.

SUN

✔ **0407.Inq.4**

TCAP TCAP Prep

Write the letter of the best answer choice.

17 When does a waning moon occur?

A between a first-quarter moon and a new moon

B when all of the Moon's near side is dark

C just after a full moon

D just after a crescent moon

SPI 0407.6.1

18 The Sun appears to move across the sky every day because Earth is

F revolving.

G waxing.

H rotating.

J waning.　　**SPI 0407.6.2**

19 The moon can be seen from Earth because it ____.

A produces its own light

B reflects sunlight

C has a rocky surface

D is smaller than Earth　　**SPI 0407.6.2**

20 The phase of the moon that directly follows a new moon is a

F last-quarter moon.

G waning crescent.

H waxing crescent.

J full moon.　　**SPI 0407.6.1**

Chapter 5

Slow Changes on Earth

LESSON 1

The sand on beaches was once rock or shells. What processes change rock into the sand?

LESSON 2

Moving water can change Earth's surface. How do rivers and ocean waves change the shape of land?

LESSON 3

Glaciers and wind are two forces that cause weathering. How do ice and wind change Earth's surface?

Fun Facts

The Appalachian Mountain range is the parent range of the Blue Ridge Mountains.

Vocabulary Preview

bay
delta
deposition
★ erosion
erratic
glacier
headland
moraine
river system
sand dune
weathering

★ = Tennessee Academic Vocabulary

 Vocabulary Strategies

Have you ever seen any of these terms before? Do you know what they mean?

State a description, explanation, or example of the vocabulary in your own words.

Draw a picture, symbol, example, or other image that describes the term.

Glossary p. H16

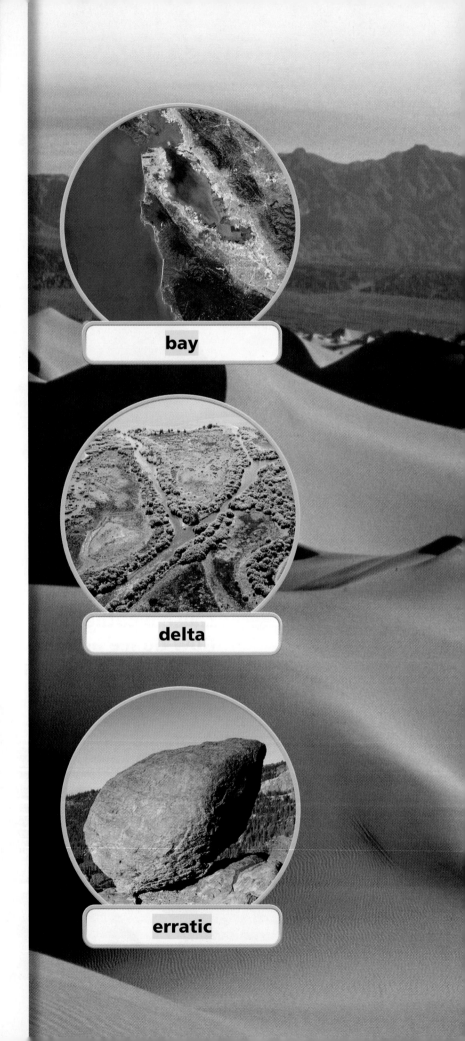

bay

delta

erratic

sand dune

Start with Your Standards

Inquiry

GLE 0407.Inq.1 Explore different scientific phenomena by asking questions, making logical predictions, planning investigations, and recording data.

GLE 0407.Inq.4 Identify and interpret simple patterns of evidence to communicate the findings of multiple investigations.

Earth Science

Standard 7 The Earth

GLE 0407.7.1 Investigate how the Earth's geological features change as a result of erosion (weathering and transportation) and deposition.

GLE 0407.7.2 Evaluate how some earth materials can be used to solve human problems and enhance the quality of life.

Interact with this chapter.

 www.eduplace.com/tnscp

Lesson 1

TENNESSEE STANDARDS

GLE 0407.7.1 Investigate how the Earth's geological features change as a result of erosion (weathering and transportation) and deposition.
GLE 0407.Inq.1 Explore different scientific phenomena by asking questions, making logical predictions, planning investigations, and recording data.

What Are Weathering and Erosion?

Building Background...

The land has many different shapes. Weathering slowly wears away rock into smaller pieces. Erosion moves these rock materials—pebbles, sand, and soil—from one place to another. Over time, these and other processes change the surface of Earth.

PREPARE TO INVESTIGATE

Inquiry Skill

Measure In some science investigations, you can estimate a measurement of weight, length, or volume.

Materials

- small plastic soft drink bottle with cap
- water
- 250-mL graduated cylinder
- funnel

Science and Math Toolbox

For step 1 and 5, review **Measuring Volume** on page H7.

Freezing Effects

Procedure

STEP 1

1. **Measure** Work with a partner. Completely fill a soft drink bottle with water. Pour the water into a graduated cylinder to find out how much water it takes to fill the bottle. In your *Science Notebook*, record this amount of water in mL. This is the volume of the liquid that the bottle can hold.

2. Refill the bottle with water. Then firmly tighten the cap on it.

STEP 2

3. Put the bottle into a freezer and allow it to remain overnight.

4. **Observe** Take the bottle out of the freezer. Observe any effects that the ice had on the bottle.

STEP 5

5. **Measure** Estimate the difference in volume between the water-filled bottle and the ice-filled bottle.

Think and Write

1. **Infer** What caused the changes you observed in the bottle?

2. **Infer** How do the effects that you observed relate to things that happen in nature?

Guided Inquiry

Ask Questions What questions would you ask about how sediment and water interact in nature? Choose one question to **research** in the library, on websites, or by asking an expert.

0407.7.1

Weathering and Erosion

VOCABULARY

★ erosion
  glacier
  weathering

GRAPHIC ORGANIZER

Sequence Use the chart like the one below to show the processes of weathering and erosion.

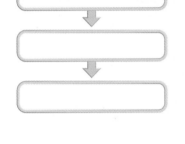

GLE 0407.7.1 Investigate how the Earth's geological features change as a result of erosion (weathering and transportation) and deposition.

Weathering

Have you ever picked up a smooth stone from the beach? If so, you have observed an example of weathering (WETH ur ihng). **Weathering** is the slow wearing away of rock into smaller pieces. Ice, plant roots, moving water, and chemicals are causes of weathering.

Weathering caused this huge boulder in Yosemite to break off from the top of the hill.▼

boulder

▲ Acid rain has damaged this stone figure on a building in Paris, France.

◄ The roots of plants can break apart large rocks.

Most rocks have tiny cracks in them. In cold climates, rainwater that enters the cracks can freeze and expand. The expanding ice makes the cracks bigger. Over time, periods of freezing and melting cause rocks to break.

A similar thing happens when plant roots grow into cracks in a rock. The growing roots widen the cracks, and the rock breaks.

Streams flow over rocks, moving them. Over and over rocks bump against other rocks. As the rocks wear down, sharp edges become smooth and the rocks get smaller.

Outer layers of rock can peel off when a forest fire or the Sun heats up the outside of a rock. When cool rainwater falls on heated rocks, it can also cause them to break.

Chemicals can weather rocks. Gases in the air react with iron in some rocks to form rust, which crumbles. Other gases in air react with rainwater to form acid rain. Acid rain weakens rock, causing it to break apart.

🎯 **FOCUS CHECK** Describe the sequence of events that might smooth down a sharp-edged rock that falls into a stream.

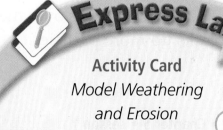

Express Lab

Activity Card
Model Weathering and Erosion

This balanced rock formation is the result of weathering and erosion.

Erosion

After a heavy rainstorm, have you ever noticed soil and pebbles being carried by running water? If so, you have seen an example of erosion (ih ROH zhuhn). **Erosion** is the movement of rock material from one place to another. The materials that result from weathering are carried away by erosion.

Water is the main cause of erosion. Suppose a drop of water splashes onto soil. The water loosens and picks up tiny particles. When the water moves downhill, it carries the tiny particles with it. As the water flows over the soil, it picks up more particles.

Weathering and erosion of rock take place over thousands and even millions of years. The water of a fast-moving river breaks down rock. Over many years, the running water carries enough weathered material away to form a deep canyon. The Grand Canyon in Arizona was formed this way.

A **glacier** (GLAY shur) is a large mass of slow-moving ice. A glacier moves so slowly that its movement is difficult to see. As it moves, a glacier causes both weathering and erosion of the rocks over which it moves. A glacier can dig out huge areas of rock and soil to form deep valleys and canyons.

Wind is another cause of weathering and erosion. Some areas have few plants to hold soil in place. In these areas, the wind carries away dry sand and soil.

⊙FOCUS CHECK How do weathering and erosion form a deep canyon?

This U-shaped valley was shaped by moving water in the form of a glacier.

Lesson Wrap-Up

Visual Summary

Plant roots cause weathering by breaking rock into smaller pieces. Plant roots grow into cracks in a rock. The growing roots widen the cracks.

Gases in air react with rainwater to form acid rain. Acid rain weakens rock, causing it to break.

This balanced rock formation is the result of weathering and erosion. The materials that result from weathering are carried away by erosion.

Check for Understanding

WIND EROSION

Prepare a demonstration to show how wind can change an area where few plants grow. Identify what tools you will need.

✓ 0407.7.1

Reading Review

❶ **MAIN IDEA** What is the slow process of wearing away rock into smaller pieces?

❷ **VOCABULARY** Use *erosion* in a sentence about acid rain.

❸ **READING SKILL:** Describe the steps involved when water and ice weather rocks.

❹ **CRITICAL THINKING: Apply** Thousands of years ago, enormous sheets of moving ice covered much of New England. Explain why large boulders litter the landscape.

❺ **INQUIRY SKILL: Observe** In what types of places could you observe weathering?

TCAP TCAP Prep

The process that moves sediment from one place to another is ____.

A weathering.
B acid rain.
C mountain building.
D erosion.

SPI 0407.7.1

Technology

Visit **www.eduplace.com/tnscp** to find out more about erosion and weathering

TENNESSEE STANDARDS

GLE 0407.7.1 Investigate how the Earth's geological features change as a result of erosion (weathering and transportation) and deposition.
GLE 0407.Inq.4 Identify and interpret simple patterns of evidence to communicate the findings of multiple investigations.

Guiding Question: How Does Water Shape the Land?

Building Background...

Moving water is one of the processes that gradually changes the shape of Earth's surface. Water wears away and reshapes rock. It moves pebbles, sand, and soil from one place to another. Moving water formed this unusually shaped island.

PREPARE TO INVESTIGATE

Inquiry Skill

Predict When you predict, you state what you think will happen based on observations of causes and effects.

Materials

- hand lens
- sediment (sand, bits of rock, soil)
- plastic soft-drink bottle with cap
- metric ruler
- water
- clock or watch
- goggles

Science and Math Toolbox

For step 2, review **Using a Tape Measure or Ruler** on page H6.

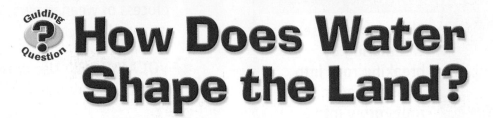

Directed Inquiry

Effects of Water on Sediment

Procedure

1. **Collaborate** Work with a partner. Use a hand lens to observe a mixture of sediment. In your *Science Notebook* record what you observe. **Safety:** Wear goggles.

2. **Measure** Make a chart like the one shown. Use a funnel to put about 2 cm of the sediment into a plastic soft drink bottle. Fill the bottle about two-thirds with water. Put the cap back on the bottle and tighten it firmly.

3. **Observe** Swirl around the material in the bottle for about 30 seconds. Then set the bottle down and do not move it again. Record what you observe.

4. **Predict** Observe the contents of the bottle every 2 hours for the rest of the day. Record what you observe each time. At the end of the day, write a prediction about how the sediment will look in 24 hours.

 Think and Write

1. **Compare** How are the observations you made before swirling the bottle similar to the ones you made after swirling it? How are they different?

2. **Infer** How do the effects you have observed relate to things that happen in nature?

✓ 0407.7.2

STEP 1

STEP 2

	Sediment with water
Start	
After 2 hours	
After 4 hours	
Prediction	

STEP 3

Guided Inquiry

Experiment Make a model to show what happens when water runs downhill over sediment. Measure the material that is moved. Repeat this three times. Average your results. **Infer** reasons for any differences.

161

Water Shapes the Land

VOCABULARY

bay
delta
deposition
headland
river system

GRAPHIC ORGANIZER

Cause and Effect Use the chart below to explain what causes beaches to become narrower.

GLE 0407.7.1 Investigate how the Earth's geological features change as a result of erosion (weathering and transportation) and deposition.

GLE 0407.7.2 Evaluate how some earth materials can be used to solve human problems and enhance the quality of life.

The Changing Coastline

You know that erosion moves bits of sand, soil, and rock. But what happens to these materials?

Recall that bits of sand, soil, and rock are called sediment. The dropping of sediment moved by water, wind, and ice is called **deposition** (dehp uh ZIHSH uhn). Wind, glaciers, and moving water are the main causes of weathering, erosion, and deposition. Along the seacoasts, ocean waves easily pick up and carry sand away. Waves also drop the sand, sometimes in new places.

◎FOCUS CHECK Name the three main causes of weathering, erosion, and deposition.

Ocean waves can separate parts of a headland to form tiny islands called sea stacks. ▼

California's Coastline

Eroded rock from land and eroded shells from the ocean form the beaches along California's coastline. Ocean waves and currents move sand along the shore.

Some beaches change with the seasons. Strong winter winds produce strong waves that remove more sand from the shore than they deposit. This erodes the beach, making it narrower. In summer, gentler waves deposit more sand on the beaches than they remove. This widens the beach.

Headlands and bays are other features of the California coastline. A **headland** is a point of land, usually high, that extends out into the water. A headland is surrounded by water on three sides. A **bay** is a body of water that is partly enclosed by land and has a wide opening. The opening, called the mouth, connects the bay to the ocean.

FOCUS CHECK During which season do the waves along California's coast remove more sand than is deposited?

▲ Strong winter waves carry beach sand away and deposit it offshore.

▲ Gentle summer waves deposit sand on the beach.

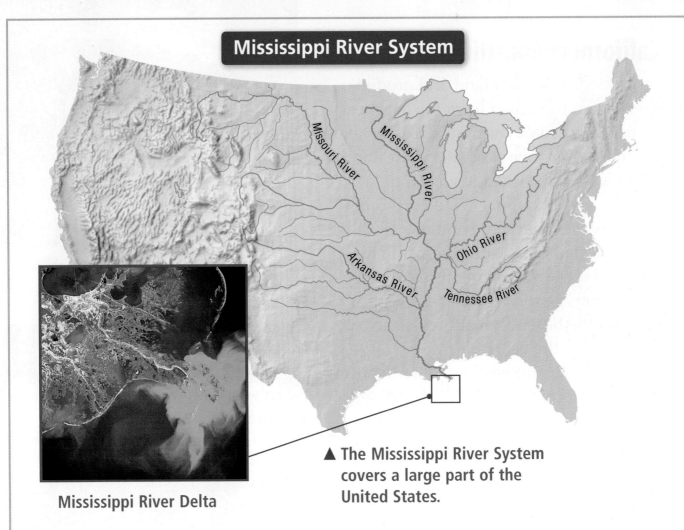

Mississippi River System

Missouri River

Mississippi River

Ohio River

Arkansas River

Tennessee River

Mississippi River Delta

▲ The Mississippi River System covers a large part of the United States.

River Systems

Rainfall on a hill or mountainside begins to trickle down the slope. Several trickles may join to form a small stream. Streams join to form a river. Small rivers can then join larger rivers. The largest river and all the waterways that drain into it are called a **river system**.

Rivers that make up the Mississippi River System begin in the Rocky Mountains in the west and the Appalachian Mountains to the east. These rivers flow into the Mississippi River. The Mississippi River flows into the Gulf of Mexico.

Deposition helps create a variety of land surface features. Some of these features occur as part of river systems. As rivers flow downhill, the fast-moving water picks up sediment. At the mouth of a river, the river empties into a lake or ocean. Here the land tends to flatten out. This flattening tends to slow the river. As the river slows, the sediment drops out of the water.

At the mouth of the Mississippi River sediments have formed a large delta that extends far into the Gulf of Mexico. A **delta** is a large mass of sediment deposited at the mouth of a river.

Another feature that river deposition can create is an alluvial fan. An alluvial fan is a fan-shaped land mass that forms after a river rushes down a steep slope and slows over a flat plain. Death Valley National Park in California is famous for its alluvial fan deposits.

As a river flows over flat land, the river tends to wind in curves called meanders (mee AND urz). The river water erodes the outside of each curve and deposits sediment on the inside.

Sometimes more water flows down a river than the normal river channel can hold. The water overflows the river's banks, or floods. Sometimes swift-flooding

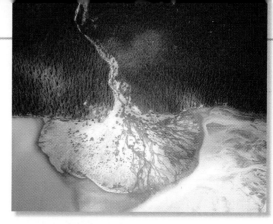

▲ This alluvial fan is at the mouth of a glacial stream in Canada.

rivers can pick up and deposit boulders in new places. The land where a river tends to flood is called a floodplain. Rivers deposit sand, silt, and clay in floodplains.

FOCUS CHECK What happens when a river or stream slows down?

As a river flows over flat land, it tends to wind in curves called meanders. ▼

Express Lab

Activity Card
Model a River

People Shape the Land

People can also shape the land. For example, when people use earth materials to build dams on rivers, they create large reservoirs and change the natural flow of the water in rivers. They also keep sediments from flowing down river.

The Watts Bar Dam is part of the Tennessee Valley Authority's flood control system. It was one of 9 dams build in the 1930s.

The Watts Bar Dam is made of concrete, which is a mixture of earth materials such as cement, sand, gravel, and water.

The dam was built with earth materials to solve a problem—how to use the Tennessee River to help the people living near it. Watts Bar Dam supplies irrigation water to farmers and has four power plants that make electricity for the counties surrounding the lake.

The reservoir formed by Watts Bar Dam is Watts Bar Lake. It provides recreational opportunities such as boating, fishing, and swimming.

FOCUS CHECK **What effect does the Watts Bar Dam have on the people of Tennessee?**

The Watts Bar Dam provides irrigation water and electricity for Tennessee.▼

Lesson Wrap-Up

Visual Summary

Moving water in the form of ocean waves deposits sand on beaches. Ocean waves can also cause beach erosion.

Deposition in river systems creates landforms such as deltas and alluvial fans.

One way people change Earth's surface is by building dams.

Check for Understanding

NATURAL RESOURCES

Research how humans impact non-renewable natural resources like water, wood, and oil. Be sure to include data from at least three informational texts, such as the internet, nonfiction books, and magazine articles.

✓ 0407.7.4

Reading Review

1 MAIN IDEA How is Earth's surface changed through deposition?

2 VOCABULARY Use the term *headland* in a sentence about the coastline.

3 READING SKILL: What causes an alluvial fan to form?

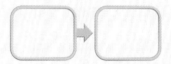

4 CRITICAL THINKING: Analyze How might dams change the effects of deposition?

5 INQUIRY SKILL: Predict What would happen if sediment builds up in a lake created by a dam.

TCAP Prep

A body of water that is partly enclosed by land but has a wide opening to the ocean is called a/an ____.

A alluvial fan.
B bay.
C headland.
D sediment.

SPI 0407.7.1

Technology

Visit **www.eduplace.com/tnscp** to find out more about how water shapes the land.

The Powell Expedition

John Wesley Powell wants to learn more about how water changes Earth's surface. He leads an expedition down the Green and the Colorado rivers and through the unexplored Grand Canyon. Over 98 days and 1,600 km, Powell rides rapids, climbs cliffs, and endures rainstorms—not bad for a man who lost an arm in the Civil War!

Characters

Professor John Wesley Powell:
geology professor and Civil War veteran

George Bradley:
expedition member and adventurer

Jack Sumner:
expedition member, hunter, trader

Narrator 1

Narrator 2

The Grand Canyon; August 1869

GLE 0407.7.1 Investigate how the Earth's geological features change as a result of erosion (weathering and transportation) and deposition.

EXTEND

Narrator 1: It's early August, 1869. Powell and his men don't know it yet but they are nearing the end of their journey.

Narrator 2: Some of his men are a bit worse for wear, as we'll see.

Professor Powell: Okay, everybody. Time to get going. We've got a lot of climbing to do before dark. I want to get high enough to see the river from above. It'll help me map our route for tomorrow.

Jack: How high do you think the canyon is here?

Professor Powell: Maybe 4,000 feet.

George: It's just one rock layer after another. [*Sighs*] It never ends!

Jack: Grumbling already, George?

George: Okay, okay. I guess I'd rather be climbing than rowing.

Professor Powell: I've got a theory that those layers you're grumbling about describe millions of years of Earth's history.

George: Millions of years? What are you talking about?

Professor Powell: Earth is millions—if not billions—of years old. The oldest rock is at the bottom of the canyon. The youngest rock is at the top.

George: It's all just a rock. Rock is rock.

Professor Powell: Oh, but the river has carved this canyon to expose different kinds of rock. From here I see shale and sandstone. Farther up, it's limestone.

POWELL points his index finger a little higher each time he mentions a layer of rock.

George: You mean the river used to be way up here?

Professor Powell: Yes, I think so.

George: I can see a difference in the color in the rocks. [*George squints.*] Does that mean something?

▲ The Colorado River carved the layers of rock in the Grand Canyon over millions of years.

Professor Powell: Different layers of rock contain different amounts and kinds of minerals. Iron is a mineral that makes rocks red.

Jack: Hey, Professor! I don't know what kind of rock this is but it's got the outline of a shell in it.

Professor Powell: What a find! That fossil helps prove another of my theories.

George: Another theory? You sure have a lot of theories! What is it this time?

Professor Powell: Well, that shell outline looks just like shells we find in the ocean. Perhaps this area used to be under the ocean. This is a great discovery! I'm going to draw a map of this area so I can find it on my next expedition.

George: Next expedition? You're planning to come back here? Count me out!

◀ A fossil from the Grand Canyon

Jack: We'll be lucky if we survive this expedition!

Professor Powell: We'll make it. I have no doubt we'll finish.

Narrator 1: And he did finish. On August 29, the Powell Expedition completed its journey through the Grand Canyon.

Rock Layers of the Grand Canyon

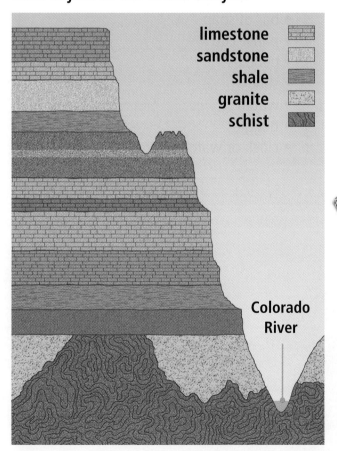

limestone

sandstone

shale

granite

schist

Colorado River

Rock layers wear away in different ways. Some rock wears away more quickly. Some layers have formed slopes and some have formed cliffs.

Narrator 2: After the trip, Powell became a national hero overnight. He conducted a second expedition in 1871.

Narrator 1: Later on, Powell was made the director of the United States Geological Survey. In that job he oversaw mapping and development of the West.

Narrator 2: He also became an expert on Native American culture as director of the Bureau of Ethnology at the Smithsonian Institute.

Narrator 1: And George, as far as we know, never signed up for another expedition again!

Sharing Ideas

1. **READING CHECK** What does John Wesley Powell think that the layers of rock tell about Earth?

2. **WRITE ABOUT IT** Describe how Powell might have felt as he was riding on the Colorado River and looking up at the canyon walls.

3. **TALK ABOUT IT** Powell considered himself a scientist in search of knowledge, rather than an explorer. Discuss how this might have affected the decisions he made during the expedition.

TENNESSEE STANDARDS

GLE 0407.7.1 Investigate how the Earth's geological features change as a result of erosion (weathering and transportation) and deposition.

GLE 0407.Inq.1 Explore different scientific phenomena by asking questions, making logical predictions, planning investigations, and recording data.

How Do Ice and Wind Shape the Land?

Guiding Question

Building Background...

Glaciers are rivers of ice. Wind and flowing water in the form of glaciers change and reshape Earth's surface. They remove sediment and other materials from one place and deposit them in other places.

PREPARE TO INVESTIGATE

Inquiry Skill

Infer When you infer, you interpret your observations

Materials

- bar of soap
- paper cup
- pebbles
- sand
- water
- goggles
- clock or watch

Directed Inquiry

A Model Glacier

Procedure

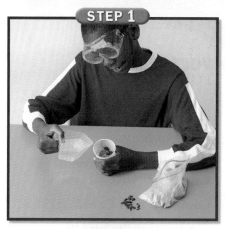

STEP 1

1. **Collaborate** Work with a partner to make a model of a glacier. A glacier is a large mass of slow-moving ice. Put about 2 cm of sand and small pebbles into a paper cup. Add water until the cup is three-fourths full. Place the cup in a freezer until the water is frozen. **Safety:** Wear goggles.

STEP 2

2. Remove the cup from the freezer. Tear away the bottom part of the paper cup from the ice block. Leave the top of the cup to use as a holder.

3. **Observe** Place your ice block with the sand side down on a bar of soap that is held in place by your partner. Grasp the cup and press down as you rub the ice block over the soap. Observe the effects of your model glacier on the soap.

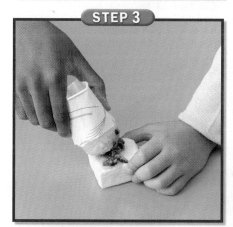

STEP 3

4. **Record Data** Record your observations in your *Science Notebook.*

Think and Write

1. **Use Models** What happened to the soap when you rubbed the ice block over it? How might your ice block be like a glacier? How is it different?

2. **Infer** Think about what you observed. What can you infer about the effects that a glacier would have on Earth's surface?

Guided Inquiry

Experiment Design a model to show how wind shapes the land. Write a list of materials you will need and how the experiment will work. **Predict** the results of your experiment.

✔ 0407.7.1

GRAPHIC ORGANIZER

Compare and Contrast
Use the chart below to compare and contrast how glaciers and wind shape the land.

GLE 0407.7.1 Investigate how the Earth's geological features change as a result of erosion (weathering and transportation) and deposition.

Ice and Wind Shape the Land

Glaciers

A glacier (GLAY shur) is a large mass of slow-moving ice that flows down a slope. Glaciers formed long ago in cold regions of Earth. Snow piled up year after year. Over time, the weight of the snow added pressure below, and the snow turned to ice.

The weight of the ice in a glacier causes it to move slowly over the land. As it moves, a glacier is a great force of erosion. Huge amounts of soil and rock are pushed ahead of the glaciers. As glaciers melt, they leave behind a changed landscape.

A glacier is a massive river of ice that moves slowly over the land. It pushes rocks and soil ahead of it. ▼

▲ A moving glacier scooped the land. Rain filled in the scooped-out area to form June Lake, in California.

What Glaciers Leave Behind

Glaciers leave signs of their past presence on Earth's surface. They shape the land through erosion and deposition. As they move across the land, they carry away tons of material. When glaciers stop moving and begin to melt, they deposit boulders, rocks, and soil.

The long ridge formed by boulders, rocks, and soil carried and deposited by a glacier is called a **moraine**. A single large boulder moved by a glacier and deposited when the glacier melts is called an **erratic**. A bowl-shaped hollow left by a glacier is called a cirque (surk).

As a glacier moves, rocks embedded in the ice scratch across rocks lying under the ice. Large grooves left in the underlying rock can show the direction the glacier moved.

FOCUS CHECK Compare how glaciers change the land through erosion with how they change the land through deposition.

Express Lab

Activity Card
Show Wind Erosion

Erratic This large boulder dropped by a glacier is called an erratic.

Cirque This bowl-shaped hollow is called a cirque.

Moraine This rock-strewn ridge is a moraine.

Grooves Rocks embedded in glaciers make grooves in solid rock.

Evidence of Glaciers

Yosemite Valley in California was formed in a variety of ways, including glaciers. Glaciers left erratics, cirques, and moraines in the valley. And glaciers formed nearly all the lakes in Yosemite Valley.

Glaciers have helped shape mountains and carve valleys. They have also left depressions that became lakes. In high mountains, glaciers have carved out bowl-shaped hollows called cirques. Glaciers have created some of the most beautiful landscapes in the world.

Wind Carves the Land

Although it is not as strong as water, wind can change the shape of the land. Have you ever been at the beach on a windy day? Then you probably know that wind can carry sediment.

Wind easily picks up and carries beach and desert sand. The stronger the wind, the more sand the wind can carry away. Wind is even more likely to cause erosion during a dry period. Dry sand is lighter and easier for the wind to carry.

Lack of rain may kill most of the plants in an area. This makes the soil in the area more subject to wind erosion. Windbreaks such as fences, grass, shrubs, and trees can prevent or reduce wind erosion.

Sediments that the wind carries also weather Earth's surface. When windblown grains of sand and sediment are pushed along the ground, they act as sandblasters, which chip, cut, and polish.

Wind-carried sediments can help shape rock formations and their surfaces. These wind-shaped formations include buttes and sandstone towers.

FOCUS CHECK How are a moraine and erratic alike and different?

▲ Devils Tower in Wyoming was polished by the wind.

This rock formation at the Grand Canyon was shaped by wind erosion. ▶

Wind Builds Up the Land

Wind picks up sediment from one place and deposits it in another place. The place where the sediment is deposited is then built up.

Sand dunes form along seacoasts, in dry sandy plains, and in deserts. A **sand dune** is a hill or pile of sand that was formed by the wind.

Sand dunes vary in size. Small beach dunes may be 1 m to 2 m (3 to 7 ft) high. In the Sand Dunes National Park in Colorado, the sand

Dorothea Lange, a famous photographer, took this and other photographs of the Dust Bowl.

dunes cover an area that is over 80 sq. km (30 sq. mi.). Some of these dunes are as high as 230 m (754 ft).

Where winds are strong and steady, dunes may move as much as 30 m (100 ft) in a year. Dunes can bury towns, cities, and forests.

There are a number of dunes along the coast of California. The largest are the Monterey Bay dunes. California's coastal dunes formed over thousands of years.

In the 1930s, the southern plains of the United States were called the Dust Bowl. Poor farming practices and years of no rain had destroyed the ground cover. Without these plants, the soil was not held in place. Wind-blown soil covered everything.

FOCUS CHECK Compare coastal and desert sand dunes.

What causes sand dunes to form? ▼

Lesson Wrap-Up

Visual Summary

Many landforms were made by melting or moving glaciers.

Glaciers and wind shape the land through erosion and deposition.

Wind-carried sediments shape rock formations and their surfaces.

✔ Check for Understanding

DUST BOWL

Research how the southern plains of the United States recovered from the Dust Bowl. How effective were the solutions that were used? What criteria did you use to draw your conclusions?

✔ 0407.T/E.3

Reading Review

❶ MAIN IDEA How do ice and wind shape the land?

❷ VOCABULARY How is a moraine different from an erratic?

❸ READING SKILL Compare and Contrast How do sediments moved by wind compare with materials moved by glaciers?

❹ CRITICAL THINKING: Apply Suppose you interview a city planner who is concerned that the city is being threatened by a sand dune. What questions would you ask in order to learn as much as possible about the sand dune?

❺ INQUIRY SKILL: Infer How might a moving sand dune be harmful to animals?

TCAP Prep

Where do sand dunes form?

A on mountain tops
B in rivers
C in deserts
D on glaciers

SPI 0407.7.1

Go Digital Technology

Visit **www.eduplace.com/tnscp** to find out more about how ice and wind shape the land.

Galloping Glacier

What would you call this river of ice flowing down the valley? Awesome? Enormous? Whatever you call it, call it a glacier. Most glaciers move just a few inches or feet a year. But this one gallops! Meet Hubbard Glacier, one of the fastest moving glaciers in the world. It moves 10 to 100 times faster than most glaciers do.

As a glacier moves, its thick, heavy ice grinds and carves the land. A large glacier can pick up and transport billions of tons of rock and soil and deposit it dozens of miles from its origin. Whether they gallop or crawl, glaciers are a powerful force of erosion on Earth.

GLE 0407.7.1 Investigate how the Earth's geological features change as a result of erosion (weathering and transportation) and deposition.

EXTEND

Typical glaciers move a few inches to a few feet a year. The Hubbard Glacier can move 30 meters, or 100 feet, in a single day!

GLE 0407.7.1 Investigate how the Earth's geological features change as a result of erosion (weathering and transportation) and deposition. **Math GLE 0406.5.1** Collect, record, arrange, present, and interpret data using tables and various representations. **ELA GLE 0401.3.1** Write for a variety of purposes and to a variety of audiences.

Math Data Analysis

You know that if the wind is steady, a sand dune can move. In fact, sand dunes can move from 5 meters to 30 meters a year. This line graph shows the yearly movement of one sand dune over an eight-year period.

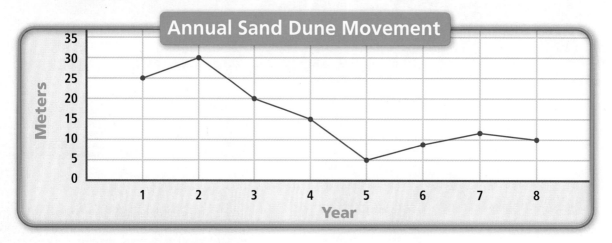

Annual Sand Dune Movement

1. In which year did the sand dune move the most? How much did it move?

2. In which year did the sand dune move the least? How much did it move?

3. How much did the sand dune move in 8 years?

 **Summary**

Research a description of weathering and erosion caused by a Tennessee river. Find out how the river has changed the land. Write a paragraph to summarize how this river, through weathering and erosion, has changed Earth's surface. Include a main idea and important details that support it.

Cartographer

Cartographers are map makers. They map many types of surface features, from the highest mountain to the ocean floor. Maps may present natural features, such as elevation and climate, or human-made ones, such as cities, roads, and crops.

Cartographers rely on physical surveys, as well as images from airplanes and satellites. They often use computers, too.

What It Takes!

- A degree in geography, geology, or art
- Drawing and computer skills

Farmer

Is farming the most important job in the world? Nearly all of the world's food comes from crops and livestock raised by farmers and ranchers. So do many other products, such as cotton, leather, and wool.

Farmers must do many tasks: operate and care for farm machinery, monitor weather conditions, prevent crop and animal diseases, care for the soil, and manage a business.

What It Takes!

- Courses in agriculture and business
- Energy for strenuous work outdoors

Vocabulary

Complete each sentence with a term from the list.

1. A body of water that is partly enclosed by land and has a wide opening to the ocean is a/an _____.

2. A hill of sand that was formed by the wind is a/an _____.

3. Movement of rock material from one place to another is _____.

4. A point of land, usually high, that extends out into the water is a/an _____.

5. A large mass of slow-moving ice is called a/an _____.

6. The wearing away of rock into smaller bits is called _____.

7. The largest river in an area and all the waterways that drain into it is called a/an _____.

8. A large mass of sediment deposited at the mouth of a river is called a/an _____.

9. A long ridge formed by boulders, rocks, and soil carried and deposited by a glacier is called a/an _____.

10. A single large boulder moved by a glacier and deposited when the glacier melts is a/an _____.

bay
delta
deposition
★ **erosion**
erratic
glacier
headland
moraine
river system
sand dune
weathering

TCAP Inquiry Skills

11. **Communicate** How do tree roots cause weathering? GLE 0407.7.1

12. **Predict** What would you predict may happen to the coastline if a glacier melted next to it? Explain. GLE 0407.7.1

Map the Concept

Complete the concept maps using the following terms.

river system
moraine
glacier
sand dune
wind
delta

GLE 0407.7.1

Cause		Effect
_____	▶	_____
_____	▶	_____
_____	▶	_____

Critical Thinking

13. Analyze What might be some of the long-term effects of building many dams along a river system?
GLE 0407.7.2

14. Synthesize What might you expect in some of the ice of a glacier?
GLE 0407.7.1

15. Analyze What is the relationship between erosion, weathering, and deposition and the formation of sand dunes?
GLE 0407.7.1

16. Evaluate Authorities are planning to build a road near the Monterey Bay sand dunes. Scientists know that sand dunes can move as much as 30 m a year. Do you think authorities should go ahead with their plans? Why or why not?
GLE 0407.7.2

Check for Understanding

Earth Materials

Building homes near landforms requires materials that can withstand erosion and weathering. Research different earth materials and list factors that determine whether or not they are appropriate to use as building materials.
0407.7.3

TCAP Prep

Write the letter of the best answer choice.

17 What is the dropping of sediment moved by water, wind, and ice?

A deposition

B weathering

C moraine

D erratic   SPI 0407.7.1

18 What area of California was partly formed by glaciers?

F Central Valley

G Monterey Bay dunes

H Yosemite Valley

J Death Valley   SPI 0407.7.1

19 What causes more erosion than any other form of weathering?

A chemicals

B plants

C wind

D water   SPI 0407.7.1

20 What helped cause the Dust Bowl of the 1930s?

F poor farming practices

G modern soil conservation

H planting too many crops at the same time

J damp, tightly packed soil

SPI 0407.7.2

Chapter 6

Using Weather Data

Lesson Preview
Note Book

LESSON 1

Planes fly through it and clouds float in it—how does Earth's atmosphere support life on the surface?

LESSON 2

From clouds to rain to water vapor—how does Earth's water change form?

LESSON 3

A warm, sunny day with gentle breezes becomes a fierce hurricane with harsh winds. What causes weather to change?

LESSON 4

Sunny tropical lands and snow-covered poles—what factors cause climates to differ?

Fun Facts

The drops of water in fog are so small that it takes 7 billion of them to fill a teaspoon.

Vocabulary Preview

air mass
air pressure
atmosphere
climate
★ condensation
★ evaporation
front
greenhouse effect
polar climate
precipitation
temperate climate
tropical climate
water cycle
weather

★ = Tennessee Academic Vocabulary

 Vocabulary Strategies

Have you ever seen any of these terms before? Do you know what they mean?

State a description, explanation, or example of the vocabulary in your own words.

Draw a picture, symbol, example, or other image that describes the term

Glossary p. H16

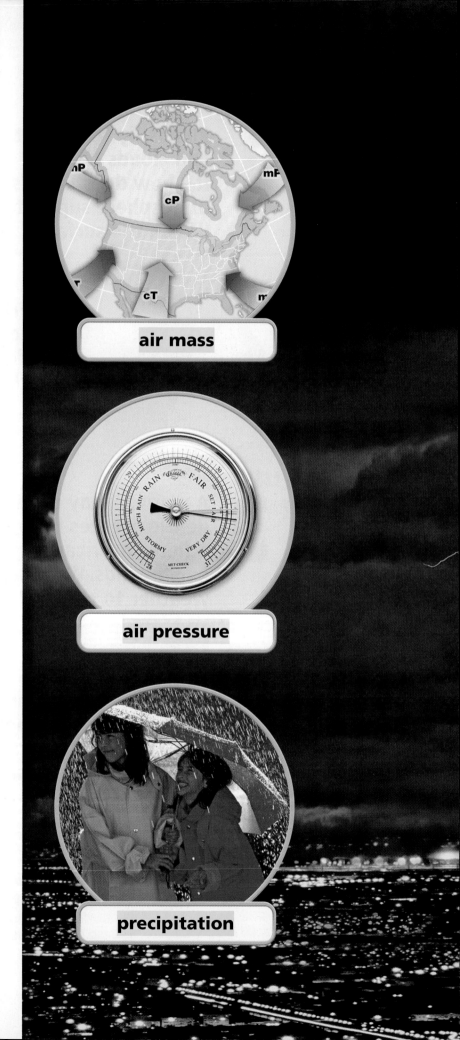

air mass

air pressure

precipitation

weather

Start with Your Standards

Inquiry

GLE 0407.Inq.1 Explore different scientific phenomena by asking questions, making logical predictions, planning investigations, and recording data.

GLE 0407.Inq.2 Select and use appropriate tools and simple equipment to conduct an investigation.

GLE 0407.Inq.3 Organize data into appropriate tables, graphs, drawings, or diagrams.

GLE 0407.Inq.4 Identify and interpret simple patterns of evidence to communicate the findings of multiple investigations.

GLE 0407.Inq.6 Compare the results of an investigation with what scientists already accept about this question.

Earth Science

Standard 8 The Atmosphere

GLE 0407.8.1 Recognize the major components of the water cycle.

GLE 0407.8.2 Differentiate between weather and climate.

Interact with this chapter.

 www.eduplace.com/tnscp

Lesson 1

TENNESSEE STANDARDS

GLE 0407.Inq.1 Explore different scientific phenomena by asking questions, making logical predictions, planning investigations, and recording data.
GLE 0407.Inq.4 Identify and interpret simple patterns of evidence to communicate the findings of multiple investigations.

What Is Air?

Guiding Question

Why It Matters...

What would it be like to float among the clouds? Ask a sky diver!

Parachutes allow sky divers to drift with the wind and fall gently to the ground. The speed is slow because air catches inside the parachute. Like birds and airplanes, sky divers depend on the air.

PREPARE TO INVESTIGATE

Inquiry Skill

Compare When you compare two things, you observe how they are alike and how they are different.

Materials

- dowel
- piece of string
- 2 balloons
- tape
- marker
- metric ruler

Directed Inquiry

Balancing Air

Procedure

1. **Collaborate** Work with a partner. Tie a string around the center of a dowel. Hold the string while your partner slides the knot along the dowel. The dowel should be balanced so that it stays exactly level.

2. **Experiment** Use a metric ruler to help you. Tape two deflated balloons exactly the same distance from the center of the dowel. Slide the knot of the string until the dowel is balanced.

3. **Predict** Use a pencil to mark the dowel at the exact place where one balloon is attached. Then remove that balloon and blow it up. Tie a knot in the neck so that no air escapes. Predict what will happen when you reattach the balloon to the dowel.

4. **Compare** Reattach the balloon to the dowel at the marked place. Compare how the dowel balanced before and after you inflated the balloon.

5. **Record Data** Record your observations in your *Science Notebook*.

Think and Write

1. **Compare** Which weighs more, an inflated balloon or a deflated balloon?

2. **Hypothesize** Write a hypothesis about what caused the change in the way the dowel balanced.

✔ 0407.Inq.4

STEP 2

STEP 3

STEP 4

Guided Inquiry

Design an Experiment
Could adding salt inside the deflated balloon be used to balance the dowel? Run an experiment to find out. What conclusion can you draw about the weights of the air and the salt?

The Atmosphere

VOCABULARY

air pressure
atmosphere
greenhouse effect
weather

GRAPHIC ORGANIZER

Draw Conclusions Use details from the lesson to show why gases in the atmosphere are important to life on Earth.

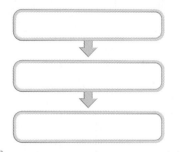

GLE 0407.8.2 Differentiate between weather and climate.

Gases in Air

Did you ever wonder what is in the air you breathe? Air is a mixture of colorless, odorless gases that surrounds Earth. Nitrogen (NY truh juhn) makes up the largest portion of air. Plants need nitrogen to grow. Oxygen (AHK sih juhn) is the second most common gas in air. Living things need oxygen to survive. Your body needs oxygen to use the energy in the food you eat. Most living things get the oxygen they need from air.

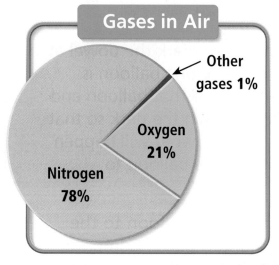

Gases in Air

Other gases 1%

Oxygen 21%

Nitrogen 78%

Living things depend on the gases in air to survive.

Nitrogen and oxygen are not the only gases that make up air. Small amounts of other substances are found in air. Two of these substances are carbon dioxide (KAHR-buhn dy-AHK syd) and water.

Carbon dioxide is a colorless, odorless gas that helps hold heat close to Earth. All animals, including people, give off carbon dioxide with every breath.

Plants take in carbon dioxide to make food. In the process of making food, plants give off oxygen. Plants transfer carbon dioxide and oxygen in just the opposite way that animals do.

FOCUS CHECK Why is carbon dioxide in the air important to plants?

Plants use carbon dioxide in air to make food. When plants make food, they release oxygen into the air.

Plants absorb nitrogen through their roots. Plants need nitrogen to grow.

Animals use oxygen to get energy from food. Animals give off carbon dioxide.

Express Lab

Activity Card
Observe Air Pressure

193

Earth's Blanket

On a cold night, it is good to have a blanket to wrap around you. Earth has a blanket, too. Earth's blanket is a layer of gases called the **atmosphere** (AT muh sfihr).

The Sun heats Earth, and the atmosphere holds the heat close to Earth's surface. This keeps Earth's surface at a comfortable temperature. The atmosphere also helps protect living things from harmful rays given off by the Sun.

Air takes up space. When you blow up a balloon, the balloon gets bigger. The air you put inside it takes up space. Air also has weight.

The weight of air presses down on Earth's surface all the time. The weight of air as it presses down is called **air pressure** (PREHSH uhr). Your body is used to air pressure, so you do not feel it. A barometer is an instrument that measures air pressure.

Suppose you travel to the top of a very high mountain. Compared with air at the base of the mountain, there are fewer particles of air and they are more spread out at the top of a mountain. Less air presses down, which means air pressure is lower on the mountaintop than at the base. Because air particles are more spread out, people sometimes say that the air is thinner.

The atmosphere has four layers. The lowest layer is called the troposphere (TROHP uh sfihr). It rises about 10 km above the surface.

As the air becomes thinner, climbers of very high mountains cannot get enough oxygen with each breath. Climbers have to breathe oxygen from a supply that they carry.

Earth's **weather** occurs in the troposphere. Weather is the conditions of the atmosphere at a certain place and time.

The layer of the atmosphere above the troposphere is the stratosphere (STRAT uh sfihr). If you have ever flown in a jet plane, you may have been in the stratosphere. Above the weather the air is calm and the airplane ride is smoother. This layer keeps a lot of the harmful part of the Sun's rays from reaching Earth.

The mesosphere (MEHZ uh sfihr) is the next layer. Most meteors burn up when they reach this layer.

The top layer of the atmosphere is called the thermosphere (THUHRM uh sfihr). Space shuttles travel in Earth's thermosphere.

FOCUS CHECK Why do jet planes fly in the stratosphere?

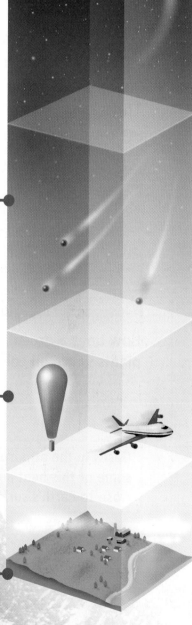

Thermosphere

The thermosphere is from 80 km (50 mi) to 700 km (430 mi). Space begins at the top of this layer.

Mesosphere

The mesosphere reaches from 50 km (30 mi) to 80 km (50 mi) above Earth. The coldest temperatures in the atmosphere are found here.

Stratosphere

The stratosphere reaches 10 km (6 mi) to 50 km (30 mi) above Earth. The Sun's powerful rays heat up the stratosphere.

Troposphere

The troposphere begins at the ground and rises to 10 km (6 mi). The temperature decreases as the height increases.

195

Greenhouse Effect

If you have ever been in a greenhouse, you know it is warm inside. The glass walls and roof of a greenhouse let in light and heat from the Sun. The glass traps the heat, letting little out. This keeps the plants inside warm.

Gases in the atmosphere keep Earth warm in much the same way. Earth's atmosphere lets in light and heat from the Sun. Some of the heat escapes into space, but most of the heat is held in by the atmosphere. More heat escapes in winter than in summer.

This natural heating of Earth is called the greenhouse effect. The **greenhouse effect** is the process by which heat from the Sun builds up near Earth's surface and is trapped there by the atmosphere.

Today, scientists are concerned by evidence that shows Earth's temperatures are rising slowly. This process is called global warming. Most scientists point to an increase in greenhouse gases, especially carbon dioxide, as the cause.

FOCUS CHECK Why is the greenhouse effect important to life on Earth?

How does a greenhouse keep plants warm on cold days?

The Greenhouse Effect

Sun

Gases in the atmosphere trap some of this heat and keep it close to Earth's surface.

Heat from the Sun passes through the atmosphere and is reflected from the surface of Earth.

Atmosphere

Lesson Wrap-Up

Visual Summary

Air is made of nitrogen, oxygen, and other gases. Living things need air to survive.

The atmosphere is a blanket of air that surrounds Earth. The air is thinner higher in the atmosphere.

The atmosphere acts as a natural greenhouse that keeps Earth warm.

✔ Check for Understanding

METEOROLOGY REPORT

Meteorology is the study of the weather. Experts in meteorology issue forecasts and teach people about weather science. Watch a weather report on television. What tools and technology do meteorologists use? How does technology improve the quality of the report?

✔ 0407.T/E.1

Review

1 MAIN IDEA How does the atmosphere support life on Earth?

2 VOCABULARY Write a sentence using the terms *atmosphere* and *weather*.

3 READING SKILL Draw Conclusions Discuss three ways that the atmosphere affects life on Earth.

4 CRITICAL THINKING: Analyze When trees burn, carbon dioxide is released into the atmosphere. What could be the long-term effect if large areas of forest were burned?

5 INQUIRY SKILL: Compare How are the troposphere and the thermosphere different?

TCAP TCAP Prep

According to many scientists, rising levels of _____ in the atmosphere are causing Earth's temperatures to rise.

A carbon dioxide
B oxygen
C nitrogen
D hydrogen

SPI 0407.8.2

Go Digital Technology

Visit **www.eduplace.com/tnscp** to find out more about Earth's atmosphere.

Lesson 2

TENNESSEE STANDARDS

GLE 0407.8.1 Recognize the major components of the water cycle.
GLE 0407.Inq.3 Organize data into appropriate tables, graphs, drawings, or diagrams.

How Does the Water Cycle Affect Weather?

Why It Matters...

Animals have their own protection against bad weather. Birds' feathers help keep them dry in the rain. Yet in heavy rains, birds likely seek shelter, just as you would.

You may not always enjoy rainy days, but nearly all of Earth's living things rely on them. Rain is part of the water cycle—the unending movement of water between atmosphere and land.

PREPARE TO INVESTIGATE

Inquiry Skill

Use Models You can use a model of an object, process, or idea to better understand or describe how it works.

Materials

- clear plastic container with lid
- water
- small resealable plastic bag
- 4–5 ice cubes
- lamp
- clock or watch
- metric ruler

Science and Math Toolbox

For step 1, review **Measuring Elapsed Time** on pages H12–H13.

Directed Inquiry

Water Cycle Model

Procedure

1. **Collaborate** Work with a partner. In your *Science Notebook*, make a chart like the one shown.

2. **Measure** Use a metric ruler to measure 1 cm of water in a plastic container. Place the lid on the container.

3. **Place** 4 or 5 ice cubes in a plastic bag. Seal the bag and place it on the lid of the container.

4. **Use Models** Put the container near a lamp so that the lamp shines on one side of the container. **Safety:** Do not touch the light bulb. It may be very hot. Do not look directly into the light.

5. **Observe** After 15 minutes, carefully observe the container. Look for any changes on the inside and the outside of the container. Record your observations in your chart. Make observations every 15 minutes for one hour.

Think and Write

1. **Analyze Data** What changes occurred on the inside of the container?

2. **Use Models** You made a model of Earth's water cycle using a lamp as a source of heat. What source of heat warms the water in lakes, rivers, and oceans on Earth?

0407.8.1

STEP 1

	Observations	
Time	Inside of Container	Outside of Container
Start		
After 15 minutes		
After 30 minutes		
After 45 minutes		
After 1 hour		

STEP 3

STEP 4

Guided Inquiry

Design an Experiment
How does temperature affect the rate that water evaporates? With your teacher's approval, design and run an experiment to find out. Include a diagram or graph to present data and observations.

199

The Water Cycle and Weather

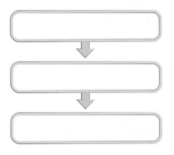
Three States of Water

About three-fourths of Earth's surface is covered by water. Water is found on Earth in three states, or forms. The states are solid, liquid, and gas.

Liquid water gathers in oceans, seas, and rivers, and it falls as rain. Ice is water in its solid state. Ice forms when heat is removed from liquid water. When temperatures fall below 0°C (32°F), liquid water freezes and becomes ice.

Water can also take the form of a gas. Water in the gas state is called water vapor (VAY pur). Water vapor is part of the air, but you cannot see it. It forms when heat is added to liquid water.

This lake is partially frozen. Which states of water can you see? Which cannot be seen?

ice

If you have ever watched ice melting, then you have observed one way that water changes state. Heat from the Sun is melting the ice on the lake shown below.

Heat can also change liquid water to water vapor. Raise the temperature of liquid water to 100°C (212°F), and you will observe water vapor bubbling throughout the sample. This is called boiling.

Yet liquid water also can become water vapor at lower temperatures. This happens in a process called **evaporation** (ih VAP uh ray shuhn), in which the surface of the water slowly changes into a gas. Even on a cold day, heat from the Sun will cause some evaporation.

Do you see the steam, or mist, in the photograph below? The steam is made not from water vapor, but from tiny drops of liquid water. The drops formed by **condensation** (kahn dehn SAY shuhn), the change of state from gas to liquid.

How does steam form above a lake? First, liquid water evaporates from the lake surface. When the water vapor meets the cold air above the lake, it condenses into tiny drops. The drops are so small that they hang in the air.

Clouds form in a similar way, only higher above the surface. Read on to learn how this happens!

FOCUS CHECK How does mist form above a lake, as shown below?

water vapor

liquid water

Express Lab

Activity Card
Create Condensation

The Water Cycle

The water on Earth changes from one form to another over and over again as it goes through the water cycle (SY kuhl). The **water cycle** is the movement of water into the air as water vapor and back to Earth's surface as precipitation (prih sihp-uh TAY shuhn). **Precipitation** is any form of water that falls from clouds to Earth's surface.

Water in oceans, lakes, and rivers evaporates and becomes water vapor. As water vapor rises in the air, it cools and condenses into water droplets. These droplets form clouds.

As more water vapor condenses, the drops become heavier and form drops which fall to Earth as precipitation.

Some precipitation flows downhill on Earth's surface as runoff. Runoff water flows toward streams, rivers, lakes, and oceans. Some precipitation flows down into the ground to become groundwater.

The water cycle cleans Earth's water supply. For example, salt and other materials in the ocean are left behind when ocean water evaporates.

Water moves into the air as a gas and back to Earth's surface as a liquid in the water cycle.

Water Cycle

precipitation
Water droplets in the cloud become heavy, and they fall as precipitation.

evaporation
Heat from the Sun causes evaporation of water from oceans, lakes, and rivers. Water vapor rises in the air and cools.

Types of Clouds

Clouds form when water vapor in the air condenses. A cloud that forms close to the ground is called fog.

Stratus (STRAT uhs) clouds are low-level clouds that form in layers. Stratus clouds usually bring steady rain.

Cumulus (KYOOM yoo luhs) clouds are fluffy and have flat bases. They form low in the sky. They usually mean fair weather.

Cirrus (SEER uhs) clouds are thin, feathery clouds made of ice crystals. They form high in the sky. Cirrus clouds indicate fair weather.

Cumulonimbus (kyoom yoo lo NIHM buhs) clouds bring thunderstorms.

FOCUS CHECK How could water from the ocean become the water that makes up a cloud?

Stratus

Cumulus

Cirrus

condensation
Cooled water vapor condenses into water droplets and forms clouds.

Cumulonimbus

Rain consists of falling drops of liquid water.

Sleet forms when rain freezes as it falls.

Snowflakes can form in many different shapes.

A hailstone can be as large as a baseball.

Forms of Precipitation

Rain is the most common form of precipitation. It rains when drops of water in clouds fall through air that is above freezing.

Sleet is rain that freezes as it falls. If the temperature near Earth's surface is below freezing, rain turns to ice before it strikes the ground.

Snow falls when the temperature in a cloud is below freezing. Water vapor in the cloud forms ice crystals known as snowflakes.

Hail forms when drops of rain freeze and strong winds carry them higher into a cloud. As hailstones fall again, more ice forms on them. They become larger. This process can happen over and over. Finally, when the hailstones are too heavy to be lifted by the wind, they fall.

◎ FOCUS CHECK Describe the repeating process that forms hail.

Lesson Wrap-Up

Visual Summary

Water exists in three states: solid ice, liquid water, and water vapor.

The water cycle is the movement of water into the air as water vapor and back to Earth as precipitation.

Different types of clouds bring pleasant weather or precipitation.

Check for Understanding

EVAPORATION TIME

Record the time, then wet a section of sidewalk, chalkboard, or other surface. Observe changes in the surface as it dries. Record the time when it is completely dry. Repeat the experiment when the surface is warmer or colder. Compare the results, and explain any differences.

✔ 0407.Inq.4

Review

❶ **MAIN IDEA** Describe the stages of the water cycle.

❷ **VOCABULARY** What does the term *precipitation* mean?

❸ **READING SKILL** Sequence During a storm, rain falls to Earth's surface. The water runs into a river and out into the ocean. What happens to the water next?

❹ **CRITICAL THINKING:** Evaluate Suppose someone tells you that snowflakes are frozen raindrops. Is this statement true? Explain.

❺ **INQUIRY SKILL:** Use Models To best model the water cycle, would you use an open cup of water, or a cup of water covered in plastic wrap? Explain.

TCAP Prep

Where does evaporation take place on a lake?

A at the bottom of the lake
B at the surface of the lake
C throughout the lake
D along the shoreline

SPI 0407.8.1

Go Digital Technology

Visit **www.eduplace.com/tnscp** to learn more about the water cycle.

Lesson 3

TENNESSEE STANDARDS

GLE 0407.8.2 Differentiate between weather and climate.
GLE 0407.Inq.2 Select and use appropriate tools and simple equipment to conduct an investigation.

Guiding Question

What Causes Weather?

Why It Matters...

Mt. Washington in New Hampshire is nicknamed "Home of the World's Worst Weather." Scientists here record weather conditions and conduct important research. The research includes testing instruments that can help improve weather forecasts.

PREPARE TO INVESTIGATE
Inquiry Skill

Analyze Data When you analyze data, you look for patterns that can help you make predictions, hypotheses, and generalizations.

Materials

- barometer
- thermometer
- precipitation gauge
- local newspaper weather map and weather forecast

Science and Math Toolbox

For step 5, review **Using a Thermometer** on page H8.

Directed Inquiry

Local Forecast

Procedure

① **Collaborate** Work in groups of 3 or 4. In your *Science Notebook*, make a chart like the one shown.

② **Measure** Set a barometer outside. Read it immediately and then again after one hour. Note whether the air pressure is rising, falling, or unchanged.

③ **Research** Look on the Internet and in reference books to learn about barometer readings. Find out what type of weather usually follows a rising or falling barometer reading. Predict the day's weather based on your barometer readings. Record your prediction.

④ **Analyze Data** Study a newspaper weather map and forecast. In your chart, record the newspaper's forecast.

⑤ **Measure** Set a thermometer and precipitation gauge outside in an open area. Check and record the temperature and the depth of any rain or snow that falls throughout the day. Also, record the cloud cover and wind conditions.

Think and Write

1. **Compare** How did your weather prediction compare to the newspaper's forecast?

2. **Predict** Did the actual weather match the newspaper's forecast? Did it match your prediction? Explain.

✔ 0407.Inq.2

STEP 1

	My Weather Prediction	Newspaper Weather Forecast	Actual Weather
Temperature			
Precipitation			
Wind			
Clouds			

STEP 2

STEP 5

Guided Inquiry

Research Use the Internet, the library, or other resources to learn how scientists forecast your local weather. Write a report about the instruments and tools they use.

Weather

Weather Factors

On a fair day, you might describe the weather with just one word, such as "sunny" or "warm." Scientists talk about many more factors when they describe the weather. Weather involves all of the conditions of the atmosphere at a certain time and place. They include temperature, amount of water vapor in the air, wind, and air pressure.

The temperature is how hot or cold the air is. The amount of water vapor in the air is called humidity (hyoo MIHD uh tee). High humidity can make the air feel wet and sticky. Wind is the movement of air. Recall that air pressure is the weight of air as it presses down on Earth's surface.

Each weather factor can be measured using a different instrument. A thermometer measures the temperature of the air. A rain gauge collects and measures precipitation. An anemometer (an uh MAHM uh tuhr) is a tool used to measure wind speed.

Air pressure is measured with a device called a barometer (buh RAH muh tur). It tells whether air pressure is high or low.

FOCUS CHECK **What are the main factors that affect weather?**

Thermometer
A thermometer measures temperature in degrees Celsius or degrees Fahrenheit.

Rain Gauge
A rain gauge measures the amount of precipitation that has fallen in an area.

Barometer
A barometer measures air pressure in units called millibars.

Anemometer
The cups on the anemometer spin in the wind. The anemometer calculates the wind speed in kilometers per hour or miles per hour.

Most cities in Tennessee receive less than 25 cm (about 10 in.) of snow per year.

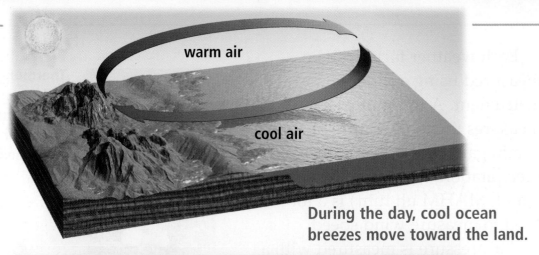

During the day, cool ocean breezes move toward the land.

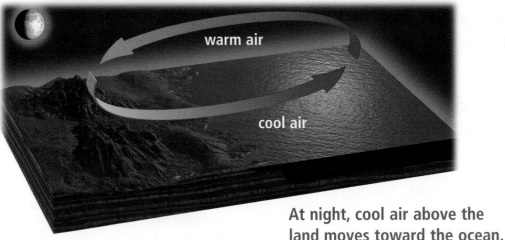

At night, cool air above the land moves toward the ocean.

Wind

What makes air move? Air flows from areas of high pressure to areas of low pressure. High-pressure areas and low-pressure areas form because the Sun heats Earth unevenly.

For example, during the day, land areas become warm very quickly. The land warms the air above it. As the air warms, it expands. This expanding of air produces an area of low pressure. The warm, light air that is above the land begins to rise.

Oceans change temperature slowly, so they do not become as warm as the land. During the day, air above the ocean is not as warm as air over the land. As the warm air above the land begins to rise, the cooler, heavier air above the ocean moves in to take its place. This flow of cool air from the ocean to the land is known as a sea breeze.

At night, the land cools off more quickly than the ocean water does. In this case, the air above the ocean is warmer and lighter than the air above the land. As the warm air rises, the cool air above the land moves toward the ocean.

Air Masses

You have seen that land and water absorb different amounts of heat from the Sun. Areas near the equator (ee KWAY tur) receive more heat from sunlight than areas near the poles. The equator is an imaginary line around Earth and is an equal distance from the North Pole and the South Pole.

Each area warms or cools the air above it, creating an air mass. An **air mass** is a large body of air that has about the same temperature, air pressure, and moisture throughout.

Air masses are described by two conditions—temperature and humidity. They are either warm or cold, as well as either moist or dry.

Air masses that form near the equator are usually warm. Those that form near the poles are cold. Air masses that form over the oceans are moist. Those that form over the land areas are usually dry. Most changes in weather occur when one air mass moves into an area and pushes out another air mass.

FOCUS CHECK **What conditions describe air masses?**

The arrows show the movement of air masses that affect the United States.

A polar land air mass brings cold, dry air to the northern Midwest during the winter.

A polar ocean air mass brings cool, moist air to the Pacific Northwest.

A polar ocean air mass in the Atlantic Ocean keeps the Northeast cool and wet.

A tropical ocean air mass brings wet winters to California and the Pacific coast.

A tropical land air mass brings extremely hot, dry air to the Southwest.

A tropical ocean air mass brings warm, wet weather from the Gulf of Mexico to the South.

Weather Patterns

As Earth rotates, air masses move. In North America, most air masses move from west to east. As they move, they bump into each other.

The place where two air masses meet is called a **front**. A front moves across Earth's surface as one air mass pushes against the other. Weather can change very suddenly when a front moves across an area. Most storms and precipitation take place along fronts.

A cold front forms as a cold air mass meets a warm air mass. The cold air moves under the warm air, pushing it up. As the warm air rises, clouds form and precipitation falls. Thunderstorms often strike along a cold front.

A warm front forms as a warm air mass pushes into a cold air mass. The warm air slowly moves up over the cold air. Layers of gray clouds and steady precipitation are common along a warm front.

The same types of air masses usually form over North America each year. They usually move in the same directions, too. This creates weather patterns that repeat with the seasons.

For example, cold air masses often move down from Canada. They meet warm air masses from the Gulf of Mexico. Every spring and summer these air masses collide over the Great Plains. The cold fronts cause violent thunderstorms and tornadoes across the region.

Data from many sources are combined on maps that can be used to forecast the weather. ▼

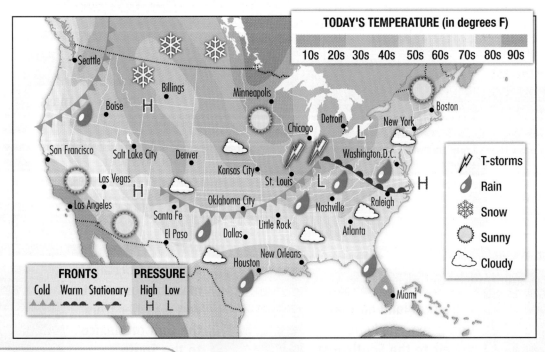

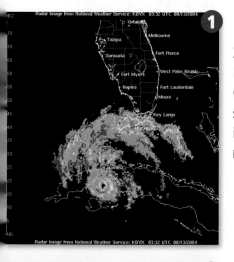

3:32 A.M. Hurricane Charley first struck Florida in the early morning.

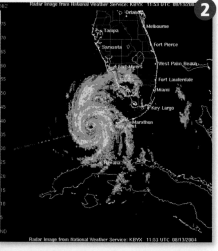

11:53 A.M. Hurricane Charley continued to move up the western coast.

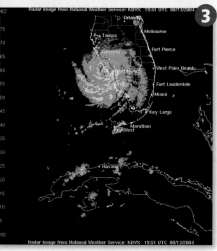

7:51 P.M. Heavy rains fell over much of Florida as the storm moved across the state.

▲ In these radar images, the swirling colored bands show that a hurricane is approaching the land. Compare these images to those on the next page.

Analyzing Weather Data

A meteorologist (mee tee uh- RAHL uh jihst) is a scientist who studies weather. Studying weather involves measuring conditions near Earth's surface and high in the atmosphere. Scientists gather data from many sources, including radar and satellites.

Meteorologists use the data they collect to identify the kinds of air masses over an area. They also predict what kind of front will form and where that front will move. This type of information is used to produce a weather map.

You can read weather maps in newspapers as part of the weather forecast. A forecast is a prediction of what the weather will be for a particular day, week, or longer period of time.

How accurate and precise can forecasts be? The answer depends on how far into the future they predict. The forecast for tomorrow's weather tells more details than the one for next week or next month.

◎**FOCUS CHECK** Where does most precipitation occur?

Express Lab

Activity Card
Forecast Weather

213

Severe Weather

Weather forecasts can help you decide if you should wear a jacket to school. But weather forecasts can also help save lives.

Hurricanes, tornadoes, thunderstorms, and snowstorms are examples of severe, dangerous weather. Hurricanes are a special threat in the southeastern United States. They can threaten lives and destroy property.

Meteorologists study storms using satellites in space and weather instruments on the ground. Forecasters issue weather warnings when severe weather approaches. These warnings can save lives by giving people time to prepare for a storm. Warnings can also allow people to leave areas that are in the path of dangerous weather.

FOCUS CHECK Identify three kinds of severe weather.

This satellite image shows the huge swirling clouds of a hurricane. The storm brings heavy rains and strong winds.▼

Lesson Wrap-Up

Visual Summary

Weather factors include temperature, moisture, air pressure, and wind.

Earth's surface heats unevenly, causing air masses to form. Fronts form where air masses collide.

Meteorologists gather and study weather data. They use this data to make forecasts and track severe weather.

✔ Check for Understanding

MAKE WEATHER INSTRUMENTS
Research how to construct simple weather instruments such a barometer, rain gauge, and weather vane. Use your instruments to collect measurements. Compare these measurements with weather reports. Draw conclusions about the accuracy of your instruments and the measurements. How can you make them more accurate?

✔ 0407.T/E.4

Review

❶ **MAIN IDEA** What factors make up the weather?

❷ **VOCABULARY** Write a sentence using the terms *air mass* and *front*.

❸ **READING SKILL Main Idea and Details** Describe the kind of information you can learn from a weather map.

❹ **CRITICAL THINKING: Apply** Suppose there is a large lake located east of where you live. During the day, the lake heats more slowly than the land. From which direction will the wind blow during the day?

❺ **INQUIRY SKILL: Analyze Data** A wam, humid, and sunny morning changes to stormy weather in the afternoon. In the evening, it is cool and dry. What type of front passed through?

TCAP Prep

To measure air pressure, you would use a/an

A anemometer.
B barometer.
C weather vane.
D thermometer.

SPI 0407.8.2

Go Digital Technology

Visit **www.eduplace.com/tnscp** to find out more about weather.

INTO THE EYE OF THE STORM

Hurricane Katrina hit the Louisiana coast in August 2005. As the storm neared, many people ran, drove, or flew away as fast as possible. But a few people flew into (yes, into) the eye, or center, of the storm. They are Hurricane Hunters, from the United States Air Force.

Hurricanes are powerful, whirling storms that form over warm oceans and cause heavy rains and high winds. The eye of a hurricane is calm. Once inside the eye of Hurricane Katrina, the Hurricane Hunters released tubes with tiny parachutes. Each tube was about the size of a can of tennis balls. Instruments inside the tubes sent back data about wind speed and other conditions.

This information helps forecasters rate hurricanes on a scale of 1 to 5. Storms with a 5 rating have the highest speeds and cause the most damage. Hurricane Katrina was a Category 5 storm.

Hurricane Katrina caused more than $80 billion in damage.

Hurricane Katrina hit with winds of up to 280 kilometers (175 mi) per hour.

The Hurricane Hunters study a hurricane from the inside of the storm.

Lesson 4

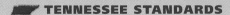

TENNESSEE STANDARDS

GLE 0407.8.2 Differentiate between weather and climate.
GLE 0407.Inq.6 Compare the results of an investigation with what scientists already accept about this question.

Guiding Question

How Does Climate Change?

Why It Matters...

Did you know that a tree stump can give you a history lesson? Each ring records one year of a tree's life. Ring widths are clues to temperature and rainfall patterns when the tree was alive.

Scientists study all sorts of evidence to learn about weather conditions of the past. They have learned that weather patterns have changed many times—and may change again in the future.

PREPARE TO INVESTIGATE

Inquiry Skill

Use Models You can use a model of an object, process, or idea to better understand or describe how it works.

Materials

- aquarium
- cardboard to cover aquarium
- black construction paper
- salt
- rolling pin
- pan
- hot water
- clock or watch
- goggles

Science and Math Toolbox

For step 4, review **Measuring Elapsed Time** on pages H12–H13.

Directed Inquiry

Land and Water

Procedure

1. **Collaborate** Work with a partner. Sprinkle a large amount of salt on a sheet of black construction paper. Use a rolling pin to grind the salt into the paper. The paper should be covered with white powder. **Safety:** Wear goggles.

2. **Use Models** Fold the black paper in half, with the salt-covered side facing out. Set the paper in an empty aquarium so it stands up in a tent shape to model a mountain.

3. **Use Models** Place a pan of hot water in the aquarium next to one side of the model mountain. Cover the aquarium with a sheet of cardboard.

4. **Observe** After 10 minutes, remove the cover. Observe each side of the mountain. Record your observations and draw a sketch in your *Science Notebook*.

Think and Write

1. **Analyze Data** What happened to the salt on each side of the mountain?

2. **Hypothesize** What might have caused the change in the way the salt appeared?

3. **Use Models** If the paper models a mountain, what might the pan of water stand for? Use your observations to describe what the weather conditions might be like in an area similar to your model.

✓ 0407.8.3

STEP 1

STEP 2

STEP 3

Guided Inquiry

Research Use an atlas or other maps to find places on Earth where the surface features look like your model. Use the Internet and the library to find out what kinds of weather conditions exist in these areas.

Climates of the World

GRAPHIC ORGANIZER

Cause and Effect As you read, write down the causes of changes in climate.

GLE 0407.8.2 Differentiate between weather and climate.

Major Climate Zones

If someone asked you what winter is like in Tennessee, what would you say? You could not say exactly what the temperature would be or how much snow or rain would fall. But you could describe winter weather in general terms, such as cool and pleasant.

Tennessee, like all other places, has a specific climate (KLY muht). **Climate** is the average weather conditions in an area over a long period of time. The climate of an area determines the kinds of plants and animals that can live there.

Skunks are hardy animals that can survive both warm summers and cold winters.

Colorful tropical fish can only survive in hot climates where the water temperature is warm.

Harp seals live in cold climates. Their thick fur keeps them warm.

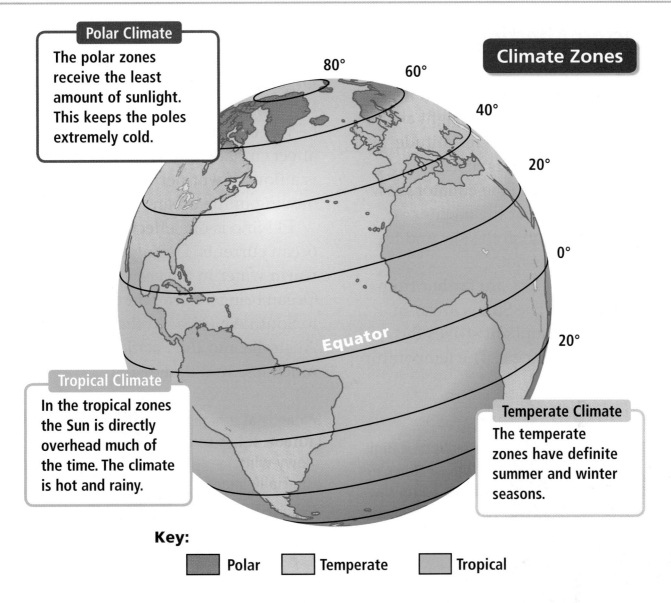

Climate Zones

Polar Climate
The polar zones receive the least amount of sunlight. This keeps the poles extremely cold.

80°   60°   40°   20°   0°   20°

Equator

Tropical Climate
In the tropical zones the Sun is directly overhead much of the time. The climate is hot and rainy.

Temperate Climate
The temperate zones have definite summer and winter seasons.

Key:

■ Polar   ■ Temperate   ■ Tropical

Earth can be divided into three major climate zones. The warmest climates are found in the tropical climate zone. A **tropical climate** is hot and rainy. The tropical climate zone is the area directly north and south of the equator. It receives strong sunlight all year.

The coldest climate zones are the areas around the North Pole and the South Pole. The poles receive the least amount of sunlight on Earth. Because of this, a **polar climate** has very cold temperatures all through the year. Most places in the polar climate zones have snow on the ground almost all year.

Most of the United States is in a temperate (TEHM pur iht) zone. The temperate zones are between the tropical zone and the polar zones. A **temperate climate** usually has warm, dry summers and cold, wet winters.

FOCUS CHECK What causes a polar climate to be so cold?

221

Factors Affecting Climate

The amount of sunlight an area receives has a large effect on its climate. How much sunlight an area receives depends on its latitude (LAT ih tood), or its distance north or south of the equator. Low latitudes are near the equator. The Sun is high in the sky and the temperature is hot.

High latitudes are farther from the equator. The Sun is lower in the sky and sunlight strikes the surface at an angle. The temperature is colder.

Oceans and other bodies of water also affect the climate of an area. A large body of water usually causes the climate of nearby land areas to be wet and mild. Ocean currents affect climate, too. An ocean current is a flow of warmer or colder water moving in the ocean.

El Niño is one effect of changing ocean currents. During El Niño, warm water in the eastern Pacific Ocean brings more rain than usual to South America. At the same time, Australia and the Pacific Islands get much less rain than usual.

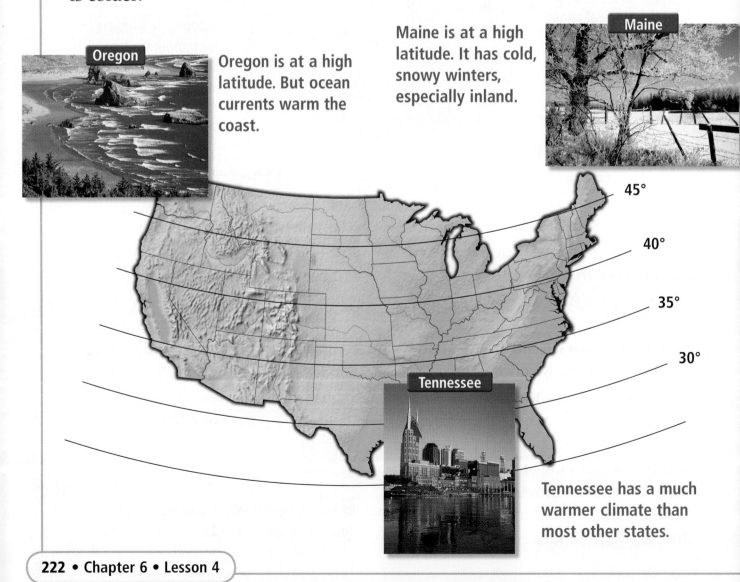

Oregon

Oregon is at a high latitude. But ocean currents warm the coast.

Maine is at a high latitude. It has cold, snowy winters, especially inland.

Maine

45°

40°

35°

30°

Tennessee

Tennessee has a much warmer climate than most other states.

Altitude (AL tih tood), or height above sea level, also affects climate. The higher you travel up a mountain, the colder it gets.

The Alps are a group of high mountains in Europe. Most of Europe has a mild temperate climate. But the altitude at the top of the Alps is great enough to keep temperatures cold. For this reason, there is a covering of snow on some of these mountaintops all year round.

Mountains can affect climate in other ways. Mountains can block the path of air masses. When a warm, wet air mass reaches a mountain, the air mass is forced upward. The air mass cools as it rises. The water vapor in the air mass condenses and falls on the mountain as precipitation.

When the air mass moves over the mountain, the air is dry. The land on the other side of the mountain might get so little precipitation that it is a desert.

FOCUS CHECK What are three factors that affect climate?

The tops of the Alps are cold and snowy. The climate at the base of the Alps is fairly mild. Different plants and animals live at different altitudes.

Express Lab

Activity Card
Study Your Climate

223

How Climates Have Changed

Tennessee's climate has stayed about the same for many years. But Earth's climates have changed many times in the distant past. They likely will continue to change in the future.

For example, about 20,000 years ago, much of North America was covered in ice. Woolly mammoths and saber-toothed tigers roamed the Great Plains. Since this period, known as an ice age, Earth's climate has become warmer. Most scientists believe that Earth's climate may still be warming.

Scientists study climate in many ways. The rings in fossil tree trunks show what the climate was like when the tree was alive. So do core samples of ice from cold places, such as Antarctica at the South Pole. This ice can be hundreds of thousands of years old. Each layer contains traces of air from long ago.

Today, scientists are concerned about rising levels of carbon dioxide in Earth's atmosphere. These gases may be causing warmer temperatures on the surface.

⊚FOCUS CHECK How has Earth's climate changed?

A protective layer of Earth's atmosphere has been damaged by certain chemicals. The damaged part, shown in purple, allows harmful rays from the Sun to reach Earth's surface. ▼

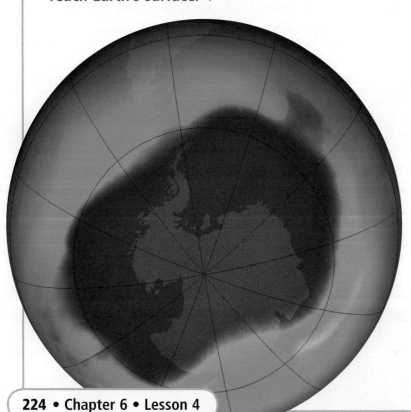

▲ Each layer of an ice core contains bits of dust, gases, and other materials. Scientists can tell what the atmosphere was like in the past by studying ice cores.

Lesson Wrap-Up

Visual Summary

Climate is the average weather conditions of an area over many years.

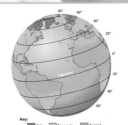

Earth is divided into three major climate zones: tropical, temperate, and polar.

Key: ■ Polar ■ Temperate ■ Tropical

Latitude, altitude, and bodies of water can affect the climate of an area. Climates change over time.

Check for Understanding

CLIMATE TRACKING

Use the Internet or library resources to research climate data for your part of Tennessee. Compare typical values for temperature and precipitation with those observed this year. Do you think the climate is changing? Cite evidence to support your answer.

✔ 0407.8.3

Review

❶ **MAIN IDEA** What are two factors that affect climate?

❷ **VOCABULARY** Write a sentence that describes a tropical climate.

❸ **READING SKILL** Cause and Effect Describe two ways that scientists study climates of long ago.

❹ **CRITICAL THINKING: Synthesize** Kilimanjaro is a tall mountain in Africa close to the equator. What do you think the climate is like at the base of Kilimanjaro? What would the climate be like at the top?

❺ **INQUIRY SKILL: Use Models** You place a lamp on a table next to a globe. Which part of the globe will warm up most?

TCAP Prep

When was Tennessee's climate much different than it is today?

A six months ago
B last year
C 100 years ago
D 20,000 years ago

SPI 0407.8.2

Go Digital Technology

Visit www.eduplace.com/tnscp to find out more about weather and climate.

An Amazing Journey!

In December 1914, Sir Ernest Shackleton left a whaling station on South Georgia Island in the South Atlantic on the ship *Endurance*. He and his crew of 27 men planned to be the first to walk across Antarctica.

Two months later, the ship was locked in ice. The men survived on the frozen ship for 10 long months, through the dark Antarctic winter. In early spring, shifting ice crushed the ship, and it sank. The crew escaped with three lifeboats, tents, and other supplies. They camped on the ice for 5 months. When the ice began to break apart, they rowed to a remote island.

Shackleton knew no one would find them. He and five men set out in a lifeboat rigged with a sail for South Georgia Island, 1,300 km away over rough ocean. They landed 13 days later—but on the wrong side of the island. They hiked over uncharted mountains to reach the whaling station. On May 19, 1916, the men finally stumbled to safety. After 4 months and several attempts, Shackleton and a rescue party reached his crew.

Even though they failed in their goal, their journey is one of the greatest survival stories in history. They battled crushing ice, freezing temperatures, gale winds, and rough seas. And every one of the 28 men who set out returned to tell the tale!

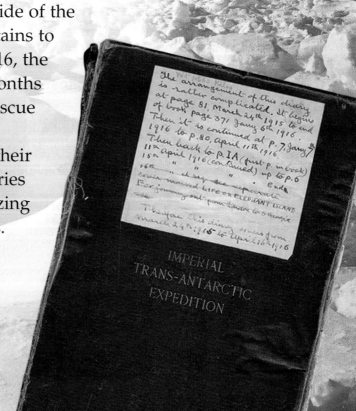

▶ **GLE 0407.T/E.1** Describe how tools, technology, and inventions help to answer questions and solve problems.

EXTEND

Antarctica proved too powerful for even this sturdy ship. Shackleton later wrote, "It was a sickening sensation, to feel the decks breaking up under one's feet, the great beams bending and then snapping...."

Frank Hurley photographed the journey. Shackleton (*left*) and some of the crew are shown here at their camp on the ice.

Sharing Ideas

1. READING CHECK What goal did Sir Ernest Shackleton hope to reach with his 1914 expedition?

2. WRITE ABOUT IT Imagine you are a member of Shackleton's crew. Write a journal entry about one day of the expedition.

3. TALK ABOUT IT What tools and technology that explorers have today would have help Shackleton's crew?

GLE 0407.8.2 Differentiate between weather and climate..
Math GLE 0406.4.2 Understand and use measures of length, area, capacity, and weight. **ELA GLE 0401.3.3** Write in a variety of modes and genres (e.g., narration, description, personal expression, imaginative writing, response to literature, response to subject matter content).

Math Storm Tracking

As the map shows, on June 13th and 14th, 2006, Tropical Storm Alberto moved across the southeastern United States. Tornadoes formed along its path. The numbers of tornadoes by state are listed in the chart.

1. Describe the path of the storm. Use place names and directions.

2. How far did the storm travel on June 13th from 5:00 P.M. to 11:00 P.M.? Measure the distance on the map in centimeters. Then use the map scale to estimate the actual distance.

3. Make a circle graph and a bar graph for the data on tornadoes. Discuss the advantages and disadvantages of the graphs and the table.

Tornadoes Reported	
State	**Number**
Florida	4
Georgia	3
North Carolina	3
South Carolina	6

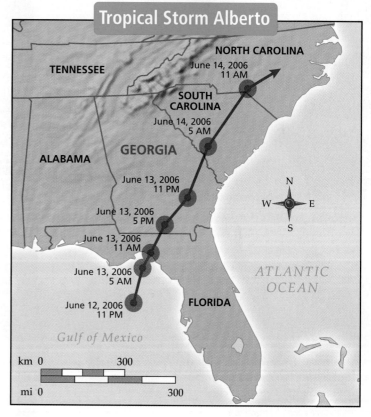
Tropical Storm Alberto

Writing
Response to Literature

Read a story that describes a hurricane, tornado, or other severe storm. Does the story accurately present the storm? Discuss this question in your report.

John Knox

Meteorologist John Knox teaches college students about the weather. He also tells lots of weather stories, both in class and in the textbooks he writes. In the paragraph below from one of his books, Dr. Knox wrote about a thunderstorm that he remembered from when he was four years old.

Dr. Knox uses stories to show how weather affects people's lives. What weather story can you tell? What more would you like to learn about the weather event in your story?

"It's a hot, muggy summer night at the baseball stadium. Midway through the game, the weather takes a violent turn. High winds suddenly blow chairs off the stadium roof. Then the sky explodes with light and sound as lightning strikes an electric transformer . . . A fireball dances along the power lines and the stadium lights go dark."

from *Tales from My Childhood*, by Dr. John Knox

Vocabulary

Complete each sentence with a term from the list.

1. The process in which liquid changes to gas is called _____.

2. Expect very cold temperatures when you visit a/an _____.

3. The place where two air masses meet is a/an _____.

4. The trapping of heat by Earth's atmosphere is called the _____.

5. A large body of air that has about the same weather factors throughout is a/an _____.

6. Any form of water that falls from clouds is called _____.

7. An area with warm, dry summers and cold, wet winters has a/an _____.

8. The change of state from gas to liquid is called _____.

9. The blanket of air that surrounds Earth is the _____.

10. The weight of air as it pushes down on Earth's surface is called _____.

air mass
air pressure
atmosphere
climate
★ condensation
★ evaporation
front
greenhouse effect
polar climate
precipitation
temperate climate
tropical climate
water cycle
weather

TCAP Inquiry Skills

11. **Compare** Compare and contrast a warm front and a cold front. What type of weather does each bring?
    GLE 0407.8.1

12. **Use Models** Describe how you could model clouds with the following materials: puffy cotton balls; thick, layered gray blankets; and thin, wispy fibers. GLE 0407.8.1

13. **Communicate** Describe the climate of your area. Include facts about latitude, landforms, bodies of water, and air masses. GLE 0407.8.2

Map the Concept

Complete the statements below with words from the list.

wind speed   air pressure
wind direction   temperature

| A wind sock measures _____ . |
| A thermometer measures _____ . |
| A barometer measures _____ . |
| An anemometer measures _____ . |

GLE 0407.Inq.2

Critical Thinking

14. Evaluate A certain kind of plant requires a great deal of water and sunlight. In which climate would it grow best: a polar climate, a tropical climate, or a temperate climate? Explain.   **GLE 0407.8.2**

15. Synthesize Hawai`i has warm, tropical weather all year long. Yet it sometimes snows at the tops of its mountains. Explain.   **GLE 0407.8.1**

16. Analyze Research data on temperature and precipitation for Tennessee and for another state in another part of the country. How do the two climates compare?   **GLE 0407.8.2**

Check for Understanding

Make a Weather Map

Make a Tennessee weather map for today or a recent day. Use the Internet, newspapers, or library resources to research weather data. Then add numbers and symbols to an outline map. Include a key and a paragraph about the day's weather.

Compare weather patterns in Tennessee to the climate.   **0407.8.2**

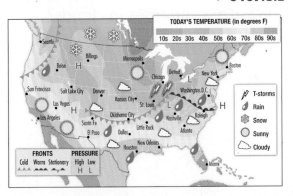

TCAP Prep

Choose the letter of the best answer choice.

17 An example of a liquid turning into a gas is

A rain water evaporating.

B ice melting into water.

C rain water turning into ice.

D water vapor condensing.   **SPI 0407.8.1**

18 Which instrument is used to measure the force of air pressing upon an object?

F barometer

G anemometer

H thermostat

J rain gauge   **SPI 0407.8.1**

19 What makes up clouds?

A tiny water droplets or ice crystals

B water vapor

C a mixture of oxygen and nitrogen

D tiny hailstones   **SPI 0407.8.1**

20 As you move south from the North Pole to the equator, the climate changes from

F tropical to temperate.

G polar to temperate to polar.

H polar to tropical to temperate.

J polar to temperate to tropical.   **SPI 0407.8.2**

7 The Earth

Performance Indicator: **SPI 0407.7.1 Design a simple model to illustrate how the wind and movement of water alter the earth's surface.**

1 What is happening to this landform?

A Wind is depositing sediment on top of it.

B Wind is carrying sediment away from it.

C Water is depositing sediment along its sides.

D Water is carrying sediment away from it.

2 Which of the following forms when rivers deposit sediment?

F mountain

G delta

H dune

J cirque

8 The Atmosphere

Performance Indicator: **SPI 0407.8.1 Identify the basic features of the water cycle and describe their importance to life on earth.**

3 In the water cycle, what happens just before water condenses in clouds?

A Water falls as rain.

B Water evaporates.

C Water vapor changes to a gas.

D Water dissolves salt in the ocean.

6 The Universe

Performance Indicator: **SPI 0407.6.1 Organize the phases of the moon in the correct sequence.**

4   A gibbous moon occurs just before or just after a full moon. Which shows a gibbous moon?

   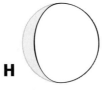   

F   **G**   **H**   **J**

5   When does a waning moon occur?

A between a first-quarter moon and a new moon

B when all of the Moon's near side is dark

C after a full moon

D just after a crescent moon

8 The Atmosphere

Performance Indicator: **SPI 0407.8.2 Distinguish between weather and climate.**

6   Which climate zone has a weather pattern of warm, dry summers and cold, wet winters?

F polar

G temperate

H tropical

J Equator

7   Where is precipitation most likely to fall?

A along a front

B in the middle of an air mass

C in the northern part of an air mass

D in the southern part of an air mass

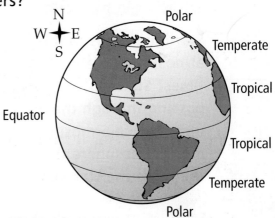

Climate Zones

Discover More

Because stars are many light-years away from Earth, they appear as points of light in the sky. What happens to that light when it finally passes through Earth's atmosphere? The answer explains why stars appear to twinkle.

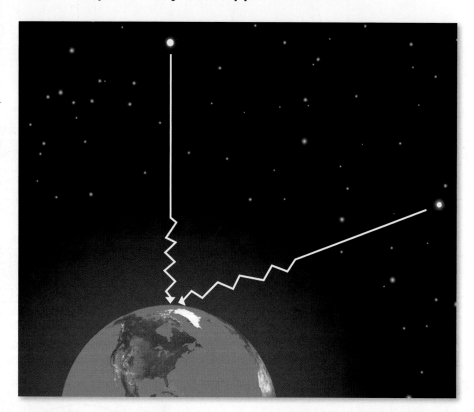

Starlight bends as it passes through Earth's atmosphere. Because the atmosphere is always moving and changing, starlight can bend many times! Stars closer to the horizon twinkle more because the starlight passing through the horizon to reach your line of sight travels through more of the atmosphere than starlight passing from directly above. The more atmosphere the starlight passes through, the more it is bent and the more the star appears to twinkle.

 Visit **www.eduplace.com** to learn more about stars.

TENNESSEE

IMAX 3-D Theater

Where can you see dolphins, sharks, and a movie all in the same trip? At the Tennessee Aquarium, you can see all of these things and more. Watching a three-dimensional (3-D) movie at the IMAX 3-D Theater is an exciting way to learn about living things. Here, viewers may experience a close encounter with a sunfish and watch a pack of lions hunt their prey.

Some of the films look like regular movies, but it's the 3-D movies that are the most popular. To watch a 3-D film, each visitor must wear a pair of glasses. Without these glasses, the film appears to be blurry, because there are two separate images on the screen. The glasses make the two images appear as one 3-D image.

GLE 0407.10.2 Investigate how light travels and is influenced by different types of materials and surfaces.

ENGAGE

The lenses in these glasses only allow light moving in a certain way to pass through.

Seeing in 3-D

You probably know that humans see in three dimensions. You also know that films such as IMAX movies appear to be in three dimensions. To make 3-D films, filmmakers must replicate how people see. Since people have two eyes, 3-D films are made by using cameras that have two lenses. The action is filmed from two different, but very similar, points of view.

So, why don't you notice the two overlapping images? The lenses of the 3-D glasses are polarized. This means that they only allow light waves oriented in a certain way to pass through to your eyes. The left lens and the right lens are polarized to be opposite from one another. This causes the viewer's right eye to see only the image on the right and the viewer's left eye to see only the image on the left.

At some place between the eyes and the screen, the viewer's brain combines the two 2-D images into one 3-D image. This point is called the point of convergence. The closer the two images are to each other on the screen, the farther away the object appears to the viewer. The farther away the two images are from each other, the closer they appear to the viewer.

Think and Write

1 **Scientific Thinking** Why does a viewer need polarized glasses to watch a 3-D movie?

2 **Scientific Inquiry** Do you think it is better to sit in the front row or the back row in a 3-D movie? Why?

Tennessee

Nashville

ICE!
at Gaylord Opryland Resort

Bundle up! This field trip is going to be cold—ice-cold. At –12°C (about 10°F), the Ice! exhibit at the Gaylord Opryland Resort and Convention Center in Nashville is one of the coolest places to be in December. The exhibit hall is filled with sculptures of snow figures, penguins, and trains, all made of ice. It even has an ice slide or two for visitors to try. Nearly 400,000 visitors in their warmest coats view the sculptures.

Each October, the Gaylord Opryland Resort brings two million pounds of ice to Tennessee. A group of 30 to 50 artists from Harbin, China, works to transform the ice into sculptures for the Ice! exhibit. Harbin holds an ice festival every year, so these artists are skilled at making ice sculptures.

A sculptor carves a block of ice.

GLE 0407.9.2 Explore different types of physical changes in matter.

ENGAGE

Visitors can experience slides made of ice.

From Water to Ice and Back

Each ice sculpture at Ice! undergoes several physical changes. The best sculptures are made from clean water. Boiling the water removes any impurities and reduces the number of bubbles that will show up in the ice. The water is frozen quickly, often with color added, and then cut into 180-kg (400-lb) blocks. In a matter of a few hours, the ice has undergone three physical changes.

The artists carve the ice blocks using chisels with blades that are designed to work on ice. To make large sculptures, a few partially formed pieces are "glued" together with water. Spraying the individual blocks with water in the cold room causes them to freeze together—another physical change.

Once the ice is carved, colored lights, music, and other decorations are added. At the end of the season, the sculptures are allowed to melt. Next year's fantasy in ice will be made from scratch.

Think and Write

❶ **Scientific Thinking** Name three examples of physical changes that the ice sculptures undergo.

❷ **Scientific Inquiry** How do you think the artists smooth and polish the ice sculptures?

239

Kayaking on the Ocoee River

Do you want an exciting experience outdoors? Try kayaking on the white-water rapids of the Ocoee River! Kayaks are small boats made for one rider to paddle. They are perfect for white-water rapids because a small kayak moves more easily than a boat or canoe through rough water.

Adventurers travel from around the world to test themselves on the Ocoee River. The 1996 Summer Olympic canoe and kayak slalom events were held on the Ocoee River because the rapids are so challenging.

GLE 0407.11.1 Recognize that the position of an object can be described relative to other objects or a background.

ENGAGE

Visitors come from around the world to conquer the Ocoee River rapids.

To determine if this kayaker is moving, you need a frame of reference.

Speed and Position

Look at the picture of the kayaker. From the picture, can you tell if he is moving? To determine whether an object is moving, you must have a frame of reference. Your frame of reference is a background that isn't moving. If you were standing on one bank of the river, the background would be the other bank. The riverbank helps you determine that the rider is changing position. An object is in motion when its position changes.

It is easy to tell the kayak is moving when there is a background. Can you tell how fast the kayak is going? Speed is the distance an object travels in a certain amount of time. How could you measure the speed of a kayak? In white-water kayak racing, the course is usually 6–10 kilometers (4–6 mi) long. The speed of the racer is found by dividing the distance by the amount of time it takes him or her to travel the course. The best racers can finish one of these courses in 25 minutes.

Think and Write

1 **Scientific Thinking** What is a frame of reference?

2 **Scientific Inquiry** What are some ways you can describe your position?

Build a Brake

Identify the Problem Your class is having a toy car race. Each student's car must go a certain distance, but the car that will win will be the one that stops closest to the finish line.

Think of a Solution You can make a brake that will stop your car at the right spot. List characteristics the brake must have in order to stop the car in the right place. For example, it will need to be applied at a certain time to stop the car at the right spot.

Plan and Build Using your list, sketch and label the parts of your brake. Think of the materials you could use. Then build your brake.

Test and Improve Test your brake. Then work to improve it, if necessary. Provide sketches and explanations of what you did.

Possible Materials

- masking tape
- rubber erasers
- toy cars
- paper clips
- craft sticks
- stopwatch
- glue
- scrap cardboard
- string
- small magnets
- hook-and-loop tape

Communicate

1. How did you decide whether your brake design was a success or not?

2. How did you decide which materials to use?

3. Explain one improvement that you made to your design.

GLE 0407.T/E.5 Apply a creative design strategy to solve a particular problem generated by societal needs and wants.

Physical Science

Tennessee

Guiding Question

How do scientists describe matter, electricity, magnetism, light, and motion?

Chapter 7
Properties of Matter

LESSON

1

Your weight on the Moon and your weight on Earth—how would it vary?

LESSON

2

The bright color of a flower or the rough texture of a tree trunk—what are some other ways to describe matter?

LESSON

3

Cut a sheet of paper to make a paper snowflake, or break a piece of candy to make smaller pieces—is the paper still paper, is the candy still candy?

Fun Facts

The Grand Guitar in Bristol is a music shop shaped like a 3-story, 70-foot-long guitar!

Vocabulary Preview

density
energy
mass
metric system
physical change
volume
weight

 Vocabulary Strategies

Have you ever seen any of these words before? Do you know what they mean?

State a description, explanation, or example of the vocabulary in your own words.

Draw a picture, symbol, example, or other image that describes the word.

Glossary p. H16

weight

physical change

volume

Start with Your Standards

Inquiry

GLE 0407.Inq.2 Select and use appropriate tools and simple equipment to conduct an investigation.

GLE 0407.Inq.3 Organize data into appropriate tables, graphs, drawings, or diagrams.

GLE 0407.Inq.4 Identify and interpret simple patterns of evidence to communicate the findings of multiple investigations.

Physical Science

Standard 9 Matter

GLE 0407.9.1 Collect data to illustrate that the physical properties of matter can be described with tools that measure weight, mass, length, and volume.

GLE 0407.9.2 Explore different types of physical changes in matter.

mass

Interact with this chapter.

 www.eduplace.com/tnscp

Lesson 1

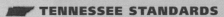

TENNESSEE STANDARDS

GLE 0407.Inq.3 Organize data into appropriate tables, graphs, drawings, or diagrams.
GLE 0407.9.1 Collect data to illustrate that the physical properties of matter can be described with tools that measure weight, mass, length, and volume.

Guiding Question

How Is Matter Measured?

Why It Matters...

Using a balance is just one way to measure the hamster shown here. How else could you measure the hamster? What tools would you use?

Scientists measure matter for many reasons, including to show the results of their experiments. Standard units of measurement allow them to understand and compare results.

PREPARE TO INVESTIGATE

Inquiry Skill

Measure When you measure, you use tools to find the length or mass of an object.

Materials

- balance
- metric ruler
- 5 small classroom objects (pencil, paper clip, chalk, eraser, coin)

Science and Math Toolbox

For step 2, review **Using a Balance** on page H9.

Directed Inquiry

Measure It

Procedure

1. **Collaborate** Work with a partner. In your *Science Notebook*, make a chart like the one shown. Select five small objects from around the classroom. For example, you might choose a pencil, a paper clip, a piece of chalk, an eraser, and a coin.

2. **Measure** Use a balance to find the mass of each object. Record your measurements in your chart. Be sure to use the correct units of measure for mass.

3. **Measure** Use a metric ruler to find the length of each object. Record your measurements in the chart. Be sure to use the correct units of measure for length.

Think and Write

1. **Communicate** Make a bar graph to show the mass of each object you measured. Make a second bar graph to show the lengths of the objects.

2. **Analyze Data** Which object has the greatest mass? Which has the least?

3. **Analyze Data** Which object is the longest? Which is the shortest?

STEP 1

Object	Mass	Length

STEP 2

STEP 3

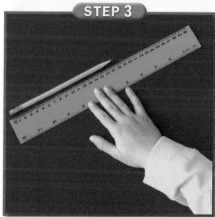

Guided Inquiry

Design an Experiment
Use a rubber band to attach 4 or 5 small objects together. Does the mass of the bound objects equal the sum of the masses of the parts? Predict the answer, then find out.

0407.Inq.3

Measuring Matter

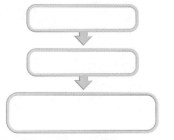
The Metric System

How could you find the exact height of a giraffe? By measuring it, of course! People have been measuring objects to describe their properties exactly for hundreds of years. At first, people used their hands or feet as measuring tools. But the measurements differed from one person to another.

Over time, scientists developed a standard system of measurement. Today, scientists all over the world use the same system, which allows them to communicate easily with one another. This system is often called the metric system.

The **metric system** is a system of measurement based on multiples of 10. The table shows how different metric units are related. Notice that they use prefixes such as *centi-*, *milli-*, and *kilo-*.

Metric Units Conversion Chart

Property Measured	Metric Unit	Converts To
Length	1 centimeter (cm)	10 millimeters (mm)
	1 meter (m)	100 centimeters (cm)
	1 kilometer (km)	1,000 meters (m)
Volume	1 liter (L)	1,000 milliliters (mL)
Mass	1 kilogram (kg)	1,000 grams (g)

Metric ruler (cm) ▼

0 1 2 3 4 5 6 7 8 9 10 11 12 13 14 15 16 17 18 1

Find centimeter, meter, and kilometer in the table. These units are metric units of length. You can see that 100 centimeters is the same as 1 meter. Both 1 and 100 are multiples of 10. You can easily convert between units simply by multiplying or dividing by a multiple of 10. This is true for all metric units.

When scientists measure objects, they use tools that measure in metric units. The ruler below measures length in centimeters. The giraffe's height is measured in meters.

To find out how much mass something has, scientists use a balance that measures grams or kilograms. Scientists use beakers or graduated cylinders marked in liters or milliliters to measure the volumes of liquids

FOCUS CHECK What metric units could be used to measure an amount of juice?

Giraffes are one of the tallest animals in the world. Many grow to more than 5.5 m tall. ▼

◄ The mass of a bowling ball can be more than 7 kg.

Mass

Suppose you hold two blocks, one in each hand. They are the same size, color, shape, and texture. However, one block feels heavier than the other.

To describe exactly the difference between these blocks, you can measure their masses. **Mass** is the amount of matter in an object. The block that feels heavier has more mass—and more matter.

As you have learned, all matter has mass. Scientists use many tools to measure mass, including balances of the kind shown below.

To measure the mass of a block, place it on one pan of a balance. Add objects with known masses, such as 1-gram or 1-kilogram standards, to the other pan. When the two pans balance, the total mass of the standard masses equals the mass of the block.

You also can use addition or subtraction to find the mass of an object made of many parts. The mass of an object equals the sum of the masses of its parts.

The standards on the left side of the balance have the same total mass as the block on the right side.

Volume

Another physical property of matter that is measured exactly is volume (VAHL yoom). **Volume** is the amount of space that matter takes up. As with mass, all matter has volume, even air and very tiny particles.

Volume is measured in different ways depending on the object. The volume of a liquid is measured directly with a beaker or graduated cylinder. Liters and milliliters are the metric units of volume.

To find the volume of a rectangular solid, such as this block, multiply together its length, width, and height. Its volume can be described in cubic centimeters. One cubic centimeter has the same volume as one milliliter.

How can you measure the volume of a rock? Carefully place the rock into a graduated cylinder partly filled with water and measure the change in water volume.

⊙FOCUS CHECK **How can you find the volume of a block?**

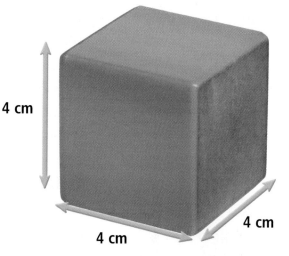

4 cm

4 cm

4 cm

▲ The volume of a rectangular solid is equal to length times width, times height. This cube has a volume of 64 cubic centimeters (64 cm^3).

300 ml
±5%
250
200

The change in water volume is the volume of the rock.

Express Lab

Activity Card
Measure Parts of a Mixture

253

▲ The spring scale measures the weight of the bear cub. Weight is a measure of the pull of gravity on an object.

Weight

How much does this bear weigh? Is its weight the same as its mass? No, it is not. Remember that mass is the amount of matter in an object.

Weight is the measure of the pull of gravity on an object. Even if this bear went to the Moon, its mass would stay the same. However, its weight changes depending on the amount of gravity pulling on it. Its weight is slightly less on top of Mount Everest compared to sea level.

On the Moon, the bear would weigh even less. Why? The Moon has less mass than Earth. So, the pull of gravity on the Moon is very weak. Objects weigh about 1/6 as much on the Moon as they do on Earth.

In contrast, on massive planets such as Jupiter, the pull of gravity is very strong. On Jupiter, the bear likely could not even lift its head!

You can experience changes in weight when you are moving up or down very quickly. Part of the fun of a roller coaster comes from feeling lighter when the coaster falls and heavier when it rises up.

FOCUS CHECK What is weight?

Weight and Mass

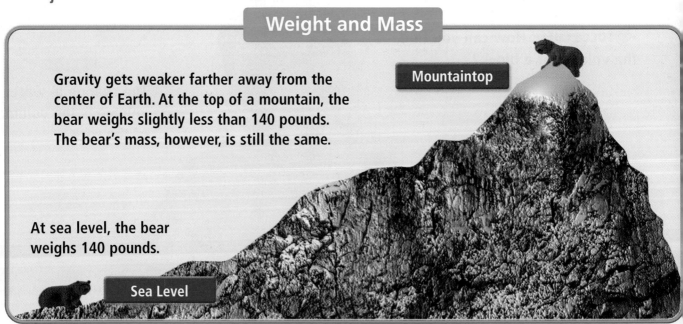

Gravity gets weaker farther away from the center of Earth. At the top of a mountain, the bear weighs slightly less than 140 pounds. The bear's mass, however, is still the same.

Mountaintop

At sea level, the bear weighs 140 pounds.

Sea Level

Lesson Wrap-Up

Visual Summary

Scientists use the appropriate units of the metric system to measure the properties of matter.

Mass is the amount of matter in an object. Volume is the amount of space an object takes up.

Weight is the pull of Earth's gravity on an object. Weight can vary; mass stays the same.

✔ Check for Understanding

MASS AND PARTS

In this lesson, you read that the mass of an object equals the sum of the masses of its parts. What evidence can you provide to show that this statement is true? Collaborate with your classmates to conduct a series of useful tests. Try working with jigsaw puzzles, building toys, or models made from parts.

✔ 0407.9.1

Review

❶ **MAIN IDEA** What units would a scientist most likely use to measure the length of a nail or another small object?

❷ **VOCABULARY** Write a paragraph about measuring matter. Use the terms *mass* and *volume* in the paragraph.

❸ **READING SKILL: Draw Conclusions** An object has a mass of 42 g on Earth. What is its mass on the Moon?

❹ **CRITICAL THINKING: Evaluate** How has the metric system helped scientists?

❺ **INQUIRY SKILL: Measure** Use the metric ruler shown in this lesson. How many centimeters long is your pen or pencil?

TCAP TCAP Prep

Which of the following could be the mass of an object?

A 5.13 centimeters
B 20 liters
C 52 cubic centimeters
D 71 kilograms

SPI 0407.9.2

 Go Digital **Technology**

Visit **www.eduplace.com/tnscp** to find out more about measurement.

TENNESSEE STANDARDS

GLE 0407.Inq.4 Identify and interpret simple patterns of evidence to communicate the findings of multiple investigations.
GLE 0407.9.1 Collect data to illustrate that the physical properties of matter can be described with tools that measure weight, mass, length, and volume.

Guiding Question

What Are the Properties of Matter?

Why It Matters...

Why are winter hats made from yarn? Perhaps it's because yarn is soft, fuzzy, and flexible. Hats would be scratchy if they were made from paper. They wouldn't hold up well in a blizzard either. A hat made from metal wouldn't fit snugly on your head. It also wouldn't keep you very warm.

PREPARE TO INVESTIGATE

Inquiry Skill

Predict When you predict, you state what you think will happen based on observations and experiences.

Materials

- 2 small, clear plastic cups
- unknown liquid A
- unknown liquid B
- masking tape
- graduated cylinder
- goggles

Science and Math Toolbox

For step 5, review **Measuring Volume** on page H7.

Directed Inquiry

Compare Liquids

Procedure

① **Collaborate** Work with a partner. In your *Science Notebook*, make a chart like the one shown.

② **Observe** Pour equal amounts of each liquid into separate clear plastic cups. Label the containers *Liquid A* and *Liquid B*. Observe how each liquid looks. Record your observations in your chart. **Safety:** Wear goggles when pouring liquids.

③ **Compare** Carefully lift each cup. Which one seems heavier? Record your observations in your chart.

④ **Predict** What do you think will happen when you pour the two liquids into the same container? Record your prediction.

⑤ **Experiment** Pour 10 mL of each liquid into a graduated cylinder. What happens? Record your observations.

Think and Write

1. **Analyze Data** How does your prediction compare with the results of your experiment?

2. **Infer** What can you infer about the mass of the two liquids based on your observations?

3. **Hypothesize** Why is it important to use an equal amount of each liquid to compare their masses?

✔ 0407.Inq.3

STEP 1

Unknown Liquid	How It Looks	How Heavy It Seems
Liquid A		
Liquid B		

STEP 2

Liquid A   Liquid B

STEP 5

Guided Inquiry

Design an Experiment
Think about how you can compare the masses of milk and fruit juice. Would you use the same method as you used in this investigation? Would you try something different?

GRAPHIC ORGANIZER

Compare and Contrast
Use the chart to compare and contrast physical properties.

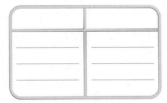

GLE 0407.9.1 Collect data to illustrate that the physical properties of matter can be described with tools that measure weight, mass, length, and volume.

GLE 0407.9.2 Explore different types of physical changes.

Properties of Matter

Physical Properties

In the morning you walk to school with your blue backpack. At lunch you eat a large sandwich. At night you sleep in your soft bed. The words "blue," "large," and "soft" all describe physical properties of matter. Any sample of matter can be described by its physical properties.

Color One way to describe matter is by color. For example, flowers may be yellow or red or yellow and red. Objects may be a single color or several colors.

Shape Another way to describe matter is by shape. An object may have an easily recognizable shape, such as a sphere or a pyramid. Many objects do not have a regular shape. How would you describe the shape of your hand?

Texture The texture (TEHKS chur) of an object describes how the object feels. Wool has a rough texture.

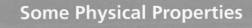

Some Physical Properties

Shape

Color

Texture

Density Differences

Each solid object sinks through a liquid less dense than itself and floats on a liquid more dense than itself. How does the density of the grape compare to the densities of the three liquids?

Oil The liquid with the lowest density is on top.

Water The liquid with neither the lowest density nor the highest density is in the middle.

Corn syrup The liquid with the highest density is at the bottom.

Luster Glass windows are smooth. Luster describes how the surface of an object looks when light shines on it. A mirror is very shiny, but a piece of black construction paper is not.

Density Another physical property that describes matter is density (DEHN sih tee). **Density** describes how much matter is in a given space, or volume. Because one cubic centimeter of steel has more mass than one cubic centimeter of cotton, steel is denser than cotton.

If you know the mass and volume of an object, you can calculate that object's density.

Density is usually described as mass per volume with the metric units grams per cubic centimeter (g/cm³).

The density of a substance determines whether it will float or sink in water or another liquid. If a substance is more dense than water, it will sink. If it is less dense than water, it will float.

FOCUS CHECK What are five physical properties that can be used to compare two samples of matter?

Express Lab

Activity Card
Observe Physical Properties

Useful Physical Properties

Every type of matter has its own set of physical properties. These properties affect how we use each type of matter. You would not use ice to make a chair. Although ice keeps its shape at very cold temperatures, it would melt in your classroom. A chair made of wood, metal, or plastic will keep its shape at room temperature.

Look at your desk. Does it look anything like the desk in the picture? Of course not! What kind of matter is your desk made of? What physical properties of this matter make it suitable for a desk? Your desk is likely made from many different kinds of matter. The legs of your desk are made of matter that is rigid and strong, like metal or wood. The top might be made of wood or plastic. They are solid, rigid, and strong. The top is also smooth so that you can easily write or draw on it. Is the color of the matter used to make your desk important? It might be if you chose a white desk over a brown one.

Properties that make matter useful for one purpose do not always make it useful for another. Glass is perfect to use for windows but not for swim goggles. It shatters too easily.

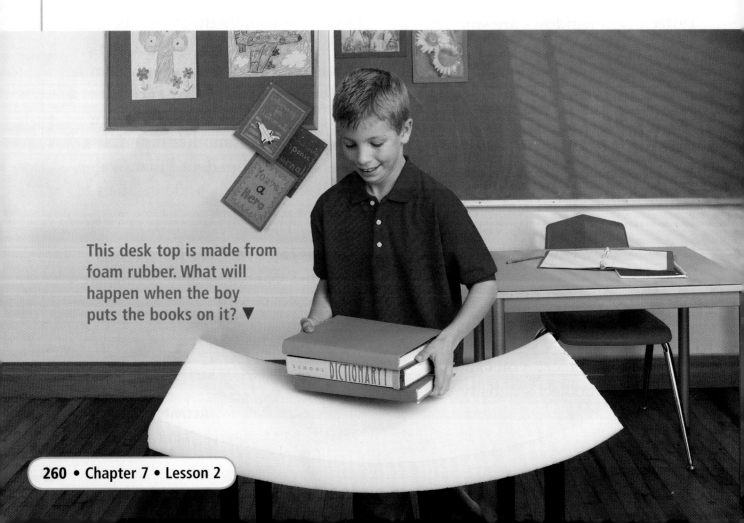

This desk top is made from foam rubber. What will happen when the boy puts the books on it? ▼

Lesson Wrap-Up

Visual Summary

Color is one way to describe matter. Objects can be a single color or several colors.

Density is the amount of matter in a given space, or volume.

Every type of matter has its own set of physical properties.

Check for Understanding

BROADCAST THE NEWS

Concrete is a material that has many uses. Scientists are looking for new ways to change the density and other physical properties of concrete. Research how technology is changing concrete. Give a news broadcast to your class about what you learn.

✔ 0407.T/E.1

Review

❶ MAIN IDEA What are some physical properties of paper that can be observed?

❷ VOCABULARY Use the term *density* in a sentence about physical properties.

❸ READING SKILL: Compare and Contrast Compare and contrast the physical properties of a log and a board cut from the log.

❹ CRITICAL THINKING: Synthesize When placed in water, object A floats and object B sinks. The objects are the same size and shape. Describe the masses of the objects.

❺ INQUIRY SKILL: Predict Suppose you drop a solid cube into a jar containing oil and water. The cube has a higher density than the oil and a lower density than the water. Predict what will happen to the cube.

TCAP Prep

One physical property is____.

A how it reacts to fire.
B density.
C how it reacts to water.
D smell.

SPI 0407.9.1

Technology

Visit **www.eduplace.com/tnscp** to find out more about chemical properties.

FIRST SNOW

The GOLDEN HOARD
MYTHS AND LEGENDS OF THE WORLD
GERALDINE McCAUGHREAN
Bee Willey

A Native American Myth

A Native American myth tells the story of a mischievous Coyote who gave snow to the First People of the World. But the People didn't know what to do with the beautiful, white powder. Coyote had to teach them. Read the excerpt below from the story "First Snow," from *The Golden Hoard* by Geraldine McCaughrean.

Coyote had filled a cooking pot with white handfuls from a drift of snow. He lit a fire and smoke curled up into the sky, fraying it to gray. He began to cook the snow. The People crowded around to see what delicious stew he was making. But as they watched, they began to shiver.

First the snow in the pot turned gray, then to transparent liquid, seething, bubbling, boiling and steaming, cooling only as the fire burned out. As it did so, the snow on the trees wept and dripped and dropped down in icy tears. The white on the ground changed to a gray slush that soaked

GLE 0407.9.2 Explore different types of physical changes in matter.

EXTEND

the children's moccasins, and the women let fall their skirtfuls of snow, crying, "Oh! Urgh! So cold! So wet! Urgh! Oh!" The old people drew their shawls about their heads and shook their wet mittens....

"Now look what you've done!" cried First Woman, wrapping herself tight in a dozen shawls. "Our lovely food has rotted away and there's nothing left but the juices. What a wicked waste! You always were a troublemaker, Coyote! In the time before the world, you were always making mischief, stealing, tricking, complaining. But this is the worst! You've made all our beautiful sky flour melt away!"

The People tried to pelt him with snowballs, but the snow only turned to water in their palms.

Coyote simply drank from the pot of melted snow, then shook his head so hard that his yellow ears rattled.

"You don't understand," he said gently. "Snow was not meant for food. It was sent down upon the five mountaintops for the springtime sun to melt, drip joining drop, dribble joining trickle, stream joining river, filling the lakes and pools and ponds, before it rolls down to the sea. Now, when you are thirsty, you need not wait for the rain, or catch the raindrops in your hands. You can drink whenever you please."

Note Book **Sharing Ideas**

1. **READING CHECK** Why does Coyote give snow to the People of the World?

2. **WRITE ABOUT IT** Imagine you are seeing snow for the first time. Write a journal entry describing what it is like.

3. **TALK ABOUT IT** Discuss the physical properties of the water in this story.

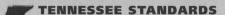

TENNESSEE STANDARDS

GLE 0407.Inq.3 Organize data into appropriate tables, graphs, drawings, or diagrams.
GLE 0407.9.2 Explore different types of physical changes in matter.

Guiding Question

What Are Physical Changes in Matter?

Why It Matters...

When you cut a piece of paper, you change the way it looks. It would be hard to make the paper look as it did before it was cut. But the paper is still paper. It has not become a new kind of matter.

PREPARE TO INVESTIGATE

Inquiry Skill

Compare When you compare two things, you observe how they are alike and how they are different.

Materials

- 2 clear plastic cups
- 2 saltine crackers
- crushed or shaved ice
- spoon
- metric ruler
- marker

Science and Math Toolbox

For steps 2–4, review **Using a Tape Measure or Ruler** on page H6.

Directed Inquiry

Matter Changes

Procedure

① In your *Science Notebook*, make a chart like the one shown. Half fill a plastic cup with crushed ice. Put two crackers in another cup.

② **Measure** Use a metric ruler to measure the height of the crushed ice and of the crackers. Mark the heights on the outside of the cups. Label the marks *Ice* and *Whole Crackers.* Record the height, shape, and state of the materials in your chart.

③ **Compare** Allow the ice to melt. Crush the crackers with a spoon. Measure the height of both materials and mark them on the cups. Label the marks *Melted Ice* and *Crushed Crackers*. Record the height, shape, and state of the materials.

④ Combine the materials in one cup and stir them together. Mark the height and label it *Mixture*. Record the height, shape, and state of the mixture.

Think and Write

1. **Analyze Data** How did each material change during each step?

2. **Infer** Were any materials taken away during the experiment? Were any new materials added?

3. **Predict** How do you think the mixture will change if you place it in a freezer?

STEP 1

Material	Height	Shape	State
Crushed ice			
Whole crackers			
Crushed crackers			
Melted ice			
Mixture			

STEP 3

STEP 4

Guided Inquiry

Design an Experiment
Allow the mixture from step 4 to dry out. Measure the height of the material that remains. Is the height close to the height of any of the materials in the Investigate?

0407.9.2

Physical Changes

VOCABULARY

energy
physical change

GRAPHIC ORGANIZER

Cause and Effect On a chart, list three examples of physical changes and the cause of each change.

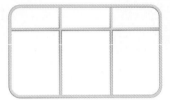

GLE 0407.9.2 Explore different types of physical changes in matter.

Size, Shape, and State

Suppose you are playing baseball with friends. You hit a home run right through the garage window. The glass shatters into hundreds of tiny pieces. Your baseball has caused a physical change in the window glass. A **physical change** is a change in the way matter looks without changing it into a new kind of matter.

Many physical changes change the size, shape, or state of matter. Breaking the window caused a change in the shape and size of the window glass, but each tiny piece of glass still has the properties of glass. No new kinds of matter were formed.

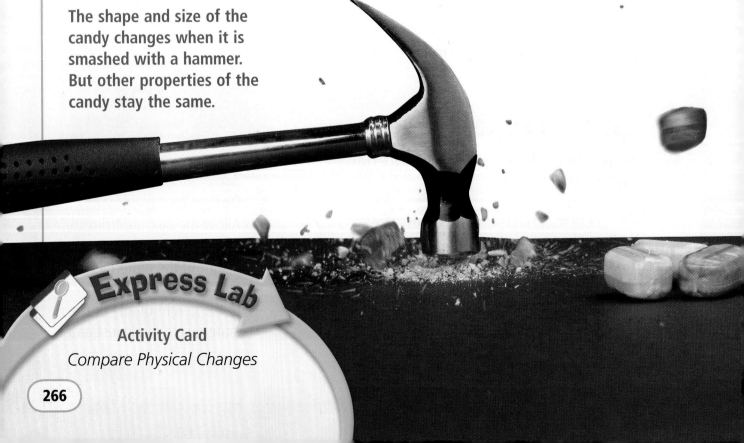

The shape and size of the candy changes when it is smashed with a hammer. But other properties of the candy stay the same.

Express Lab

Activity Card
Compare Physical Changes

▲ The melting juice bar is changing from a solid to a liquid. Changes of state are physical changes.

The melted part of this juice bar looks different from the frozen part. If you could taste the melted part of the juice bar, you would observe that it tastes the same as the frozen bar. The melted juice bar is not a new kind of matter. It still tastes like a juice bar—it has only changed from a solid to a liquid. A change in state is a physical change.

Suppose you smashed the juice bar with a hammer in the same way as the hard candy in the picture was smashed. How would smashing the juice bar change it? The juice bar would likely break into smaller pieces as

the hard candy did. The hard candy would not melt as easily as the juice bar would. Not all matter changes in the same way when conditions are the same. For example, at 0°C, pure water freezes but salt water does not.

◎ FOCUS CHECK How does matter change in a physical change?

When this balloon is blown up, it looks bigger, but it is still made of the same kind of matter. A change in size is a physical change. ▶

Common Physical Changes

The art supplies on the table have been cut, molded, and colored. You know that these changes are physical changes because the art supplies have not been changed into something new. A student has cut the paper, molded the clay, and drawn on the paper.

Whenever matter is moved or changed, energy (EHN ur jee) is always involved. **Energy** is the ability to cause change. Sometimes energy must be added to matter to cause a change. For example, a glue stick melts in a hot glue gun when heat is added. Heat is one form of energy.

Sometimes energy is given off by matter when it changes. Suppose a paper clip is quickly bent back and forth several times. The paper clip will feel warmer than it did before it was bent. That is because you added energy by bending the clip.

Think about physical changes that happen around you every day—melting ice, breaking glass, or building a sand castle. These changes in form, size, and shape cannot occur without energy. Heat from the Sun melts ice. The energy of a moving baseball breaks glass. You use energy in your muscles to form sand into a sand castle.

◎ FOCUS CHECK **What form of energy causes ice to melt?**

This student has caused many physical changes while making this art project.

Lesson Wrap-Up

Visual Summary

A physical change involves a change in size, shape, or state. No new kinds of matter are formed.

All changes in matter involve energy. Energy may be added, or it may be given off.

Check for Understanding

DO ORIGAMI

Japanese origami is a way of physically changing a piece of paper into complex shapes by folding it. Find some origami instructions in a book or on the Internet. Try to make some shapes. As you fold, keep a log of geometric shapes that you notice.

✓ 0407.9.2

Review

❶ **MAIN IDEA** How do you know that melting ice is a physical change?

❷ **VOCABULARY** Use your own words to describe what energy is.

❸ **READING SKILL: Cause and Effect** What type of energy causes a rain puddle to disappear on a sunny day?

❹ **CRITICAL THINKING: Analyze** A plumber uses a torch to heat a copper pipe in order to bend it. Is this change a physical change? Explain.

❺ **INQUIRY SKILL: Compare** Compare the properties of broken and unbroken glass. Explain why breaking glass is a physical change.

TCAP Prep

Which of the following is <u>not</u> a physical change?

A A dish of water set out in the Sun becomes dry.

B Wood burns in a campfire to form charcoal.

C A sandwich is cut into four smaller pieces.

D Chocolate melts in your pocket on a hot day.

SPI 0407.9.3

Go Digital Technology

Visit **www.eduplace.com/tnscp** to learn more about physical changes.

EXTREME Science

How Cool Is That?

You've heard of "boiling hot." Well, what about "boiling cold?"

This rose was "boiled" in one of the coldest liquids known—liquid nitrogen. Liquid nitrogen boils at a temperature so cold it can instantly freeze anything that contains water, such as this rose, or even your skin.

Nitrogen (N_2) is more familiar to us as a gas. It's very familiar, in fact. About 78% of the air we breathe is nitrogen. But when nitrogen is compressed and cooled, it turns to liquid.

How cold is liquid nitrogen? Think how cold an ice cube feels. That's 0°C. Now imagine something 196 degrees colder! Nitrogen liquefies at -196°C. At room temperature, it boils away like water on a hot stove!

GLE 0407.9.2 Explore different types of physical changes in matter.

EXTEND

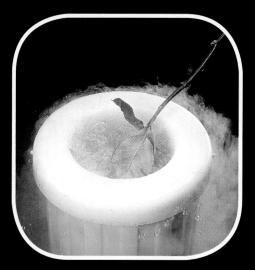

A rose, like most living tissue, is largely made of water. That's why it's soft and flexible at room temperature.

The liquid nitrogen absorbs heat from the rose and boils furiously as it returns to a gas.

After one swift dip in the liquid nitrogen, the rose is frozen solid. It's so brittle, it shatters like glass!

GLE 0407.9.2 Explore different types of physical changes in matter.
Math GLE 0406.5.1 Collect, record, arrange, present, and interpret data using tables and various representations. **ELA GLE 0401.3.3** Write in a variety of modes and genres (e.g., narration, description, personal expression, imaginative writing, response to literature, response to subject matter content).

Math Changes of State for Water

Heat is added slowly to a beaker of ice. The ice first melts to liquid water, then boils to become water vapor. The graph shows the temperature of the water over time.

1. How does the temperature of water change when heat is added? Use the graph to support your answer.

2. At what temperature does ice melt? At what temperature does liquid water boil?

3. Convert the answers to question 2 from degrees Celsius (°C) to degrees Fahrenheit (°F). Use the formula: °F = (1.8 × °C) + 32.

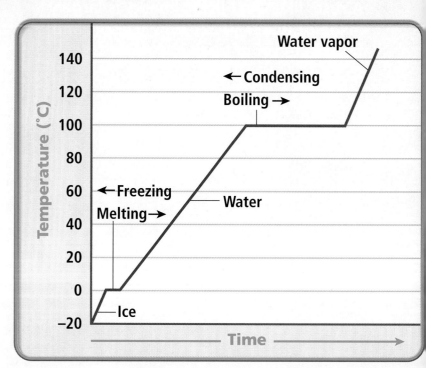

 **Narrative**

Present the three states of water in a short story. Characters should use or be affected by water in interesting ways.

Fire Investigator

It's a fire investigator's job to figure out exactly how and why a fire started. Fire investigators work at the scene of a fire. They observe damage, take photographs, collect evidence, and interview witnesses. Then they test materials in a lab and write reports on their findings.

What It Takes!

- A degree in fire science
- Skills in problem solving and an interest in chemistry
- Experience as a firefighter

Food Science Technician

Food science technicians work in labs where food is tested for quality and safety. They test to see that nutrition labels on food are correct. They check the taste and smell of the food. They use microscopes to check food for organisms that could cause disease.

Food science technicians need good listening and speaking skills. Many of these technicians work as assistants to food scientists.

What It Takes!

- A high-school diploma
- Additional job-related courses
- An interest in working in a laboratory

Chapter 7 — Review and TCAP Prep

Vocabulary

Complete each sentence with a term from the list.

1. The measure of the pull of gravity on an object is its _____.

2. A change in the way matter looks without changing it into a new kind of matter is a/an _____.

3. The _____ of an object is the amount of matter it contains.

4. The physical property that describes how much mass is in a given space, or volume, is called _____.

5. The _____ of a sample of matter is the amount of space it takes up.

6. _____ is the ability to cause change.

7. Meters, grams, and liters are units of the _____.

density
energy
mass
metric system
physical change
volume
weight

TCAP Inquiry Skills

8. **Compare** Is an object's weight the same as its mass? GLE 0407.9.1

9. **Infer** An ice cream sandwich has melted on the kitchen counter. What can you infer happened? GLE 0407.9.2

10. **Observe** What is one way you can observe a physical property?
GLE 0407.9.1

11. **Predict** A pot of water is being heated on a stove. Will the physical properties of the water change? Explain. GLE 0407.9.2

12. **Measure** What is the volume of the liquid? GLE 0407.9.1

Map the Concept

Use terms from the list to complete the concept map.

Solid
States of Matter
Liquid
Gas

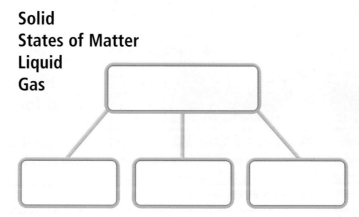

GLE 0407.9.2

Critical Thinking

13. Apply Compare the mass of an astronaut on Earth with the mass of the same astronaut on the Moon. Then compare the weight of an astronaut on Earth with the weight of the same astronaut on the Moon. **GLE 0407.9.1**

14. Synthesize A liquid has a volume of 1000 mL. It is placed into a different container and its volume is 1 L. What can you conclude about how the volume of this liquid changed? Explain.

GLE 0407.9.2

15. Evaluate You are given two cubes that are the same size and have the same texture. You are told that the cubes are identical. How could you test to see if this statement is correct?

GLE 0407.Inq.2

16. Analyze Why does describing texture use a different sense than describing color? **GLE 0407.9.2**

 **for Understanding**

Physical Properties

Obtain a block of wood from your teacher. Describe and measure as many physical properties of the block of wood as you can.

 0407.9.1

TCAP Prep

Write the letter of the best answer choice.

17 Weight is a measure of _____.

A the amount of space an object takes up

B how fast the particles in an object move

C the amount of matter in an object

D the pull of gravity on an object

SPI 0407.9.1

18 The ability to _____ is <u>not</u> a physical property.

F burn

G float

H melt

J sink **GLE 0407.9.2**

19 The metric system is _____.

A used only to measure the mass of objects

B used only to measure the height of objects

C not used by scientists

D based on multiples of 10

SPI 0407.9.2

20 Texture is an example of a _____.

F measurment

G physical property

H size

J mass **GLE 0407.9.2**

275

Chapter 8

Electricity and Magnetism

LESSON 1

A small shock from a doorknob, a giant bolt of lightning—is static electricity the cause?

LESSON 2

A tiny flashlight bulb and three million light bulbs in the Empire State Building—what do you need to make all the bulbs light?

LESSON 3

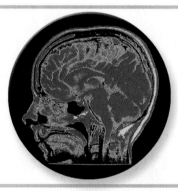

A bar magnet, Earth, and an MRI scan of the brain—what do they all have in common?

LESSON 4

From the generator in a car to the giant generators in power plants—how can motion produce electricity?

Fun Facts

A spark of static electricity can measure up to three thousand volts!

conductors
electric cell
electric charges
electric circuit
electric current
electromagnet
generator
insulators
magnet
magnetic poles
motor
★ parallel circuit
★ series circuit
static electricity

★ = Tennessee Academic Vocabulary

Vocabulary Strategies

Have you ever seen any of these words before? Do you know what they mean?

State a description, explanation, or example of the vocabulary in your own words.

Draw a picture, symbol, example, or other image that describes the word.

Glossary p. H16

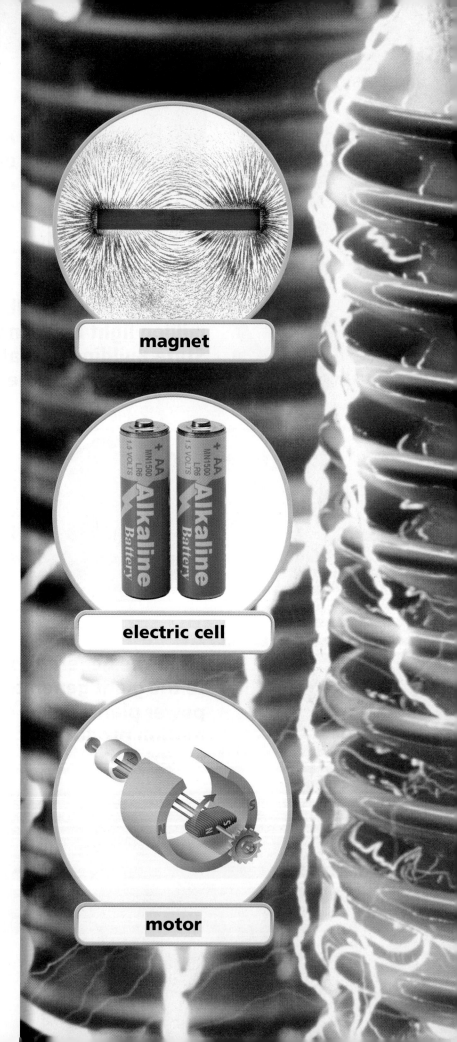

magnet

electric cell

motor

static electricity

Start with Your Standards

Inquiry

GLE 0407.Inq.1 Explore different scientific phenomena by asking questions, making logical predictions, planning investigations, and recording data.

GLE 0407.Inq.2 Select and use appropriate tools and simple equipment to conduct an investigation.

Physical Science

Standard 12 Forces in Nature

GLE 0407.12.1 Explore the interactions between magnets.

GLE 0407.12.2 Observe that electrically charged objects exert a pull on other materials.

GLE 0407.12.3 Explain how electricity in a simple circuit requires a complete loop through which current can pass.

Interact with this chapter.

 www.eduplace.com/tnscp

TENNESSEE STANDARDS

GLE 0407.Inq.1 Explore different scientific phenomena by asking questions, making logical predictions, planning investigations, and recording data.

GLE 0407.12.2 Observe that electrically charged objects exert a pull on other materials.

Guiding Question

What Is Static Electricity?

Why It Matters...

On dry days, your hair stands on end when you comb it. Sometimes, doorknobs give you shocks. These events are caused by static electricity. Scientists have used their understanding of static electricity to invent machines such as photocopiers and devices that help keep air clean.

PREPARE TO INVESTIGATE

Inquiry Skill

Infer When you infer, you use facts you know and observations you have made to draw a conclusion.

Materials

- 2 balloons
- 2 pieces of string
- metric ruler
- wool
- plastic wrap

Science and Math Toolbox

For step 1, review **Making a Chart to Organize Data** on page H10.

Directed Inquiry

Build a Charge
Procedure

1. **Collaborate** Work with a partner. Blow up two balloons. Knot the neck of each balloon and tie with a string. In your *Science Notebook*, make a chart like the one shown.

2. **Observe** Hold one string. Have your partner hold the other string so that the two balloons hang about 10 cm apart. Observe any movements the balloons make. Record your observations.

3. **Record Data** Rub each balloon with the wool cloth. Again, hold the balloons so they hang about 10 cm apart. Observe and record any movements they make.

4. **Record Data** Let the balloons touch. Then rub both balloons with plastic wrap and let them hang next to each other. Record your observations.

5. **Observe** Repeat step 4, but this time rub one balloon with plastic wrap and one with the wool cloth.

Think and Write

1. **Analyze Data** Rubbing a balloon with wool or plastic wrap gives the balloon an electric charge. Based on your data, how would you describe an electric charge?

2. **Infer** Based on your data, infer whether there is more than one kind of electric charge. How do your results support your inference?

✔ 0407.12.1

STEP 1

Balloon Setup	Results
No treatment	
Each balloon rubbed with wool	
Each balloon rubbed with plastic wrap	
One balloon rubbed with wool, the other with plastic wrap	

STEP 2

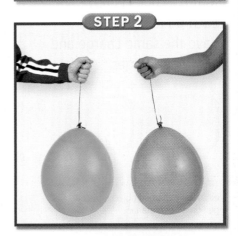

STEP 3

Guided Inquiry

Design an Experiment
Rub one balloon with wool. Choose other materials to rub another balloon with. For each new material, predict what will happen when the balloons are brought close to each other. Record your findings.

281

Static Electricity

Electric Charges

Does your hair ever stand on end after you comb it? Have you ever felt a shock from a metal doorknob after walking on a carpet?

You have learned that all matter, including hair and combs, is made up of tiny particles called atoms. Atoms are made up of even tinier particles. Many of these very tiny particles carry units of electricity called **electric charges.** These charges can make your hair stand on end or they can give you a shock.

There are two kinds of electric charges, positive ➕ and negative ➖. Charges that are the same are called like charges. Charges that are different are called unlike charges. Most matter is electrically neutral. This means it has an equal number of positive and negative charges.

VOCABULARY

electric charges
static electricity

GRAPHIC ORGANIZER

Cause and Effect Use a chart to show the effect that two objects have on each other when they have the same charge and different charges.

GLE 0407.12.2 Observe that electrically charged objects exert a pull on other materials.

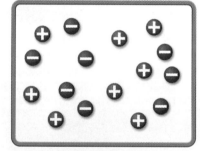

Electrically Neutral
Matter that has the same number of positive and negative charges

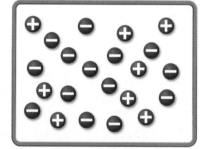

Negatively Charged
Matter that has more negative than positive charges

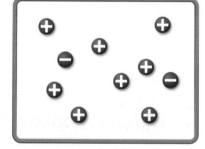

Positively Charged
Matter that has more positive than negative charges

Express Lab

Activity Card
See the Effects of Static Electricity

How Charges Behave

Electric charges can affect each other, even without touching. For instance, like charges repel, or push away from, each other. Unlike charges attract, or pull toward, each other. Two objects with the same charge will push away from each other. Two objects with opposite charges will pull toward each other.

Particles that have a negative charge can move more easily from one material to another than particles with a positive charge can. Remember that negative charges are attracted to positive charges. So, negative charges are more likely to move to a material or object that has an overall positive charge.

On their own, negative charges do not usually move toward an object that is electrically neutral. However, negative charges can be made to move. Rubbing can move negative charges from one neutral object to another. For example, when you rub a balloon with a piece of wool cloth, it causes negative charges to move from the cloth to the balloon.

⊙FOCUS CHECK How do like charges affect each other? How do unlike charges affect each other?

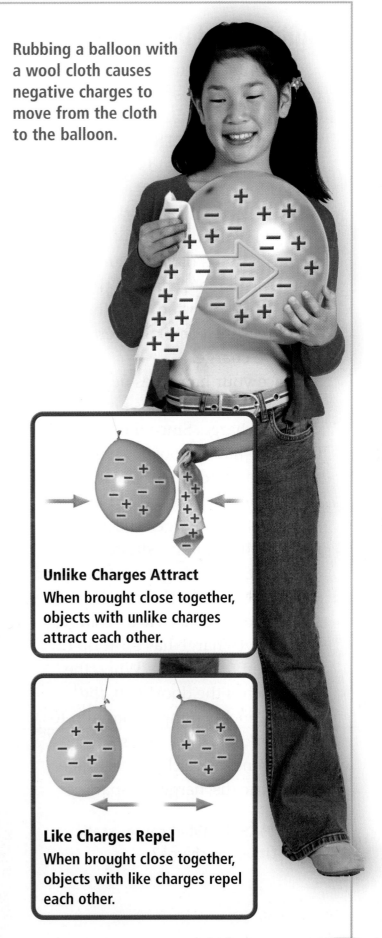

Rubbing a balloon with a wool cloth causes negative charges to move from the cloth to the balloon.

Unlike Charges Attract
When brought close together, objects with unlike charges attract each other.

Like Charges Repel
When brought close together, objects with like charges repel each other.

Buildup and Discharge

Sometimes a charge builds up on a material. This built-up electric charge is called **static electricity** (STAT ihk ih lehk TRIHS ih tee). When your hair stands on end and moves toward a plastic comb, that is static electricity at work. Combing your hair rubs the teeth of the comb against strands of your hair. As a result, negatively charged particles move from your hair onto the comb. This gives the comb an overall negative charge.

Once your hair loses negatively charged particles, it has an overall positive charge. Since the hair and the comb have opposite charges, they attract each other. At the same time, each strand of hair has a positive charge. The strands repel each other and stand up.

You sometimes get a shock when you touch a metal doorknob. The shock is due to electric discharge. A negative charge has built up on the boy in the picture. When the boy touches the doorknob, the charge quickly jumps from him to the doorknob. This release of the built-up negative charge is called an electric discharge, or spark.

FOCUS CHECK What causes static electricity to discharge?

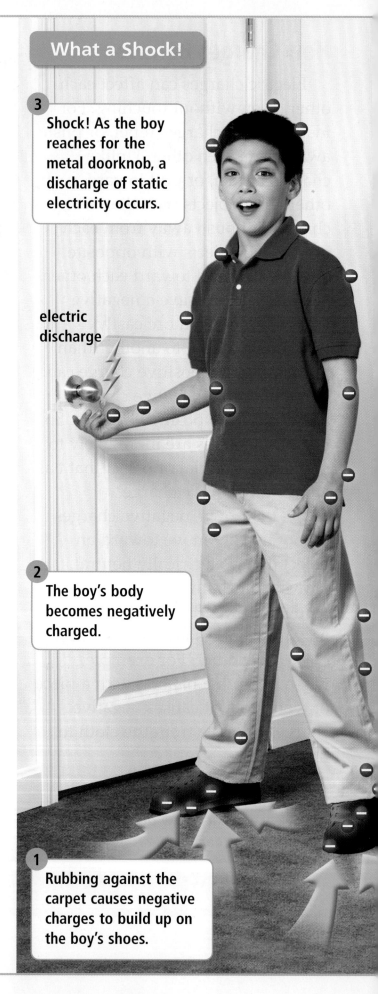

What a Shock!

3 Shock! As the boy reaches for the metal doorknob, a discharge of static electricity occurs.

electric discharge

2 The boy's body becomes negatively charged.

1 Rubbing against the carpet causes negative charges to build up on the boy's shoes.

Lesson Wrap-Up

Visual Summary

Atoms are made up of tiny particles, many of which carry electrical charges.

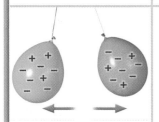

Objects with like charges repel each other. Objects with unlike charges attract each other.

Static electricity can discharge when a negatively charged object comes near another object.

Check for Understanding

RESEARCH SCRUBBERS

Research how static electricity is used in devices that control smokestack pollution. These devices are called scrubbers. Make a poster that shows in a simple way how a scrubber works.

✔ **0407.T/E.1**

Review

❶ **MAIN IDEA** When does an object have an overall positive charge?

❷ **VOCABULARY** Write a short paragraph using the terms *static electricity* and *electric discharge*.

❸ **READING SKILL: Cause and Effect** Explain how rubbing an object with a piece of cloth could change the overall charge of the object.

❹ **CRITICAL THINKING: Apply** Suppose you pull a shirt from the dryer. It has a sock stuck to it. Explain why this happens.

❺ **INQUIRY SKILL: Infer** Object A has a positive electric charge. Object A and Object B attract each other. What can you infer about the overall electric charge of Object B?

TCAP Prep

A built-up electric charge is ____.

A electrically neutral.
B static electricity.
C always positive.
D an electric discharge.

SPI 0407.12.2

Technology

Visit **www.eduplace.com/tnscp** to learn more about static electricity.

 **TENNESSEE STANDARDS**

GLE 0407.Inq.3 Organize data into appropriate tables, graphs, drawings, or diagrams.

GLE 0407.12.3 Explain how electricity in a simple circuit requires a complete loop through which current can pass.

Guiding Question

What Is Electric Current?

Why It Matters...

You flip a switch and the lights come on. You press a button and your computer screen comes to life. For the lights and computer to work, electric charges must move in a continuous flow. Understanding how electric charges move lets people safely produce and use electricity.

PREPARE TO INVESTIGATE

Inquiry Skill

Predict When you predict, you state what you think will happen based on observations and experiences.

Materials

- dry cell (size D)
- dry-cell holder
- electrical tape
- flashlight bulb
- insulated wires (20 cm each, stripped on ends)

Directed Inquiry

Make a Bulb Light

Procedure

1. **Collaborate** Work with a partner to connect the battery, wires, and bulb as shown in Diagram A. In your *Science Notebook*, record whether the arrangement of materials in Diagram A makes the bulb light. **Safety:** The wires may be sharp.

2. **Observe** Repeat step 1 for Diagram B.

3. **Predict** Predict whether the arrangement of materials in Diagram C will make the bulb light. Record your prediction.

4. **Experiment** Test your prediction. Make the connections shown in Diagram C. Record the results and compare them with your prediction.

5. **Experiment** Test other ways to arrange the materials so that the bulb lights. Make a drawing of each arrangement and record all the results.

Think and Write

1. **Analyze Data** Which arrangement caused the bulb to light?

2. **Hypothesize** When you made the bulb light, you made an electric circuit. Think about the arrangement of materials when the bulb lit and when it did not. Form a hypothesis about what an electric circuit is.

✔ **407.Inq.3, 407.12.3**

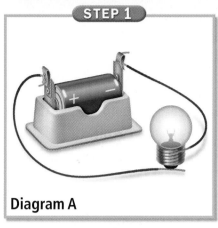

STEP 1

Diagram A

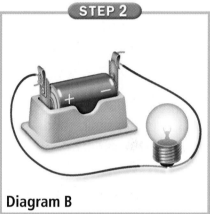

STEP 2

Diagram B

STEP 3

Diagram C

Guided Inquiry

Design an Experiment
Use what you learned in the Investigate to design a circuit that will make two bulbs light. Draw your design. Then test your design.

Electric Current

GRAPHIC ORGANIZER

Compare and Contrast
Use a Venn diagram to tell how conductors and insulators are similar and how they are different.

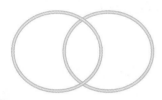

GLE 0407.12.3 Explain how electricity in a simple circuit requires a complete loop through which current can pass.

How Charges Move

Perhaps you wake up to a beeping alarm clock. Later you flip on a light switch and then you toast a piece of bread. This means you start your day using the energy of moving charged particles.

You have learned that static electricity is produced when charged particles build up on a material. However, the charges that make up static electricity either stay in one place or jump from one place to another in a sudden discharge. Such energy is not very useful.

For the energy of moving charged particles to be useful, it must be controlled. Suppose, instead of building up on a material, charged particles continuously move, or flow, through it. The energy of these particles can be controlled and used. Such a continuous flow of electric charges is called **electric current.**

Toasting Bread

1 When the toaster is turned on, electric charges flow from the outlet, through one copper wire, to heating coils in the toaster.

◀ Electric charges move from the outlet, through the cord, to coils in the toaster. The heated coils toast the bread.

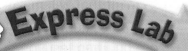

Express Lab

Activity Card
Light a Bulb

Conductors and Insulators

Negatively charged particles move easily through certain materials called **conductors** (kuhn-DUHK tuhrz). Electric current easily passes through metals such as copper, aluminum, gold, and silver. These metals are good conductors.

Electric charges also flow through water. This means that water is a conductor. The cells that make up all living things contain water. So living plants and animals are conductors, too.

Materials that electric charges do not flow through easily are called **insulators** (IHN suh lay tuhrz). Some examples of insulators are plastic, rubber, glass, air, and wood.

Conductors and insulators are used to control and direct the flow of electric charges. The power cord of an appliance controls and directs the movement of electric current. It contains both conductors and insulators.

A power cord is usually made of metal wires surrounded by a rubber or plastic covering. Each metal wire is a conductor that carries electric current between the electrical outlet and the appliance. The outer covering is an insulator. It prevents the current from escaping.

FOCUS CHECK How is electric current different from static electricity?

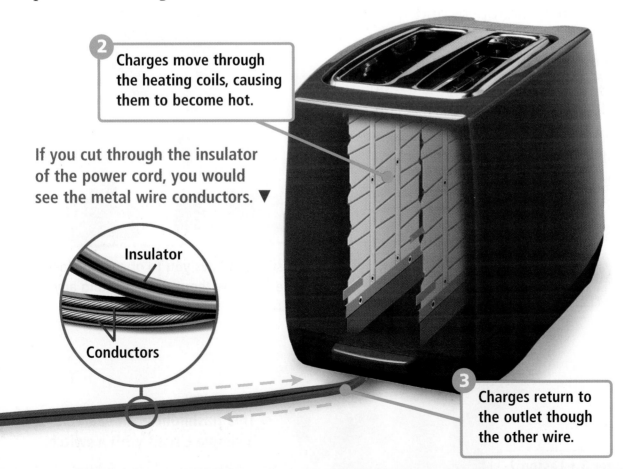

2 Charges move through the heating coils, causing them to become hot.

If you cut through the insulator of the power cord, you would see the metal wire conductors. ▼

Insulator

Conductors

3 Charges return to the outlet though the other wire.

Circuits and Switches

The pathway that electric current follows is called an **electric circuit** (SUR kiht). A circuit is a closed, or complete, path that does not have any gaps or openings.

You can use wire, a battery, and a light bulb to make a simple electric circuit. You create a closed circuit by connecting these items without gaps. When charges flow through the closed circuit, the light bulb will light.

If there is a gap in the circuit, you have an open or incomplete circuit. When a circuit is open, electric charges cannot flow and the bulb will not light.

Most circuits include a device called a switch that opens and closes the circuit. A switch allows you to turn a light bulb on and off. When you flip the switch to turn on the bulb, you close the circuit. When you flip the switch to turn off the bulb, you open the circuit. Pushing the button of a doorbell also closes a circuit and causes the bell to ring.

Simple Circuit

When the parts of the circuit are connected with no gaps, the bulb will light.

Simple Circuit With a Switch

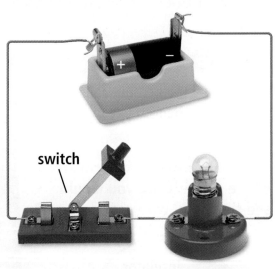

switch

A switch allows you to open and close the circuit without disconnecting any wires.

◀ This flashlight is an example of a simple circuit with a switch.

Circuit Pathways

Series Circuit

If you remove one part from the circuit, you create a gap. Current no longer moves through any of the parts.

Parallel Circuit

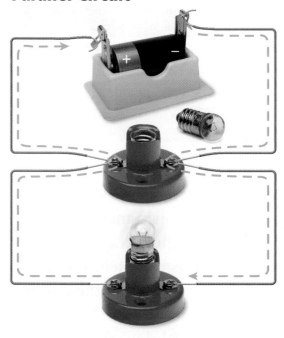

If you remove one part from the circuit, current can still move through the other parts.

Two Types of Circuits

Every working circuit has at least three parts:

- a power source, such as a battery;
- a conductor, usually wire;
- and an object that uses electric current, such as a light bulb.

When a circuit has just these three parts, there is only one pathway for the current to follow. However, a circuit can have more parts. It can have a switch, more than one battery, and more than one object using the current.

There are two ways to arrange the pathways of a circuit with many parts. In a **series circuit**, the parts are connected so that electric current passes through each part, one after another, along a single pathway. In a **parallel circuit**, the parts are connected so that current passes along more than one pathway.

🎯 **FOCUS CHECK** What is the difference between a series circuit and a parallel circuit?

▲ Party lights are usually connected in a parallel circuit. If one bulb burns out, the others stay lit.

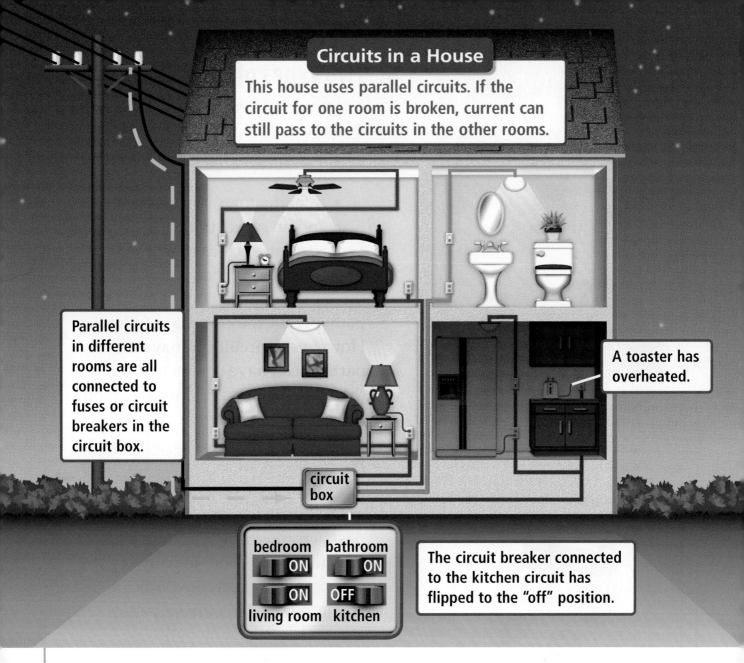

Circuits in a House

This house uses parallel circuits. If the circuit for one room is broken, current can still pass to the circuits in the other rooms.

Parallel circuits in different rooms are all connected to fuses or circuit breakers in the circuit box.

A toaster has overheated.

circuit box

bedroom ON
bathroom ON
living room ON
kitchen OFF

The circuit breaker connected to the kitchen circuit has flipped to the "off" position.

Electricity in the Home

The electric wiring in a house is connected in parallel circuits. Different circuits control current in different parts of a house. Each circuit is connected to a central circuit box. The box connects all the circuits to an outside source of electric current.

If too much current passes through a circuit, the wires can overheat. Home circuits have a safety device, such as a fuse or a circuit breaker. A fuse contains a metal strip. The strip melts when it overheats, opening the circuit. A circuit breaker is a switch. It opens, or breaks, a circuit when the circuit overheats.

Some electrical devices are battery-powered. A battery is made up of one or more electric cells. An **electric cell** is a device that changes chemical energy into electrical energy.

Lesson Wrap-Up

Visual Summary

Electrical wiring is made from conductors such as copper or gold.

If one light burns out in a parallel circuit, the other lights stay lit.

Electric circuits usually have a switch that opens and closes the circuit.

Check for Understanding

ELECTRIC CARS

Electric cars run on batteries instead of gasoline. Research how electric cars work. Then write an ad for an electric car. Include benefits these cars have over gas-powered cars, such as being cleaner to operate. Also include any drawbacks to using electric cars. ✔ **0407.7.4**

Review

1 MAIN IDEA Explain why a switch might be added to a circuit. Give examples.

2 VOCABULARY What is a conductor?

3 READING SKILL: Compare and Contrast Why is the wiring in a house usually connected in parallel circuits and not in series circuits?

4 CRITICAL THINKING: Analyze At public swimming pools, swimmers are not allowed in the water during a thunderstorm. Why do pools have this rule?

5 INQUIRY SKILL: Predict Suppose an outlet is part of a circuit containing a circuit breaker. Predict what would happen if too many appliances were plugged into the outlet.

TCAP Prep

An electric cell is a device that ____.

A opens and closes circuits.
B cannot be used in a parallel circuit.
C cannot be used in a series circuit.
D changes chemical energy into electrical energy.

SPI 0407.12.2

 **Technology**

Visit **www.eduplace.com/tnscp** to learn more about electric current.

Lesson
3

TENNESSEE STANDARDS

GLE 0407.Inq.3 Organize data into appropriate tables, graphs, drawings, or diagrams.
GLE 0407.12.1 Explore the interactions between magnets.

What is a Magnet?

Why It Matters...

The sculpture below isn't held together with glue or tape. The animal's "body" is a magnet, and its legs, tail, and other parts are objects that stick to magnets. The ability of magnets to attract certain materials has many uses. Magnets can help you find your way on a hike and help doctors look for diseases. Magnets also are an important part of electric motors.

PREPARE TO INVESTIGATE

Inquiry Skill

Hypothesize If you think you know why something happens, you can make an educated guess, or hypothesize, about it.

Materials

- bar magnet
- iron or steel nail
- bag containing cork, paper clip, glass marble, penny, plastic button, rubber band, pencil eraser, paper, small steel spring, wooden cube, sponge, aluminum foil, 15 brass paper-fasteners

Science and Math Toolbox
For step 1, review **Making a Chart to Organize Data** on page H10.

Directed Inquiry

Pick It Up

Procedure

1. **Collaborate** Work in a small group. Open the bag and spread the objects out on the desk. In your *Science Notebook,* make a chart like the one shown.

2. **Observe** Move a magnet near each object. Observe what happens as the magnet gets close to each object. Record each observation in your chart. Write "yes" if the object was attracted to the magnet. Write "no" if it was not.

3. **Record Data** Move an iron or steel nail near each object. Observe what happens as the nail gets close to each object. Record each observation in your chart.

4. **Predict** Now stroke the nail 60 times with one end of the magnet. Be sure to stroke in one direction only. Predict what will happen when the nail gets close to each object. Record your predictions.

5. **Record Data** Move the stroked nail near each object. Record your observations.

Think and Write

1. **Hypothesize** Based on your data, form a hypothesis about the kinds of objects that magnets attract.

2. **Hypothesize** Form a hypothesis to explain what happened to the nail when you stroked it with the magnet.

✔ **0407.Inq.3**

STEP 1

Object	Attracted to Magnet	Attracted to Nail
cork		
paper clip		
marble		
penny		

STEP 2

STEP 4

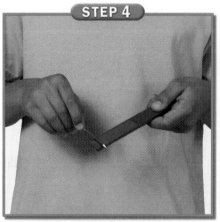

Guided Inquiry

Design an Experiment
Find out if the number of times you stroke a nail affects its magnetic strength. Get five new nails. Make a plan and record your predictions. Test your plan and record all results.

VOCABULARY

magnet
magnetic poles

GRAPHIC ORGANIZER

Main Idea and Details
As you read, write down details that describe magnets.

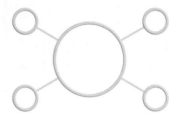

GLE 0407.12.1 Explore the interactions between magnets.

Particles of matter act like tiny magnets. If the particles making up an object line up, the object is a magnet.

Express Lab

Activity Card
Show Magnetic Fields

Magnets

Properties of Magnets

If you place a magnet (MAG niht) on a refrigerator door, it will stay there. A **magnet** is an object that attracts certain metals, mainly iron. This property of attracting iron and certain other metals is called magnetism. The force of magnetism on objects decreases as the distance from the magnet increases.

Magnets stick to most refrigerators because the doors are made of steel, which contains iron. Magnets do not attract most other metals or materials such as plastic, wood, and rubber.

Some magnets are permanent magnets. They keep their magnetism for a long time. Some magnets are temporary and lose their magnetism after a short time. You can magnetize some objects to make them temporary magnets. For example, you can stroke an iron nail with a permanent magnet to make it a temporary magnet. Increasing the number of strokes makes a temporary magnet stronger.

bar magnet

eraser

Magnetic Fields

The space in which the force of a magnet can act is called its magnetic field (MAG nehtik FEELD). In the top picture on the right, you can see the magnetic field in the pattern made by iron filings around a bar magnet.

Notice that the iron filings in the picture are thicker and closer together at each end of the magnet. The force of a magnet is greatest at two areas called the **magnetic poles.** On a bar magnet and a horseshoe magnet, the magnetic poles are at the ends.

When a bar magnet is allowed to swing freely, one end always points toward the north. This end of the magnet is the north-seeking pole, or north pole. The other end of the magnet always points south. This end is the magnet's south-seeking pole, or south pole.

Recall what you learned about electric charges. Unlike charges attract, or pull toward, each other. Like charges repel, or push away from, each other. Magnets act in a similar way. The unlike poles of two magnets attract each other. The like poles of two magnets repel each other.

FOCUS CHECK What will happen if you bring the unlike poles of two magnets near each other?

Magnetic Behavior

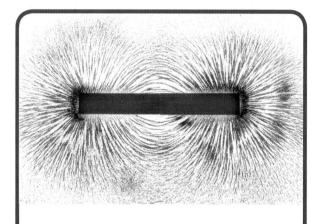

Magnetic field Iron filings trace the lines of force around the magnet.

Unlike poles attract When brought close together, the unlike poles on the ends of these bar magnets pull together until they touch.

Like poles repel When brought close together, the like poles on the ends of these bar magnets push apart.

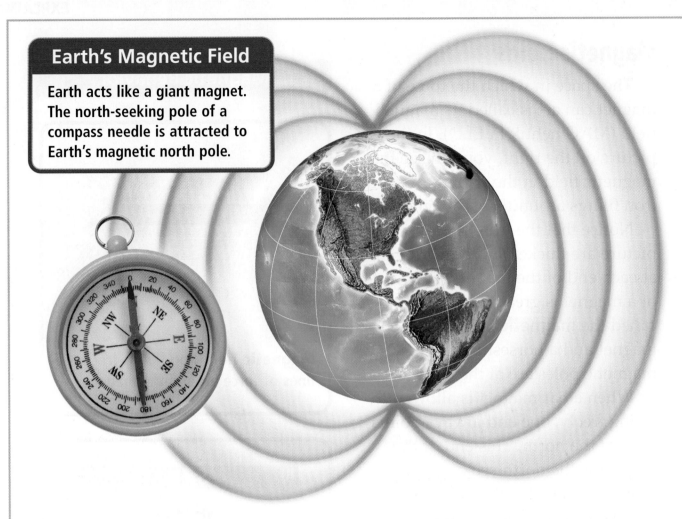

Earth's Magnetic Field

Earth acts like a giant magnet. The north-seeking pole of a compass needle is attracted to Earth's magnetic north pole.

Earth As a Magnet

Earth's center is made up mostly of molten iron. As Earth spins, electric currents in the liquid iron core produce Earth's magnetic field. As a result, Earth behaves like a giant bar magnet with two magnetic poles. Like all magnets, Earth is surrounded by a magnetic field with lines of force.

The needle of a magnetic compass is a permanent magnet. The needle is set so it can turn freely. The north-seeking pole of the compass needle will turn until it points toward the magnetic north pole of the Earth.

In the past, sailors used magnetic compasses to find their way across oceans. Today's sailors still use compasses as well as other equipment, such as radar and satellites.

You can make a compass by first changing a needle into a temporary magnet. Then float a small cork in water and place the needle on the cork. The needle causes the cork to turn so that the north-seeking pole of the needle points to Earth's magnetic north pole.

FOCUS CHECK How is Earth like a magnet?

Lesson Wrap-Up

Visual Summary

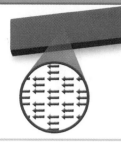

When particles in a piece of iron line up, the iron becomes a magnet.

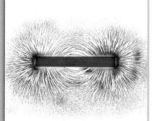

A magnetic field surrounds a magnet and has lines of force, which are strongest at the magnet's poles.

The north-seeking pole of a compass needle will point to the magnetic north pole of Earth.

✔ Check for Understanding

DESIGN A TOOL

Landfills are full of metal scraps, but the metal is hard to separate from the other stuff in the landfill. Design a new tool that can be used to separate metal scraps in a landfill. This can be a large tool or a small tool. Use magnets and small objects that are attracted to them to test if your tool is a success.

✔ 0407.T/E.2

Review

❶ MAIN IDEA Why don't magnets attract wooden objects?

❷ VOCABULARY Use the terms *magnetic field* and *magnetic poles* in a sentence.

❸ READING SKILL: Main Idea and Details When two bar magnets are placed end to end, they repel each other. Explain why the magnets behave this way.

❹ CRITICAL THINKING: Analyze Astronauts navigate by using stars or information sent from Earth. Why would magnetic compasses not work in space?

❺ INQUIRY SKILL: Hypothesize Suppose a metal nail is stroked 100 times with a magnet. When the nail is brought near a pile of metal paper clips, it fails to pick up any of the paper clips. Hypothesize why the nail did not pick up the clips.

TCAP Prep

Magnets attract objects made of ____.

A brass.
B copper.
C iron.
D plastic.

SPI 0407.12.1

Go Digital Technology

Visit **www.eduplace.com/tnscp** to learn more about magnets.

Benjamin Franklin
Flies a Kite!

What is lightning? The setting is a cluttered laboratory on a gloomy, rainy day in Philadelphia. It's June 1752. Forty-six-year-old Benjamin Franklin is hard at work on a new theory. He believes that lightning is electrical and that electricity can be collected. And he's come up with a very creative way to test his idea.

Characters

Benjamin Franklin:
scientist, printer, writer

Deborah Reed Rogers:
Benjamin Franklin's wife

William:
Benjamin Franklin's
21-year-old son

Narrator 1

Narrator 2

GLE 0407.12.3 Explain how electricity in a simple circuit requires a complete loop throuch which current can pass.

EXTEND

Benjamin: Well done is better than well said, I always say. *[He ties a string to a homemade kite.]* This experiment may be a little bit— er—unusual, but I can't worry about what others think!

Enter DEBORAH

Deborah: What are you mumbling about, Benjamin?

Benjamin: Isn't it a lovely day to fly a kite, my dear?

Deborah: Are you teasing, Benjamin? It's about to rain!

Benjamin: That's what makes it a perfectly marvelous day!

Deborah: I know everyone thinks you're a genius, what with all those science experiments and the brilliant articles and so forth. But sometimes, Benjamin, I do wonder about you.... Well, I'll leave you to your ever-interesting thoughts. I'm off to the market before the rain starts.

Benjamin: Good-bye, my dear.

Exit DEBORAH

Enter WILLIAM, in a rush, wearing his rain jacket.

William: Father, what on Earth are you doing with that kite?

Benjamin: I'm going to fly it. Would you like to come along?

William: But—it's starting to rain!

Benjamin: Exactly! I'm going to use the kite and the rain clouds to prove that lightning is electrical and that electricity can be collected.

William: What? Electrical, you say? But Father...

Benjamin: I'll explain when we get to the field. We can stand in that old shed and stay out of the rain.

BENJAMIN, with WILLIAM following, leaves the laboratory and walks quickly toward a nearby field. They arrive at the shed.

Benjamin: William, help me tie this ribbon and this key to the end of the kite string.

William: What for? And what's this pointed wire at the top of the kite?

Benjamin: The wire at the top of the kite will gather electricity from a passing cloud. The wet string will act as a conductor and guide the electricity down to the metal key, which will collect the charge of electricity.

William: I'm baffled. Conductor? Charge?

Benjamin: M-my new electrical terms! Catchy, eh? Everything will make sense to you soon enough.

William: But Father, aren't you worried the electricity will hurt you? Remember that time you were knocked unconscious?

Benjamin: I do remember, William. That's why I'm going to make sure I stay as dry as possible. Here goes! Fly kite, fly!

How Lightning Forms

3 Friction between raindrops and ice crystals causes electric charges to build up and separate.

2 Swirling air currents develop in the cloud.

4 The ground and objects on it become positively charged.

1 Warm, moist air rises and cools, producing a tall, dark storm cloud.

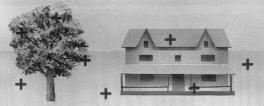

Two hours later, WILLIAM is dozing on the ground while BENJAMIN holds his kite string and scans the sky.

William [*waking up*]: You've been holding that kite string for ages. Nothing's happening! Let's go home.

Benjamin: Wait! See how those loose threads of silk kite string are standing up and away from each other? Watch what happens when I touch the key with my knuckle.

William: A spark! I saw a spark!

Benjamin: What you saw, my son, was electric fire!

Narrator 1: That day, Benjamin Franklin proved that lightning was indeed electric.

Narrator 2: He did it in a way that lots of people considered, well, unsafe. Scientists always need to find new ways to test their ideas.

Narrator 1: In other words, scientists need to come up with new approaches and even new language! Franklin invented new electrical words such as charge and conductor.

Narrator 1: That Ben Franklin was great. Talk about a spark of genius!

5 The difference in charge between the cloud and the ground continues to grow.

6 Finally lightning, a powerful discharge, occurs.

Sharing Ideas

1. **Reading Check** What idea was Ben Franklin trying to test with his kite experiment?

2. **Write About It** What clues led Franklin to believe his experiment was successful?

3. **Talk About It** Discuss why Franklin's experiment should never be repeated.

303

Lesson 4

TENNESSEE STANDARDS

GLE 0407.Inq.3 Organize data into appropriate tables, graphs, drawings, or diagrams.
GLE 0407.12.1 Explore the interactions between magnets.

Guiding Question

How Do Electromagnets Work?

Why It Matters...

Magnetism and electricity work together in electromagnets. You may never have seen electromagnets, but you depend on them every day. Electromagnets run many common appliances and machines, such as fans, refrigerators, and the generators that make electricity.

PREPARE TO INVESTIGATE

Inquiry Skill

Record Data When you record data, you write measurements, predictions, and observations about an experiment.

Materials

- insulated wire (stripped on ends, 125 cm)
- metric ruler
- iron or steel nail
- 10 metal paper clips
- dry cell (size D) in holder

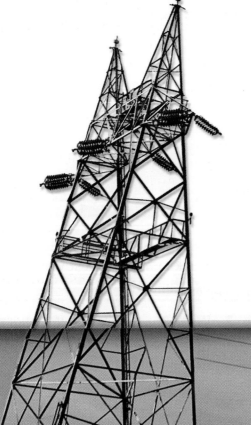

> **Science and Math Toolbox**
> For step 1, review **Using a Tape Measure or Ruler** on page H6.

Directed Inquiry

Stick to It!

Procedure

1. **Measure** Work with a partner. Measure about 20 cm from one end of a 125-cm length of insulated wire. **Safety:** Wire may be sharp.

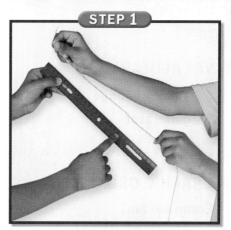

STEP 1

2. Starting at the 20-cm point, wrap 25 turns of the wire around a nail. Leave a length of free wire at both ends of the nail.

STEP 2

3. **Predict** Make a small pile of paper clips. With your partner, predict what will happen when you bring the nail close to the paper clips. Record your prediction and then test it. Record your observations.

4. **Predict** Attach each end of the wire to a different end of the dry cell. Predict what will happen if you now bring the tip of the nail toward the paper clips. Record and test your prediction.

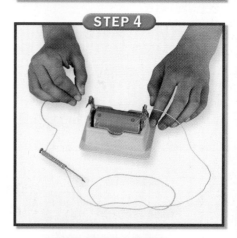

STEP 4

5. **Record Data** Disconnect the wire ends from the dry cell. Bring the tip of the nail close to the paper clips. Record your observations.

Think and Write

1. **Analyze Data** How do your predictions about the nail and paper clips compare with your observations?

2. **Infer** How did electric current flowing through the wire affect the nail?

✔ 0407.12.2

Guided Inquiry

Design an Experiment
Find out what happens if you double the number of times the wire is wrapped around the nail. Make predictions and then experiment. Record all your predictions and results.

VOCABULARY

electromagnet
generator
motor

GRAPHIC ORGANIZER

Compare and Contrast Use a Venn diagram to tell how motors and generators are similar and how they are different.

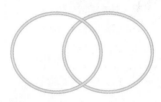

GLE 0407.12.1 Explore the interactions between magnets.

Electricity and Magnetism

Electromagnets

Whenever you play a video or turn on a hair dryer, you are putting electromagnets (ih lehk-troh MAG nihts) to work. You have learned that you can make a weak temporary magnet by stroking a piece of iron with a permanent magnet. You can make a strong temporary magnet by using electricity to produce magnetism. An **electromagnet** is a strong temporary magnet that uses electricity to produce magnetism.

How does electricity produce magnetism? When electric current passes through a wire or other conductor, the current produces a weak magnetic field around the wire. If the wire is wrapped around a piece of iron, the iron becomes magnetized. The magnetic field also becomes stronger.

The nail acts as an electromagnet when the circuit is closed and electric current flows through the wire. ▶

Express Lab

Activity Card
Make a Magnetic Field

306

Using Electromagnets

Like other magnets, electromagnets attract materials made of iron. They are also surrounded by magnetic fields.

The magnetic force of an electromagnet can be controlled. Increasing the number of wire coils or increasing the amount of current moving through the coils will increase the strength of the electromagnet. An electromagnet can be quite strong and still be small enough to fit in your hand.

An electromagnet can be turned on and off. It acts like a magnet only while electric current moves through the wire. As soon as the electric current is turned off, the electromagnet loses its magnetism.

To see how electromagnets can be useful, look at the picture of the crane. Cranes with very strong electromagnets are used to pick up cars and other heavy objects that contain iron.

Many objects in your home have electromagnets in them. Small electromagnets are located inside such devices as blenders, computer disk drives, and doorbells.

FOCUS CHECK How are a bar magnet and an electromagnet alike? How are they different?

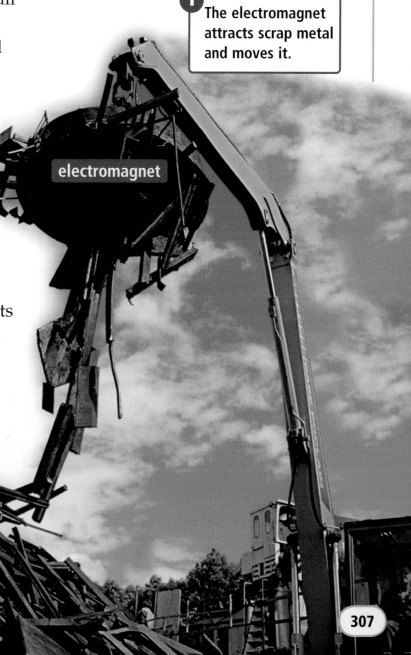

1 The electromagnet attracts scrap metal and moves it.

electromagnet

2 When the current is turned off, the crane is no longer magnetized and the metal drops into the pile.

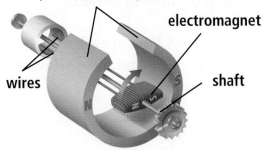

permanent magnet

electromagnet

wires

shaft

1 In a motor, electricity passes through an electromagnet. The direction of current keeps reversing.

2 As the current changes direction, the poles of the electromagnet keep reversing. The permanent magnet repels and attracts the electromagnet, turning the shaft of the motor.

3 As the shaft turns, electrical energy changes to energy of motion.

Motors

What do refrigerators, mixers, and ceiling fans have in common? They all have an electric motor. An electric **motor** is a device that changes electrical energy into energy of motion.

How does an electric motor work? All electric motors contain electromagnets and permanent magnets. Recall that an electromagnet is formed when a conductor is wrapped around an iron core and electric current runs through the conductor.

Now recall how magnetic fields interact with each other. Like poles repel, and unlike poles attract. When a motor is turned on, electric current passes through a wire that is wrapped around an iron core. The magnetic field of this electromagnet interacts with the magnetic field of a permanent magnet. The like poles of each magnet repel each other and the unlike poles attract each other, producing motion.

Generating Electricity

You have learned that an electric motor uses magnetism to convert electrical energy into energy of motion. A **generator** does the opposite. A generator (JEHN uh-ray tuhr) is a device that uses magnetism to convert energy of motion into electrical energy.

Giant generators produce the electricity that lights up cities and runs machinery. These generators have powerful magnets and huge coils of wire. Electric current is produced in the wires when the coils move across the magnetic field of the magnet.

There are two ways to increase the amount of electricity a generator produces. One way is to use stronger magnets. A second way is to increase the number of coils of wire.

Where does the energy to move the coils of a generator come from? In many power plants, energy released by nuclear fuels or by burning coal or oil heats water to produce steam. The pressure of the steam moves the coils. Energy to move the coils can also come from falling water or blowing wind.

FOCUS CHECK How are electric motors and generators different?

From Generator to Customer

Energy source Energy from falling water or burning fuels turns generator coils, producing electricity.

Electric power lines Power lines carry electricity to customers.

Homes and businesses Although generated far away, electricity is as close as the nearest light switch.

The Cost of Using Electricity

Using electricity costs money. Your monthly electric bill is based on the total amount of electricity used in your home each month.

The cost of using an electric device depends on the amount of time it is used and the amount of electrical energy it needs to run. Some devices, such as fans and washing machines, use electricity only part of the time. Others, such as refrigerators and clocks, use electricity 24 hours a day. The graph shows the average monthly cost of using some common electric devices.

Some electric devices use electricity even when they are not being used. If a computer were left on "standby" or "sleep" mode for an entire year, it would use about $40 worth of electricity. Some appliances, such as DVD players and stereos, have built in clocks. The clocks run on electricity even when the appliance is turned off.

Follow these tips to save electricity:

- Use a surge protector to plug in TVs, DVD players, and other appliances. When the surge protector is shut off, no electricity reaches the appliances.
- Turn your computer off instead of keeping it on standby.
- Turn off lights, TVs, and stereos when you are not in the room.

⊘ FOCUS CHECK How do a refrigerator and a washing machine differ in their use of electricity?

A computer still uses electricity when it is in standby mode or turned off. ▼

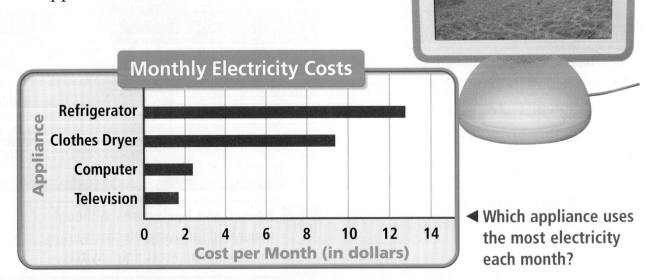

Monthly Electricity Costs

Appliance: Refrigerator, Clothes Dryer, Computer, Television

Cost per Month (in dollars): 0 2 4 6 8 10 12 14

◄ Which appliance uses the most electricity each month?

Lesson Wrap-Up

Visual Summary

Electric current in a conductor creates a magnetic field, which can be used to produce an electromagnet.

An electric motor uses magnetism and electricity to produce energy of motion.

In a generator, magnetism and energy of motion are used to produce electricity.

✔ Check for Understanding

REPORT ON MAGLEV

In December 2002, the official test run of the world's first commercial maglev train service took place in Shanghai, China. A trip of 30 km took only 8 minutes. The same trip by bus takes at least 45 minutes. Do Internet research to find out more about maglev trains. Write a paragraph summarizing what you learn.

✔ 0407.T/E.1

Review

❶ MAIN IDEA How do permanent magnets and electromagnets differ? How are they similar?

❷ VOCABULARY Use the term *generator* in a sentence.

❸ READING SKILL: Compare and Contrast how do electric motors and generators use magnetism?

❹ CRITICAL THINKING: Synthesize Use what you know about electromagnets and magnetism to explain how recycling centers use electromagnets to separate discarded materials.

❺ INQUIRY SKILL: Record Data Make a chart to record these data: an electromagnet with 25 turns of wire picks up 5 paper clips; one with 35 turns picks up 7 paper clips; one with 45 turns picks up 9 paper clips.

TCAP TCAP Prep

Electric motors are not found in a _____.

A ceiling fan.
B light bulb.
C power drill.
D refrigerator.

SPI 0407.12.3

Go Digital Technology

Visit **www.eduplace.com/tnscp** to learn more about electricity and magnetism working together.

EXTREME Science

Nature's Living Battery

Yow! You wouldn't want to bump into an electric eel while swimming. It can jolt other animals with over 600 volts of electricity! That's more than enough to stun or even kill its prey.

The electric eel uses thousands of specialized muscles to produce its charge. These muscles cause a powerful electric current to flow from the eel's body through the water—and through whatever it wants to zap.

Shocker! Electric eels use their electrical power to hunt small fish, shrimp, frogs, and water birds.

GLE 0407.12.3 Explain how electricity in a simple circuit requires a complete loop through which current can pass.

EXTEND

The long tail is the negative pole.

The head of the eel is the positive pole.

"Wow! It would take about 400 flashlight batteries to produce the same charge as an adult electric eel!"

1.5 V

GLE 0407.12.3 Explain how electricity in a simple circuit requires a complete loop through which current can pass. **Math GLE 0406.5.1** Collect, record, arrange, present, and interpret data using tables and various representations. **ELA GLE 0401.4.1** Conduct research to access and present information.

Math The Battery Test

"Ace" and "Be Bright" are two brands of flashlight-sized batteries. To test them, students connected a battery from each brand into two identical circuits. They measured the current in both circuits every hour for 12 hours. The graph shows their results.

1. What do the results show about the batteries?

2. When was the current about equal in both circuits? Explain how you know.

3. Would a bar graph have been a better choice for displaying the data? Would a circle graph have been better? Explain.

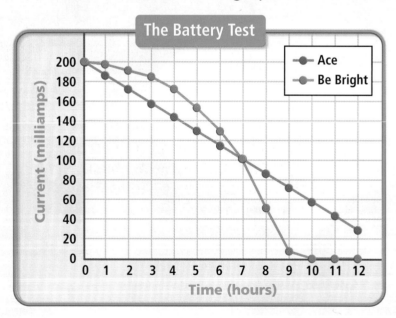

 **Informational**

Is it possible to get electricity from a lemon? How about an orange or a grapefruit? Research how certain fruits can be used as batteries. Describe the process in your report.

Robotics Engineer

Robots are used for everything from delivering medicine in hospitals to exploring other planets. Designing and producing robots is the job of a robotics engineer.

For many years robots have been used to help build cars, and handle dangerous materials. Today you can even buy a robot to vacuum a rug. Some robotics engineers are working on technology to help robots make complicated decisions. Robots in daily life are no longer the stuff of science fiction!

What It Takes!

- A degree in engineering
- Courses in computer science

Electrician

Electricians install electrical systems and devices in new homes, schools, and factories. An electrician must make sure the systems they install meet safety codes. Electricians also rewire old buildings. Some work at power stations that supply electricity to cities.

What It Takes!

- High-school diploma
- Apprentice in a training program
- Pass a licensing exam (most states)

Vocabulary

Complete each sentence with a term from the list.

1. Current can move along only one path in a/an _____.

2. The two ends of a bar magnet are its _____.

3. In an electric power plant, a giant _____ uses magnetism to convert energy of motion into electricity.

4. Electric current can pass easily through _____.

5. Chemical energy changes into electrical energy in a/an _____.

6. Electric current cannot pass easily through _____.

7. The buildup of electric charge on a material is called _____.

8. A device that is made by wrapping wire, through which electric current can flow, around a piece of iron is a/an _____.

9. An electric current can move along more than one path in a/an _____.

10. The pathway that an electric current follows is a/an _____.

conductors
electric cell
electric charges
electric circuit
electric current
electromagnet
generator
insulators
magnet
magnetic poles
motor
★ parallel circuit
★ series circuit
static electricity

TCAP Inquiry Skills

11. **Hypothesize** Write a hypothesis about which is more useful in industry for lifting heavy metal objects, a permanent magnet or an electromagnet. Give reasons for your hypothesis. **GLE 0407.Inq.1**

12. **Infer** Al creates a circuit that has one battery and two flashlight bulbs. When both bulbs are connected to the circuit, they are both lighted. When Al removes one of the bulbs from the circuit, the other bulb does not light. Based on this information, infer whether Al's circuit is a series circuit or a parallel circuit. Explain your answer. **GLE 0407.Inq.4**

Map the Concept

The chart shows two categories. Classify each object on the list into one category.

iron nail   plastic spoon
steel knife   wooden pencil

Attracted to a magnet	Not attracted to a magnet

GLE 0407.12.1

Critical Thinking

13. Evaluate A friend says that magnets are fun to play with but are not very useful. How would you respond to this statement? **GLE 0407.12.1**

14. Synthesize Suppose your home were wired entirely with series circuits. Describe some effects this would have on daily life in your home. **GLE 0407.12.3**

15. Apply You reach for a doorknob and receive a small shock. Use what you know about static electricity to explain why this happened. **GLE 0407.Inq.4**

16. Analyze Explain how a fuse helps protect against fire that could be caused by overheated wires. **GLE 0407.Inq.5**

 for Understanding

Draw a Circuit

Draw a diagram of a parallel circuit that includes two light bulbs, a battery, and wires. Label your diagram. ✓ **0407.12.3**

TCAP TCAP Prep

Write the letter of the best answer choice.

17 Two objects that attract each other have opposite _____.

  A electromagnet cores.
  B electric circuits.
  C electric charges.
  D electric motors. **SPI 0407.12.1**

18 The continuous flow of electric charges is a(n) _____.

  A magnetic field.
  C conductor.
  B temporary magnet.
  D electric current. **SPI 0407.12.2**

19 An object that attracts certain metals, mainly iron, is a(n) _____.

  A electric cell.
  B electric circuit.
  C magnet.
  D insulator **SPI 0407.12.1**

20 A device in which an electromagnet and a permanent magnet change electrical energy to energy of motion is called a _____.

  A generator.
  C motor.
  B temporary magnet.
  D battery **SPI 0407.12.1**

Chapter 9

Light

LESSON

1

Light can make the Moon shine or cast a shadow on a fence. Yet you cannot hold it or touch it. Just what is light?

LESSON

2

Light rays change direction when they strike a mirror or pass through a lens. How else can light change?

LESSON

3

Flowers come in every color of the rainbow. When you look at a red flower, what makes it appear red?

Fun Facts

Sunlight can penetrate clean ocean water to a depth of about 240 feet.

Vocabulary Preview

absorb
lens
light
opaque
prism
reflect
refract
shadow
translucent
transparent

 Vocabulary Strategies

Have you ever seen any of these words before? Do you know what they mean?

State a description, explanation, or example of the vocabulary in your own words.

Draw a picture, symbol, example, or other image that describes the word.

Glossary p. H16

opaque

translucent

transparent

reflect

Start with Your Standards

Inquiry

GLE 0407.Inq.1 Explore different scientific phenomena by asking questions, making logical predictions, planning investigations, and recording data.

GLE 0407.Inq.3 Organize data into appropriate tables, graphs, drawings, or diagrams

GLE 0407.Inq.4 Identify and interpret simple patterns of evidence to communicate the findings of multiple investigations.

GLE 0407.Inq.5 Recognize that people may interpret the same results in different ways.

Physical Science

Standard 10 Energy

GLE 0407.10.1 Distinguish among heat, radiant, and chemical forms of energy.

GLE 0407.10.2 Investigate how light travels and is influenced by different types of materials and surfaces.

Interact with this chapter.

 www.eduplace.com/tnscp

321

Lesson 1

TENNESSEE STANDARDS

GLE 0407.Inq.4 Identify and interpret simple patterns of evidence to communicate the findings of multiple investigations.

GLE 0407.10.2 Investigate how light travels and is influenced by different types of materials and surfaces.

Guiding Question

What Is Light?

Why It Matters...

Light shines from the Sun. It also shines from fires, fireflies, and electric light bulbs. Right now, you are using light to read this book.

Just what is light? Light is a form of energy that can travel through space. By applying knowledge of light, people have made and used light in many ways.

PREPARE TO INVESTIGATE

Inquiry Skill

Collaborate When you collaborate, you work with others to carry out investigations and share data and ideas.

Materials

- paper
- flashlight
- transparent tape
- sharpened pencil
- metric tape measure

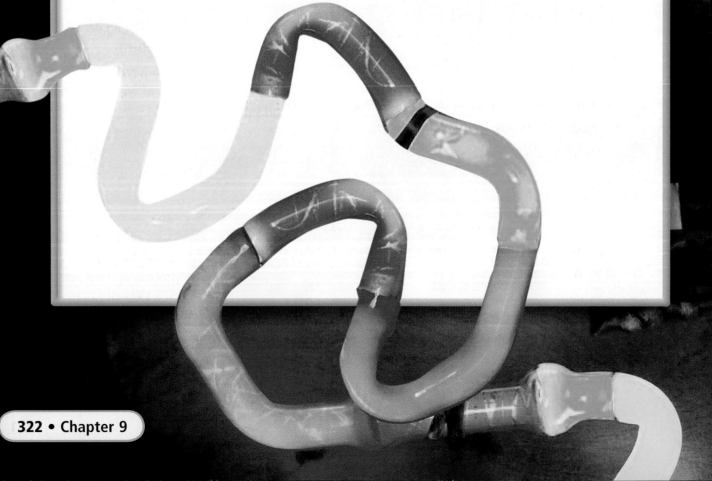

Directed Inquiry

Shadow Shapes

Procedure

1 **Collaborate** Work with a partner. Push a table or desk against a wall. Tape a sheet of white paper to the wall above the table.

2 **Measure** Have your partner hold the end of a tape measure at the wall. Stretch the tape measure out along the table past 80 cm. Use transparent tape to mark *5 cm, 40 cm*, and *80 cm* on the table. Label each piece of tape.

3 Hold a flashlight above the 80-cm mark so it points toward the paper. Have your partner hold a pencil above the 40-cm mark.

4 **Observe** Turn on the flashlight. Observe the size, shape, and edge of the pencil's shadow on the paper. Draw the shadow in your *Science Notebook*.

5 Turn off the flashlight. Have your partner move the pencil so it is above the 5-cm mark. Repeat step 4.

STEP 2

STEP 3

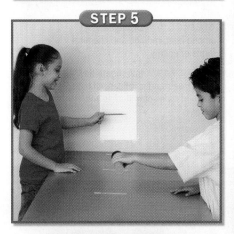

STEP 5

Think and Write

1. **Compare** How did the shadow look different when the pencil was held at the 40-cm and 5-cm marks?

2. **Infer** How does the distance an object is from the light affect how its shadow looks?

Guided Inquiry

Design an Experiment
Repeat the steps with paper cutouts of a square and a circle. Compare the shapes of the cutouts with the shapes of their shadows. Are their shadows sharp or fuzzy?

✔ 0407.Inq.3

Light

Energy You Can See

Look around. You can see the things around you because of light. **Light** is a form of energy that you can see. Energy is the ability to cause change. Light and sound are forms of energy that travel in waves. Light waves travel in straight lines in all directions, away from their source.

Light waves can travel through certain kinds of matter, such as air or clear glass. Light also can travel through empty space. This is how light from the Sun reaches Earth and other planets.

A few objects, such as lamps and fireflies, can give off their own light. Yet most objects do not do this. You see them because light from another source bounces off them.

VOCABULARY

light
opaque
shadow
translucent
transparent

GRAPHIC ORGANIZER

Main Idea and Details
Use a chart to explain two things that could happen to light when it hits an object.

GLE 0407.10.1 Distinguish among heat, radiant, and chemical forms of energy.

GLE 0407.10.2 Investigate how light travels and is influenced by different types of materials and surfaces.

In this baseball stadium, powerful lights make night seem like day. ▼

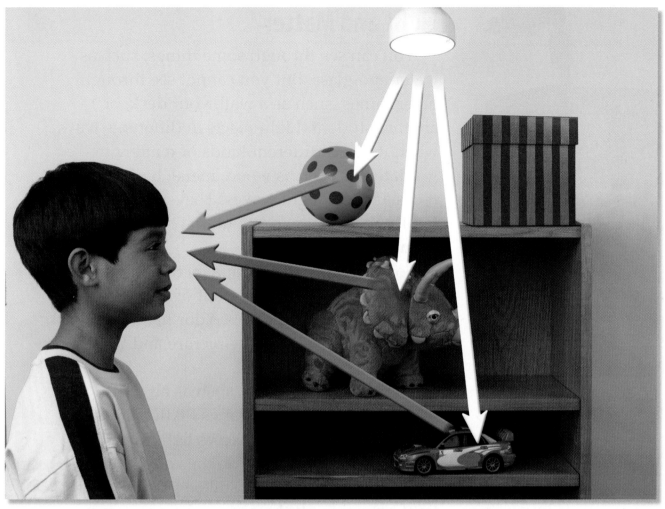

▲ The boy sees the objects when light waves bounce from their surfaces to his eyes.

Look at the picture. Light waves from the light bulb strike objects in the room, including a ball, stuffed animal, and toy car. Some of the light waves bounce from the objects to the boy's eyes. That's why he can see these objects.

As you might guess, the eye is a very special sense organ. It contains parts that focus light and control the amount of light that enters. Cells in the back of the eye receive the light and send messages to the brain.

Unlike most animals, humans have two eyes that both face forward. By combining the images from each eye, humans can form a broad, three-dimensional picture of what they see.

◎ **FOCUS CHECK** How do you see objects?

Activity Card
Categorize Objects

opaque

translucent

transparent

Light and Matter

You can see through some things, such as water and glass. But you cannot see through other things, such as a wall, your desk, or another student. Light reacts in differents ways when it meets different kinds of matter.

Materials such as wood, metal, bones, and rocks all block light waves. They are **opaque** (oh PAYK). An opaque material blocks light from passing through it.

For an example, look at a picture on a wall. Now place your hand in front of your eyes so you cannot see the picture. Your hand will block any light bouncing off the picture and traveling toward you.

Some kinds of matter, such as air and glass, are **transparent** (trahns PAIR uhnt). A transparent material allows light to pass through it. If the picture on the wall had glass in front of it, you would still be able to see any light bouncing off the picture. Windows are made from transparent glass or plastic to allow sunlight to shine through them.

Certain materials are **translucent** (trahns-LOO suhnt). A translucent material allows some light to pass through it, but scatters the light in many directions. Frosted glass is translucent. Objects seen through translucent materials appear blurry.

As the matter in an object changes, the way light reacts to it may change as well. Transparent glass may become translucent over time. Rub cooking oil into a sheet of wax paper, and it will become more transparent.

◀ Light passes through transparent and translucent materials, but not through opaque ones.

Shadows

Did you see your shadow today? Shadows occur when light strikes opaque objects, such as your body.

Light waves travel in straight lines from their source. If you stand in sunlight, some of the light waves strike your body. Your body blocks these light waves.

Other light waves do not strike your body. They continue past your body until they strike an opaque surface, such as the ground.

Your body causes a **shadow**, or an area where light does not strike. The shadow is shaped like you, because only the light waves that strike your body are blocked. Other light waves travel past you and shine on the ground.

FOCUS CHECK What kinds of objects cast shadows—opaque, transparent, or translucent?

An opaque object blocks all the light that strikes it. The shadow takes the shape of the outline of the object. ▼

Light waves that strike the girl's body are blocked. Other light waves go past her. ▶

327

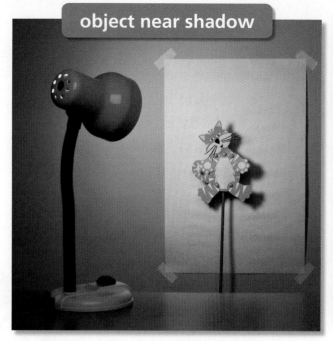

object near shadow

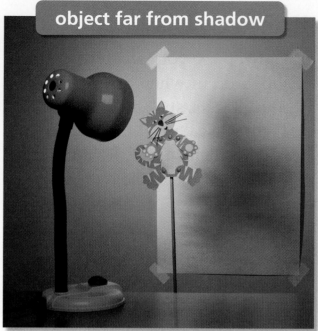

object far from shadow

▲ The nearer an object is to the shadow it casts, the sharper the shadow edges will be.

Sharp Shadows, Blurry Shadows

When an object blocks light, a shadow forms in the shape of that object. Sometimes the edges of the shadow are clean and sharp.

Look at the photos above. In both photos, the lamp is the same distance from the wall. In the photo on the left, the puppet is only 5 cm (2 in.) from the wall. The shadow it casts has clean, sharp edges. The size of the shadow is similar to the size of the puppet.

In the photo on the right, the puppet was moved to 15 cm (6 in.) from the wall. The shadow it casts is blurry and larger than the puppet. The farther an object is from the shadow it casts, the larger the shadow and the blurrier its edges.

🎯 **FOCUS CHECK** Where should you hold your hands to produce a clear, sharp shadow on the wall?

Lesson Wrap-Up

Visual Summary

You see an object when light traveling from the object enters your eye.

Opaque objects block light. Transparent objects allow light to pass through. Translucent objects allow some light to pass through.

A shadow is an area where light does not strike. Sunlight can be blocked to produce shadows.

Check for Understanding

TOOLS WITH MIRRORS

Build a tool from mirrors, cardboard tubes, and other materials. The tool should help you do something useful, such as see around a wall or a corner. Or use the tool to send coded messages to a partner.

✓ 407.T/E.2

Review

❶ **MAIN IDEA** How do you see objects?

❷ **VOCABULARY** Use the words *light* and *shadow* in a sentence.

❸ **READING SKILL: Main Idea and Details** Provide examples of the following main idea: *When light travels, it is blocked by some materials.*

❹ **CRITICAL THINKING: Synthesize** Is water opaque, transparent, or translucent? Or does the answer depend on a property of the water? Explain.

❺ **INQUIRY SKILL: Observe** Classify at least three different objects in the classroom as opaque, transparent, and translucent.

TCAP Prep

Which object is opaque along its edges, but transparent in the center?

A the Pacific Ocean
B a donut
C a cat's head
D a bottle of cooking oil

SPI 0407.10.3

Technology

Go Digital

Visit **www.eduplace.com/tnscp** to find out more about light.

Lasers Make the Cut.

Imagine an operation where the doctor doesn't have to touch the patient. Impossible? Not with lasers! Every year, thousands of people have surgery using laser light. Lasers cut with such amazing exactness that doctors can use them to perform the most delicate of operations, such as the eye surgery shown here.

What's so special about a laser beam? Unlike regular light, laser light is extremely concentrated and tightly organized. In a laser beam, the light waves move in time with each other, like people marching in rows. These properties make laser light an extremely useful tool for making precision measurements and such products as computer chips.

Lasers are both precise and powerful. Here one is used to cut a length of pipe.

GLE 0407.10.2 Investigate how light travels and is
influenced by different types of materials and surfaces.

EXTEND

Laser Surgery

Doctors use laser beams to make a microscopic cut through the eye's transparent cover, or cornea. The laser will then shave off parts of the lens to reshape it. When the cornea heals, the patient will enjoy better vision.

Sharing Ideas

Note-Book

1. **READING CHECK** How is laser light different from ordinary light?

2. **WRITE ABOUT IT** Computer chips are only about a quarter inch wide, but have many tiny wires and other parts. Why are lasers good for making computer chips?

3. **TALK ABOUT IT** What do you think are some uses for lasers that are not mentioned here?

331

Lesson 2

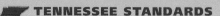
TENNESSEE STANDARDS

GLE 0407.Inq.1 Explore different scientific phenomena by asking questions, making logical predictions, planning investigations, and recording data.

GLE 0407.10.2 Investigate how light travels and is influenced by different types of materials and surfaces.

Guiding Question

How Is Light Reflected?

Why It Matters...

When you look in a mirror you see yourself. Light strikes your body and bounces off. Some of the light bouncing off your body strikes the mirror and bounces back to your eyes. If light could not bounce off surfaces, you could not see yourself, or anything else, in a mirror.

PREPARE TO INVESTIGATE

Inquiry Skill

Ask Questions You ask questions to find out how or why something that you observe happens. Questions can lead to scientific investigations.

Materials

- flashlight
- mirror
- black construction paper
- piece of cardboard
- spray bottle with water
- safety goggles

Ways of Reflecting

Procedure

STEP 1

1. **Collaborate** Work with a group. The room should be dim. Place a mirror on the table. Hold a lighted flashlight at an angle and point it at the mirror. Record your observations. **Safety:** Do not shine the flashlight into anyone's eyes. Wear goggles.

STEP 2

2. **Predict** As you hold the lit flashlight, another student will spray a mist of water through the rays of light. Predict what the path of the light will be. Then test your prediction. In your *Science Notebook,* make a diagram to show what you observe about the path of the light.

STEP 3

3. **Observe** Have another student hold a sheet of black construction paper so the light coming from the mirror shines on the paper. In your *Science Notebook*, make another diagram to show what you observe.

Think and Write

1. Did the light travel in a curved path or in a straight line after striking the mirror?

2. **Compare** How did the light's path change when black paper was held up in step 3?

2. **Ask Questions** With your group, brainstorm a list of questions about mirrors and the effect they have on light.

Guided Inquiry

Ask Questions What materials behave like mirrors? Make a list of some examples and ask questions about them. Identify traits they share that cause them to act like mirrors.

✔ 0407.Inq.3

Paths of Light

VOCABULARY

lens

reflect

refract

GRAPHIC ORGANIZER

Problem and Solution

Use the chart to list some problems that lenses could solve. List what kind of lenses could solve these problems.

Problem	Solution

GLE 0407.10.2 Investigate how light travels and is influenced by different types of materials and surfaces.

Reflection

Light waves travel in straight lines. How they behave when they strike an object depends on the object's surface.

Light waves **reflect** (rih FLEHKT), or bounce, off the surfaces of most objects. When you look at a mirror, the light waves reflect off its smooth, shiny surface. If you look directly at the mirror, the waves bounce back to your eyes. That's why you see yourself.

Yet other objects are not smooth and shiny. When light waves strike them, they bounce back in many directions. Thus, you see the object itself, not your reflection.

When the surface of water is very smooth, it reflects light like a mirror. The drawing (inset) shows how light rays bounce off a mirror-like surface.

Refraction

Light waves **refract** (rih FRAKT) when they move at an angle from one transparent material to another, such as from air to glass or to water. To refract is to bend.

People put refraction to good use by making lenses. A **lens** is a piece of curved glass, plastic, or other material that refracts light. Two types of lenses are concave lenses and convex lenses, as shown.

With the proper design, one or more lenses will enlarge or refine an image. Hand lenses and microscopes use lenses in this way. Eyeglasses use lenses to correct fuzzy images that an eye sees. A telescope uses lenses to make faraway images appear closer.

FOCUS CHECK What problems can mirrors and lenses solve?

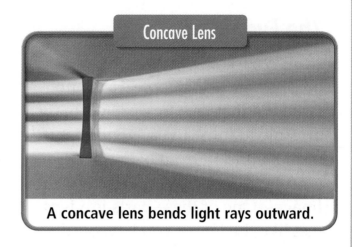

Concave Lens

A concave lens bends light rays outward.

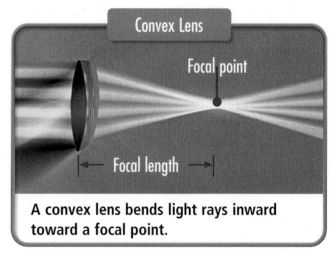

Convex Lens

Focal point

Focal length

A convex lens bends light rays inward toward a focal point.

Study how light waves change when they pass through a concave or convex lens. Lenses are used to change the image of an object.

1935

POSTFRIMÆRKE
10 ØRE
DANMARK

◀ Light is refracted by this magnifying glass. How is this useful?

Express Lab

Activity Card
Bend a Pencil with Light

The Eye

As you know, eyes are the sense organs that help people see. With two eyes that face forward, humans are able to form a very good picture of the world in front of them.

An eye uses many parts to form images. One of these parts is a lens, just like the lenses you have just studied. The lens in an eye is behind the cornea and the pupil. Find these parts in the drawing below.

When you look at an object, light reflected from it enters your eye. The cornea and the lens bend the light. An image of the object appears on the retina, at the back of your eye. Nerves in your retina send the image to your brain.

In the drawing, do you notice anything odd about the image of the flower? It is upside down! Your brain receives such images, then turns them upright for you to understand.

⊙FOCUS CHECK Would the eye work without a lens? Explain why or why not.

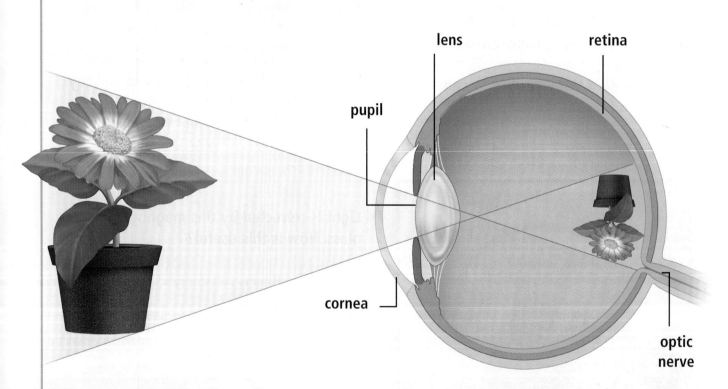

Like other lenses, the lens of your eye bends light rays to form an image. The image forms upside down on the back of the retina.

Visual Summary

Mirrors and other smooth surfaces reflect all the light that strikes them.

Light can refract, or bend, when it passes through air, water, and glass.

The lenses in your eyes refract light to form images on your retinas. Your brain interprets those images.

Check for Understanding

EXPLORE LENSES

Examine a convex lens and a concave lens. Draw and label a picture of each. Look at a small object through each lens, and move the lens back and forth until a clear image forms. What does each lens do to the appearance of the object? Report your findings.

✔ 0407.10.2

Review

❶ **MAIN IDEA** How do you see your image reflected in a mirror?

❷ **VOCABULARY** What is the difference between *reflect* and *refract*?

❸ **READING SKILL: Problem and Solution** Describe what lenses do, and three uses for lenses.

❹ **CRITICAL THINKING: Analyze** You drop a coin in a deep puddle. But each time you reach for the coin, you miss touching it. What is causing this problem?

❺ **INQUIRY SKILL: Ask Questions** Suppose you stand between two mirrors. Write two questions about what the image would be like in each mirror. Use two pocket mirrors to help you find answers to your questions.

TCAP TCAP Prep

A lens works by _____ light.

A absorbing
B refracting
C reflecting
D blocking

SPI 0407.10.2

Go Digital Technology

Visit **www.eduplace.com/tnscp** to find out more about mirrors and lenses.

337

EXTREME Science

Mighty Mirrors

What do all these mirrors do? They reflect the sunlight from a huge area and focus it onto a very small one. The place where all this sunlight comes together gets extremely hot.

How hot is this place? Would you believe 4,000°C (7,200°F)?! That's hot enough to melt diamond, the hardest natural substance on Earth.

The photograph shows a solar furnace—a huge sunlight collection and concentration system. Scientists can use the extreme heat of a solar furnace to test the effects of high temperatures on different materials.

This small solar reflector acts as a solar oven. The collected sunlight provides enough energy to cook food.

GLE 0407.10.1 Distinguish among heat, radiant, and chemical forms of energy.
GLE 0407.10.2 Investigate how light travels and is influenced by different types
of materials and surfaces.

EXTEND

The Odeillo solar furnace in the Pyrenees Mountains of France is the world's largest. The curved face of the collector is over 36 meters high. It uses 1,830 individual mirrors to focus sunlight.

TENNESSEE STANDARDS

GLE 0407.Inq.1 Explore different scientific phenomena by asking questions, making logical predictions, planning investigations, and recording data.

GLE 0407.10.2 Investigate how light travels and is influenced by different types of materials and surfaces.

Guiding Question

What Is Color?

Why It Matters...

You see objects of different colors all around you. Sometimes you can see a rainbow of colors when you look at an object, such as this cut glass ball.

When light strikes an object, it affects how the object looks. Different colors of light striking an object can affect the colors you see.

PREPARE TO INVESTIGATE

Inquiry Skill

Predict When you predict, you state what you think will happen based on observations and experiences.

Materials

- flashlight
- blue cellophane
- red cellophane
- piece of white paper

Directed Inquiry

Colored Lights

Procedure

STEP 2

1. Place a sheet of white paper on a table. The room should be dim.

2. **Observe** Shine a flashlight on the paper. Record in your *Science Notebook* the color that the paper appears to be.

STEP 3

3. **Experiment** Hold a piece of blue cellophane in front of the flashlight lens. Shine the light on the paper. Record the color that the paper appears to be.

4. **Predict** Hold a piece of red cellophane in front of the flashlight lens. Predict the color that the paper will appear to be. Test your prediction. Compare your prediction with what you observe.

STEP 4

 Think and Write

1. **Infer** How does the color of the cellophane affect the color of the light that you see coming from the flashlight?

2. In steps 3 and 4, how does the color of the light affect the color that the white paper appears to be?

3. **Predict** In step 3, suppose you shined the flashlight on a sheet of green paper. What color do you think the paper would appear to be? If possible, test your prediction.

Guided Inquiry

Design an Experiment
Test other combinations of colored cellophane and colored paper. Predict the outcome of each test before you carry it out. Compare your results with your predictions.

0407.10.2

Color

▶ **VOCABULARY**

absorb

prism

▶ **GRAPHIC ORGANIZER**

Sequence Use the chart to explain how you see the color of an object.

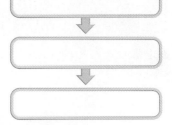

GLE 0407.10.2 Investigate how light travels and is influenced by different types of materials and surfaces.

The Colors of Sunlight

Look at the colored bands! They show that sunlight, also called white light, is really a collection of light waves of different colors.

A **prism** is a piece of glass or other transparent material that separates white light into colors. A triangle-shaped piece of glass can act as a prism. So can tiny water droplets that hang in the air after a rainfall. These natural prisms form bands of colored light called a rainbow!

Notice that the colored bands from a prism are always arranged in the same order. Red is on the outside, then orange, yellow, green, blue, indigo, and violet. This happens because a prism bends each color at a specific angle.

In 1665, Isaac Newton passed the colored bands from one prism into a second prism. The colors combined into white light! This proved that sunlight is made of colored parts.

Both a triangle-shaped glass and tiny raindrops can act as prisms. Both break white light into bands of colors.

▲ An orange absorbs most of the light from sunlight. But it reflects orange light. This is the color you see.

Seeing Colors

Most objects will **absorb** (uhb SAWRB), or take in, some of the light that strikes their surface. A colored object absorbs some colors of light but reflects other colors. You can see only the reflected colors.

Bananas, for example, look yellow because they reflect yellow light. They absorb other colors. A lime looks green because it reflects green light. It absorbs the other colors of light.

Some objects absorb nearly all the light that strikes them. They appear black! In contrast, white objects reflect all of the colors that strike them.

FOCUS CHECK What happens to sunlight after it strikes a banana?

Express Lab

Activity Card 15
Investigate Absorption

Colored Light

The color of an object depends on the color of light it reflects. It also depends on the color of the light shining on it.

White light is made up of all the colors of the rainbow. White objects reflect all of these colors. If you shine white light on a white sneaker, it will reflect all of the colors in the light. It will look white. Yet if you shine red light on the sneaker, it will reflect the red light and look red. Shine a blue light, and the sneaker will look blue.

To see this effect for yourself, tape a piece of colored cellophane across a flashlight. Then shine that flashlight in a dark room. How do you think objects will appear?

FOCUS CHECK **How could a white golf ball appear blue, red, or yellow?**

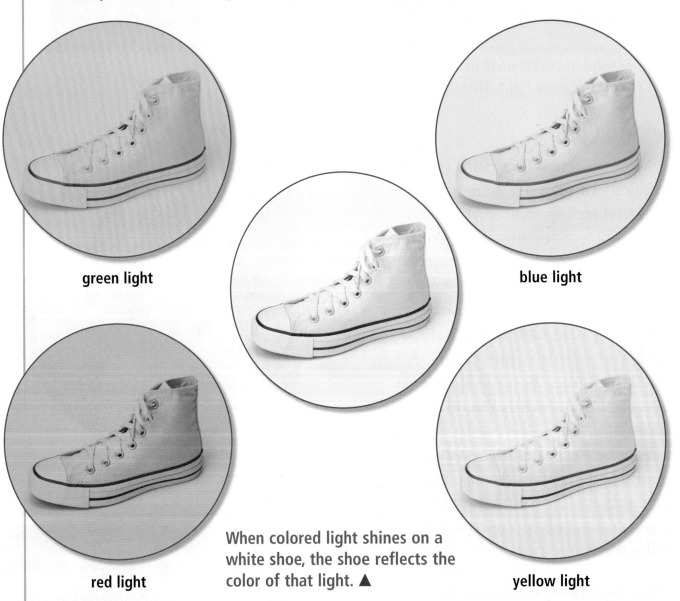

green light

blue light

red light

When colored light shines on a white shoe, the shoe reflects the color of that light. ▲

yellow light

Lesson Wrap-Up

Visual Summary

A rainbow forms when sunlight separates into colors as it passes through raindrops.

When white light strikes an object, you see only the reflected colors. The other colors are absorbed.

Light affects how an object looks. White objects appear to change color under colored light.

Check for Understanding

REFLECTION AND ABSORPTION

Cover the bases of several thermometers with colored construction paper. Choose both light and dark colors. Place the thermometers in direct sunlight, then record the temperatures every 5 minutes for 30 minutes. Use the results to explain how different colors reflect and absorb light. Include a graph to show your data.

✔ 0407.10.2

Review

❶ **MAIN IDEA** Explain how a prism changes sunlight.

❷ **VOCABULARY** Use the terms *absorb* and *reflect* in a sentence that describes light.

❸ **READING SKILL: Sequence** List the steps that produce a rainbow.

❹ **CRITICAL THINKING: Evaluate** Your friend tells you that red apples would look blue in red light. How would you evaluate this statement?

❺ **INQUIRY SKILL: Predict** You shine green light through a prism. Would other colors emerge? Explain.

TCAP TCAP Prep

When sunlight passes through a prism, colored bands exit the prism in

A one order only.

B one of two orders.

C one of seven orders.

D alphabetical order.

SPI 0407.10.2

Go Digital Technology

Visit **www.eduplace.com/tnscp** to find out more about color.

GLE 0407.10.2 Investigate how light travels and is influenced by different types of materials and surfaces. **Math GLE 0406.4.1** Understand and use the properties of lines, segments, angles, polygons, and circles. **ELA GLE 0401.4.3** Present research results in a written report.

Math Refraction of Light

The diagrams show how light rays travel through a convex lens and a concave lens. The light rays are labeled A to J.

1. For each lens, which light rays bend the most? Which bend the least?

2. Describe how each lens bends light. Use the terms parallel and angle in your answer.

3. Converge means to bring together. Diverge means to spread apart. Use these words to describe the lenses.

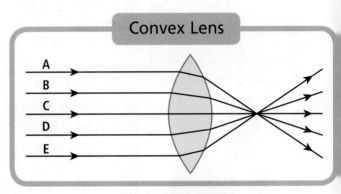

Convex Lens

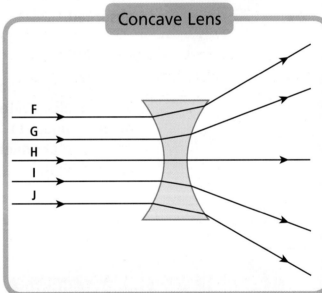

Concave Lens

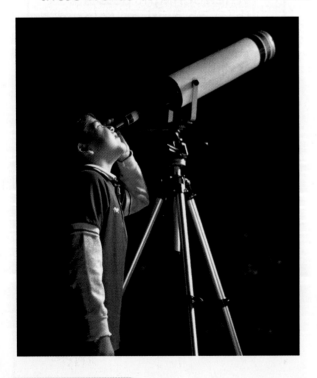

 **Informational**

What kinds of devices use convex lenses or concave lenses? Research this question. Present your findings in an essay.

Eve Higginbotham

Glaucoma is the name for a set of diseases that damage the optic nerve. This nerve carries visual signals from the eye to the brain. Glaucoma usually acts slowly and without warning. It is one of the most common causes of blindness.

Preventing and treating glaucoma is the goal of Dr. Eve Higginbotham. She is one of the world's leading experts on glaucoma. She also is dean of the Morehouse School of Medicine in Atlanta.

In the 1990s, Dr. Higginbotham began a program called Student Sight Savers. In this program, medical students screen for glaucoma in their communities. By 2004, students had screened over 30,000 people. Many were referred to eye doctors for treatment. The students' work saved the sight of many people, most of whom did not know they had an eye disease.

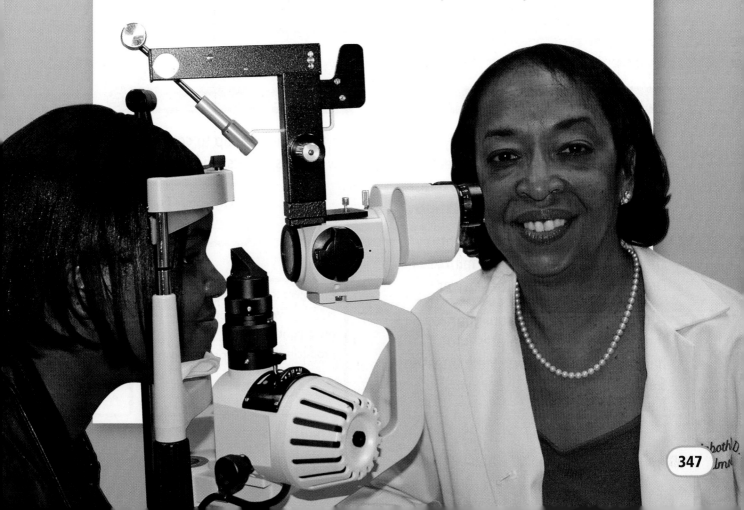

Vocabulary

Complete each sentence with a term from the list.

1. Material that allows light to pass through is _____.

2. When light waves bounce off an object, they _____.

3. A material that blocks light is _____.

4. When an object blocks light, it creates a/an _____.

5. To take in light is to _____ it.

6. An object that lets some light through but scatters it in many directions is _____.

7. To bend light is to _____ it.

8. A form of energy that you can see is called _____.

9. A thin piece of glass that refracts light is a/an _____.

10. Something that separates white light into colors is a/an _____.

absorb
lens
light
opaque
prism
reflect
refract
shadow
translucent
transparent

TCAP Inquiry Skills

11. **Observe** How could you identify whether a material was transparent, translucent, or opaque? Describe a test you could conduct. **GLE 0407.10.2**

12. **Communicate** How does a light ray change when it strikes a flat mirror? Draw a sketch to show the answer. **GLE 0407.10.2**

13. **Analyze Data** When sunlight passes through a prism, it separates into bands of different colors. State a reason for this finding. **GLE 0407.10.2**

Map the Concept

Use the concept map to compare and contrast how mirrors, lenses, and prisms change light.

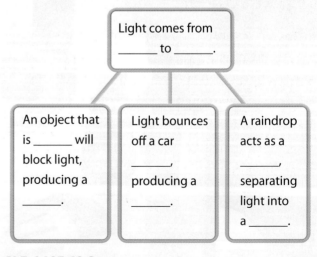

Light comes from _____ to _____.

An object that is _____ will block light, producing a _____.

Light bounces off a car _____, producing a _____.

A raindrop acts as a _____, separating light into a _____.

GLE 0407.10.2

Critical Thinking

14. **Apply** You are going outside at night and want to be visible to drivers. Should you wear a shirt that absorbs light or reflects light? Explain

    GLE 0407.10.2

15. **Synthesize** You want to see into a dark closet. A light above you is aimed in the wrong direction and too high to reach. How could you make this light shine into the closet? GLE 0407.10.2

16. **Evaluate** A flower is in a glass vase filled with water. Your friend says the stem appears bent because the glass is broken. Could there be another reason? Explain.

    GLE 0407.10.2

17. **Analyze** List items that reflect light. For each item, list something similar that does not reflect light. Compare the properties of each group of items.

    GLE 0407.10.2

✓ Check for Understanding

Research Uses for Lenses

Research a tool or instrument that uses lenses, such as eyeglasses, telescopes, microscopes, or cameras. Find out how the tool or instrument works, how it was invented or developed, and the types of lenses inside it. Summarize your findings in a paragraph.

✓ 0407.T/E.1

TCAP TCAP Prep

Choose the letter of the best answer.

18 A ping-pong ball bouncing off a flat table is most like a light ray

   F reflecting off a mirror.

   G refracting through a lens.

   H refracting through a prism.

   J being absorbed by a dark object.

   SPI 0407.10.2

19 In a light microscope, lenses are used to

   A direct sunlight into the microscope.

   B separate white light into colors.

   C enlarge the image of a distant object.

   D enlarge the image of a small object.

   SPI 0407.T/E.1

20 A thin piece of transparent glass with one curved side might be useful as a

   F convex lens only.

   G concave lens only.

   H convex lens or concave lens.

   J prism only.   SPI 0407.10.3

Chapter 10

Motion and Machines

LESSON 1

From the slow crawl of a glacier to the fast-beating wings of a hummingbird—how can motion be measured?

LESSON 2

Skydivers are pulled toward Earth and bicyclists are slowed by wind—what forces are acting?

LESSON 3

From slicing red peppers to turning a doorknob—how do people use simple machines every day?

Fun Facts

The Atlantic ghost crab is the fastest crustacean in the world, and it even runs sideways!

force

★ friction

gravity

inclined plane

lever

motion

position

pulley

screw

★ simple machine

speed

velocity

wedge

wheel and axle

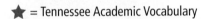 ★ = Tennessee Academic Vocabulary

 Vocabulary Strategies

Have you ever seen any of these words before? Do you know what they mean?

State a description, explanation, or example of the vocabulary in your own words.

Draw a picture, symbol, example, or other image that describes the word.

Glossary p. H16

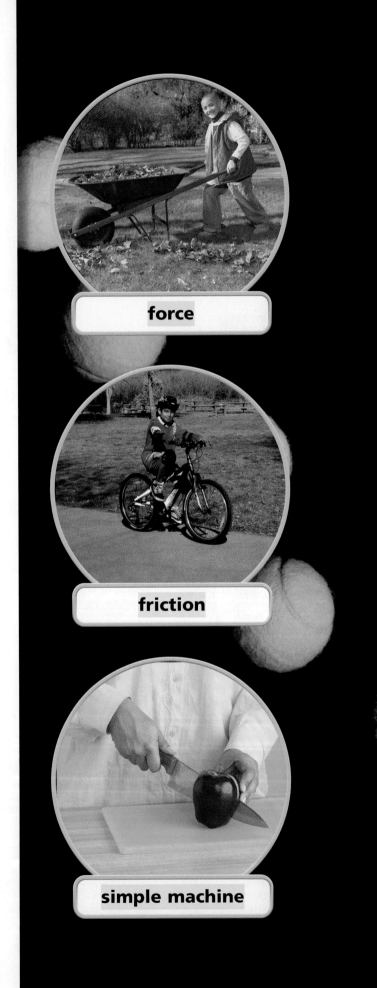

force

friction

simple machine

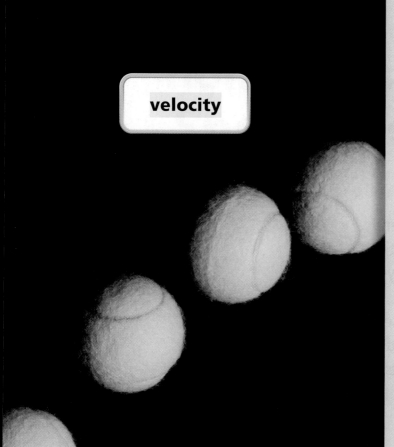

velocity

Start with Your Standards

Inquiry

GLE 0407.Inq.2 Select and use appropriate tools and simple equipment to conduct an investigation.

GLE 0407.Inq.3 Organize data into appropriate tables, graphs, drawings or diagrams.

GLE 0407.Inq.4 Identify and interpret simple patterns of evidence to communicate the findings of multiple investigations.

Physical Science

Standard 11 Motion

GLE 0407.11.1 Recognize that the position of an object can be described relative to other objects or a background.

GLE 0407.11.2 Design a simple investigation to demonstrate how friction affects the movement of an object

GLE 0407.11.3 Investigate the relationship between the speed of an object and the distance traveled during a certain time period.

Interact with this chapter.

 www.eduplace.com/tnscp

Lesson 1

TENNESSEE STANDARDS

GLE 0407.Inq.2 Select and use appropriate tools and simple equipment to conduct an investigation.

GLE 0407.11.3 Investigate the relationship between the speed of an object and the distance traveled during a certain time period.

Guiding Question

How Can Motion Be Described?

Why It Matters...

An amusement park ride sends you spinning in different directions. You are safely buckled in, but you feel as though you are flying.

Rides like this "tea cup" use motion for fun. Whatever you do— travel, do chores, or play sports— you can describe and measure the motion you experience.

PREPARE TO INVESTIGATE

Inquiry Skill

Collaborate When you collaborate, you work with others to share ideas or data.

Materials

- masking tape
- tape measure
- sponge ball
- stopwatch

Science and Math Toolbox

For step 3, review **Measuring Elapsed Time** on page H12.

Directed Inquiry

Keep It Rolling!

Procedure

1. **Measure** Work with a partner. Measure 2 m from a wall. Mark this position with a line of masking tape on the floor.

2. **Record Data** Make a chart like the one shown. Record your measurement in the blank under Short Distance.

3. **Experiment** Slowly roll a ball straight toward the wall. This is Roll 1. Have your partner start a stopwatch just as the ball crosses the tape and stop the stopwatch just as the ball strikes the wall. Record the time in the chart.

4. **Collaborate** Change places with your partner. Have your partner roll the ball faster than you rolled it. Time this roll. Record this time as Roll 2 in the chart.

5. **Use Variables** Take several steps back from the line of masking tape. Mark a second line with masking tape. Measure the distance between the wall and the second line. Record this distance under Long Distance. Repeat steps 3 and 4 for the longer distance.

STEP 1

STEP 2

	Short Distance: ___	Long Distance: ___
Roll 1 Time		
Roll 2 Time		

STEP 3

Think and Write

1. **Collaborate** For each distance, compare the time of your roll to the time of your partner's roll. Whose rolls took less time?

2. **Analyze Data** How does distance affect the time it takes the ball to reach the wall?

0407.11.5

Guided Inquiry

Solve a Problem The fire department wants to shorten the time it takes fire trucks to travel from the firehouse to a fire. Describe two ways that fire trucks could reach fires more quickly.

Describing and Measuring Motion

Position and Motion

GLE 0407.11.1 Recognize that the position of an object can be described relative to other objects or a background.

GLE 0407.11.3 Investigate the realtionship between the speed of an object and the distance traveled during a certain time period.

How would you describe the position (puh ZIHSH uhn) of your desk? **Position** is an object's location, or place. For example, the position of your desk might be 2 meters away from the east wall of the classroom and 3 meters away from the north wall.

What happens to the position of the desk if you were to move it? **Motion** (MOH shuhn) is a change in an object's position as compared to objects around it. If you move your desk, its position changes as compared to the east and north walls of the classroom.

The car is moving. As its position changes, its position moves farther and farther from the sign.

An object can appear to be moving when compared to certain objects but not to others. The objects you use for comparison become your frame of reference.

Look at the photo of the two children in the car. Compared to each other and to the car, the children are not moving. However, when compared to objects outside the car, the children are moving. Someone viewing them from the side of the road would see them move by very quickly.

Even when you are standing still, Earth is moving. You do not sense this motion because you are moving right along with Earth. An astronaut in space has a different frame of reference. From space, Earth seems to move because its position changes when compared to other objects in space.

FOCUS CHECK How can the same person be described as either moving or not moving?

The children in the car may not think they are moving unless they look out the windows and see that they are passing signs and trees.

Measuring Motion

How long would it take you to walk 10 kilometers? How long would it take you to travel the same 10 kilometers in a car? You can travel the same distance in a shorter amount of time in a car because a car can move at a higher speed.

Speed is a measure of the distance an object travels in a certain amount of time. Speed is measured using units of distance and time, such as kilometers traveled in an hour or meters moved in a second.

You can find the speed of an object if you know the distance the object traveled and how long it took to travel that distance. Divide distance by time to find speed. If a car travels 100 km in 2 hours, its speed is 100 km divided by 2 hours, or 50 km in 1 hour (50 km/hr).

The runners shown travel the same distance. However, they finish the race at different times. A runner who finishes the race in a shorter amount of time has a faster speed.

Each runner runs the same distance. The fastest runner has the shortest time.

Every motion has a speed. Some objects move very slowly. For example, most glaciers move downhill just a few meters in a year. Other objects move very quickly. The wings of a hummingbird move up and down so fast that they are just a blur. The speed at which light travels is even faster. It travels almost 300,000 km in a second through empty space. Compare how much farther light can travel in a year to the distance a glacier can travel in that same amount of time.

FOCUS CHECK **What information do you need to measure speed?**

A runner's speed is measured using units of distance and time.

2-km Race Results

Runner 1	8 min 32 s
Runner 2	10 min 50 s
Runner 3	11 min 59 s

Actvity Card
Plot a Graph

The bicyclists are traveling around a curve. They are constantly changing direction as they go around the curve. This is a change in their velocity.

Describing Direction

Each motion has a direction as well as a speed. Direction tells you which way an object is moving. You can describe direction using words such as *east, west, north, south, right, left, up,* or *down.* Speed and direction together determine the velocity (vuh LAHS ih tee) of an object. **Velocity** is a measure of speed in a certain direction.

The bicyclists shown use forces to change direction as they go around the curve. Even if their speed does not change, their change of direction causes their velocity to change. Forces such as friction and gravity can also change the velocity of moving objects.

FOCUS CHECK What forces can change the velocity of a moving object?

Lesson Wrap-Up

Visual Summary

Motion is a change in an object's position compared to objects around it.

Speed is the distance that a moving object travels in a certain time.

Velocity includes both the speed and direction of a moving object.

Check for Understanding

SINKING SPEED

Fill a tall bottle or cylinder with water. Your task is to find an object that sinks very slowly, then calculate the speed that it sinks. Try a button, a plastic thimble, or a small cork stuck with pins. Compare data with classmates to idenitfy the slowest sinker.

 0407.11.2

Review

❶ **MAIN IDEA** What two properties describe the motion of an object?

❷ **VOCABULARY** Write a definition for the term *position*.

❸ **READING SKILL: Main Idea and Details** What does velocity measure? Compare velocity and speed.

❹ **CRITICAL THINKING: Apply** Describe a situation in which you moved when using one frame of reference but did not appear to move when using another frame of reference.

❺ **INQUIRY SKILL: Collaborate** With a partner, write instructions to explain how to get from the entrance of your school to your classroom. Use words to describe position, such as "next to the library," and words to describe direction, such as "turn left."

TCAP Prep

A car traveled 120 km in 2 hours. Using this data, you can calculate its

A speed.
B velocity.
C position.
D mass and volume.

SPI 0407.11.3

Technology

Visit **www.eduplace.com/tnscp** to learn more about motion.

Lesson 2

TENNESSEE STANDARDS

GLE 0407.Inq.4 Identify and interpret simple patterns of evidence to communicate the findings of multiple investigations.

GLE 0407.11.2 Design a simple investigation to demonstrate how friction affects the movement of an object.

Guiding Question?

What Are Gravity and Friction?

Why It Matters...

A luge is a type of sled that runs on an icy track. The luge gains speed because of gravity. It slows down because of friction.

These two natural forces— gravity and friction—affect not only luge rides, but every other motion on Earth. You may not realize it, but you apply these forces every day.

PREPARE TO INVESTIGATE

Inquiry Skill

Compare When you compare objects or events, you observe how they are alike and how they are different.

Materials

- several thick books
- wooden board
- toy car
- wooden block
- metric tape measure

Science and Math Toolbox

For step 3, review **Using a Tape Measure or Ruler** on page H6.

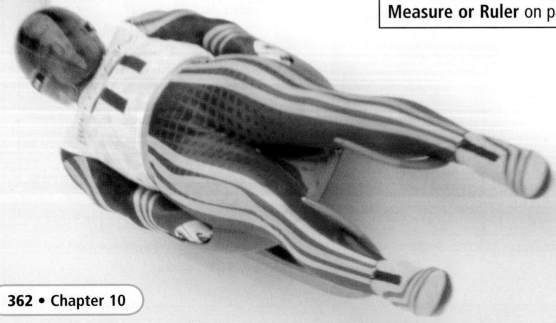

Directed Inquiry

Away You Go!

Procedure

STEP 1

1. **Experiment** Stack several books on top of one another. Place one end of a wooden board at the edge of the stack of books to form a ramp.

2. **Experiment** Hold a toy car at the top of the ramp. Do not push the car down the ramp. Allow it to roll by itself.

STEP 2

3. **Use Models** Measure the distance from the top of the ramp to the front end of the car at the location where the car stopped rolling. Record this distance in your *Science Notebook*.

4. **Collaborate** Repeat steps 2 and 3 using a wooden block instead of the toy car. Put the block onto the ramp, but do not push it down the ramp.

STEP 4

Think and Write

1. **Infer** You put the toy car and wooden block onto the ramp. What caused the car and block to move down the ramp?

2. **Compare** Which traveled farther—the toy car or the wooden block?

3. **Hypothesize** State why you think the toy car and wooden block traveled different distances.

Guided Inquiry

Research Research the work of Isaac Newton, Galileo, or another scientist who studied the motion of objects. Report on the ideas or theories that the scientist developed.

0407.11.4

Forces and Motion

VOCABULARY

force
★ friction
gravity

GRAPHIC ORGANIZER

Cause and Effect
Use a chart to write the cause and effect of a force.

GLE 0407.11.1 Recognize that the position of an object can be described relative to other objects or a background.

Pushes and Pulls

You push a heavy box across a floor. You pull a wagon behind you. You use pushes and pulls to cause these and other objects to change their motion.

A **force** is a push or a pull. A push is a force that moves an object away. A pull is a force that moves an object nearer. Look at the people shown on these pages. They are using forces to push a wheelbarrow and pull a rake.

Pull As the girl pulls on the rake, the leaves move toward her.

pull

Push As the boy pushes the wheelbarrow, the wheelbarrow moves away from him.

push

A force can change the motion of an object. A force can start an object moving, change the direction or speed of the object, or stop the object from moving.

Think again about moving a heavy box across the floor. The box has no motion until you push it. It moves slowly in one direction as you push it in that direction.

To change the speed of the box, you must apply a different force. You must push the box harder to move it faster. A box with a greater mass also requires you to push it harder in order to move it.

To change the direction of the box, you must again apply a different force. You must push the box from another angle or different side. To stop the box, you must change the force yet again. You must stop pushing the box in order to stop it from moving.

What force stops the box from continuing to slide across the floor after you stop pushing it? The force is friction (FRIHK shuhn). You will learn about this force next.

FOCUS CHECK What causes a change in motion?

▲ There is friction between the edge of the metal brake and the rubber wheel on the wheelchair. Friction stops the wheel from turning when the brake is applied.

brake

friction

Friction

The force that stops a box from sliding when you stop pushing it is friction. **Friction** is a force that slows or stops motion between two surfaces that are touching.

Friction exists between any two surfaces that touch. However, there is more friction between rough surfaces than between smooth surfaces. So there is more friction between a box and a rough concrete floor than there is between a box and a smooth tile floor.

Friction can be useful. Without friction, we would slip and slide on every surface. For example, without friction between your pencil and your fingers, you would not be able to hold the pencil and write. It would slip from your grasp. Without friction between the brake and wheel of a wheelchair, the wheelchair would not stay in place.

There is even something like friction between objects and the air. This is called air resistance. You may feel air resistance on a bike.

Friction slows and stops movement. As you have seen, this can be useful. However, sometimes less friction is better. For example, the small amount of friction between a snowboard and the snow lets the snowboard go faster.

One way to create less friction is to put slippery substances on surfaces that touch. For example, to reduce friction between a snowboard and the snow, you can put wax on the bottom of the snowboard. This makes the snowboard more slippery.

Wheels also reduce friction. They roll, rather than slide, over a surface. Some machines use small rolling metal balls between their moving parts to reduce friction. These balls are called ball bearings.

Some moving objects are designed to have less air resistance in order to move faster. Race cars and airplanes have sleek shapes that help the air pass over them. Runners wear smooth, tight-fitting clothing for the same reason.

⊙ FOCUS CHECK What is one way to reduce friction?

You can slide down a hill on a snowboard because there is very little friction between the snow and the snowboard.

Express Lab

Activity Card
Measure Forces

Gravity pulls these skydivers toward Earth.

Gravity

A group of skydivers leaps out of an airplane and falls toward Earth. You know that a force must be acting on the skydivers because they are moving. That force is gravity (GRAV ih tee).

Gravity is a force that pulls objects toward each other. For example, Earth's gravity pulls the skydivers toward the ground. Earth's gravity also keeps your book on your desk. It makes rain fall from the clouds and causes rivers to flow downhill.

While friction acts on objects that are touching, gravity can act on objects at a distance. For example,

Earth's gravity acts on the skydivers high above the ground. Earth's gravity even acts on objects in space. It holds space shuttles and the Moon in orbit around Earth.

Objects with greater mass have greater gravity. Earth has a larger mass than the Moon, so its gravity is stronger than the Moon's gravity. When astronauts landed on the Moon, they could jump higher, lift heavier objects, and hit golf balls farther than they could on Earth. That is because the Moon's gravity is weaker than Earth's gravity.

FOCUS CHECK **What keeps the Moon in orbit around the Earth?**

Lesson Wrap-Up

Visual Summary

A force is a push or a pull. Forces change the motion of an object.

Friction is a force that slows or stops motion between two surfaces that are touching.

Gravity is a force that pulls objects toward each other. Gravity can act on objects at a distance.

✓ Check for Understanding

PARACHUTE DROP

You can observe the forces that affect falling objects by making a model parachute.

- Cut open and flatten a plastic bag.
- Make a parachute by tying 4 pieces of string to each corner of the bag. Then tie their other ends to a washer or other weight. Drop the parachute and time its fall.
- Change the size of the bag or the attached weights.
- Use your data to identify the forces that affect how a parachute falls.

✓ 0407.11.4

Review

1 MAIN IDEA Give two examples of forces.

2 VOCABULARY What is friction?

3 READING SKILL: Cause and Effect Suppose you are pushing a wheelbarrow. What would be the effect if you applied a greater pushing force to the wheelbarrow?

4 CRITICAL THINKING: Analyze When you swing, you push your feet against the ground to start moving. To stop, you drag your feet on the ground. Describe each force that changes your motion on the swing.

5 INQUIRY SKILL: Compare What is the difference between a push and a pull?

TCAP TCAP Prep

Where can the force of Earth's gravity be demonstrated?

A only on Earth's surface
B only in Earth's atmosphere
C only in outer space
D anywhere on or near Earth

SPI 0407.11.2

Technology

Visit **www.eduplace.com/tnscp** to find out more about forces and motion.

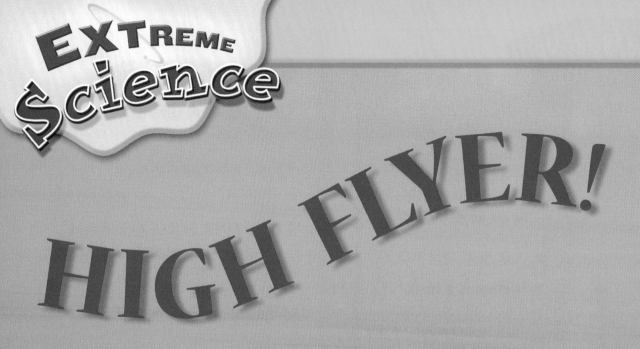

EXTREME Science

HIGH FLYER!

No pilot, no fuel tanks, no engine pollution. Meet Helios, one of the highest-flying airplanes ever made. Steered by remote control and powered by the Sun, Helios (named after the Greek sun god) is one extreme machine!

Helios can reach altitudes three times higher than most jet planes. How does Helios overcome the force of gravity? The secret is the extreme design.

Helios is basically one giant wing. The larger the wing, the more lift, or upward push. Because of Helios' huge lift and its light weight, Helios can fly high even when very little air supports it against gravity's pull.

GLE 0407.T/E.4 Recognize the connection between scientific advances, new knowledge, and the availability of new tools and technologies.

EXTEND

A Boeing 747 jet is one of the largest jet airplanes in the world. How does it compare to Helios?

	Helios	Boeing 747
Wingspan	247 ft	211 ft
Weight	1,322 lbs	875,000 lbs
Airspeed	19-25 mph	565 mph
Cruising Altitude	100,000 ft	35,000 ft
Jet Fuel	none (solar powered)	57,285 gallons

Solar cells across the top of the wing gather energy from the Sun. They change sunlight into electricity, which powers the propellers.

Lesson 3

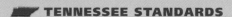 **TENNESSEE STANDARDS**

GLE 0407.Inq.3 Organize data into appropriate tables, graphs, drawings, or diagrams.
GLE 0407.11.1 Recognize that the position of an object can be described relative to other objects or a background.

Guiding Question

How Do Simple Machines Work?

Why It Matters...

You might not think of a paddle as a machine, but it is. Like all machines, a paddle changes a force to help people do work. It is far easier to move a kayak with a paddle than with your hands.

A paddle is an example of a simple machine. Combinations of two or more simple machines make other tools and machines you use.

PREPARE TO INVESTIGATE

Inquiry Skill

Use Numbers You use numbers when you count, measure, estimate, and calculate.

Materials

- masking tape
- metric ruler
- triangular wooden block
- small self-stick notes

Science and Math Toolbox

For step 1, review **Making a Chart to Organize Data** on page H10.

Directed Inquiry

Balancing Act

Procedure

① In your *Science Notebook*, make a chart like the one shown.

② **Use Numbers** Count out two stacks of 25 self-stick notes. Place one stack on the left end of a metric ruler. Place the other stack on the right end of the ruler. Be sure the numbers on the ruler are face up.

③ **Experiment** Make a loop of masking tape and press it onto the tip of a triangular wooden block. Balance the ruler on the tip of the block at the 15-cm mark. Record the number of self-stick notes on each end of the ruler.

④ **Experiment** Reposition the ruler at the 18-cm mark. Place additional self-stick notes on the right end of the ruler until the ruler balances again. Record the number of self-stick notes on each end.

⑤ **Experiment** Repeat step 4, but this time reposition the ruler at the 21-cm mark.

Think and Write

1. **Analyze Data** As you moved the ruler, how did it affect the number of self-stick notes you needed to balance the ruler?

2. **Predict** Predict how you could balance the ruler if you moved it so that the 10-cm mark was over the tip of the block.

STEP 1		
Ruler Balance Point	Number of Notes on Left	Number of Notes on Right
15 cm		
18 cm		
21 cm		

STEP 3

STEP 4

Guided Inquiry

Solve a Problem
A construction crane has an arm balanced on a tower. Draw a diagram to show where you would attach the weight and place the arm of the crane to most easily lift a heavy object.

Simple Machines

Six Simple Machines

VOCABULARY

inclined plane
lever
pulley
screw
★ simple machine
wedge
wheel and axle

GRAPHIC ORANIZER

Problem-Solution
Use a chart to write a problem and the simple machine you can use to solve the problem.

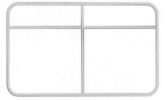

GLE 0407.T/E.1 Describe how tools, technology, and inventions help to answer questions and solve problems.

GLE 0407.T/E.3 Identify appropriate materials, tools, and machines that can extend or enhance the ability to solve a specified problem.

Have you ever opened a can using a pull tab? If so, you were using a machine. A machine is any tool that makes work easier.

A **simple machine** (SIHM puhl muh SHEEN) is a simple device that changes a force. Simple machines, like other machines, let you use less force to move an object. They do this by increasing the distance over which the force is applied. Some simple machines change the direction of the force.

Inclined Plane An **inclined plane** (ihnn KLYND playn) is a simple machine made up of a slanted surface. Ramps are examples of inclined planes.

An inclined plane increases the distance over which a force is applied. This makes it easier to raise an object. For example, it is easier to push a heavy box up a long ramp than to lift it straight up to the top of the ramp.

This ramp is an inclined plane. Using the ramp makes it easier to raise the box to the top of the ramp. ▶

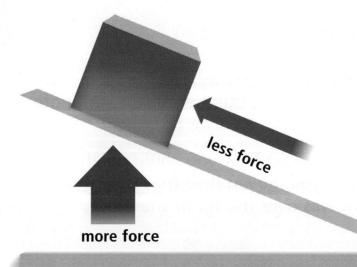

less force

more force

downward force

outward force

Wedge A simple machine made up of two inclined planes is called a **wedge** (wehj). It is V-shaped, like the knife shown here. A wedge changes a downward force to an outward force. This helps to cut or split apart objects.

Screw A simple machine made up of an inclined plane wrapped around a column is called a **screw** (skroo). It changes a weak circular force to a strong downward force.

Turning a screw with a screwdriver forces the screw to push into the wood. It is easy to turn the screw because the force is spread out over many turns.

⊙**FOCUS CHECK** What simple machine could be used to split a log into smaller pieces?

The threads of the screw form an inclined plane. The turning force of the screw easily pushes it into the wood. ▼

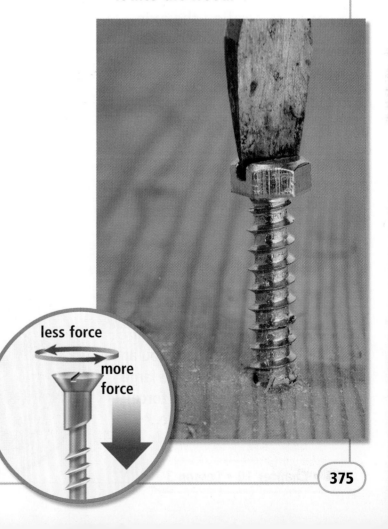

less force

more force

375

Lever A simple machine made up of a stiff bar that moves freely around a fixed point is called a **lever** (LEHV ur). The fixed point is the fulcrum (FUL kruhm). The fulcrum is usually placed so that one end of the bar is longer than the other.

Examples of levers include seesaws and can openers. Levers are often used to help lift objects. A small force is applied to the long end of a lever. This results in a large force at the short end.

Wheel and Axle A simple machine made up of two cylinders that turn on the same axis is called a **wheel and axle** (hweel and AK suhl). The outer cylinder is called the wheel. It is larger than the inner cylinder, which is called the axle.

Examples of wheels and axles include car steering wheels and doorknobs. A small force is applied to turn the large wheel. This results in a large force that turns the small axle. By using a wheel and axle, less force is needed to steer a car or to open a door.

more force

less force

▲ This screwdriver is being used as a lever. A lever makes it easier to lift the lid.

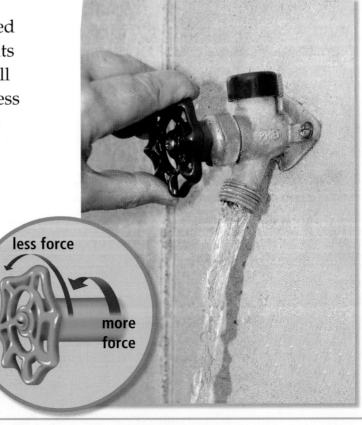

less force

more force

A faucet is a wheel and axle. To get water, you apply a small force to the large wheel and a large force turns the small axle. ▶

Pulley A simple machine made up of a rope fitted around the rim of a fixed wheel is called a **pulley** (PUL ee). Some pulleys increase the force that is applied to them. Others change the direction of the force. Pulleys are used to raise and lower elevator cars, to move clotheslines back and forth, and to lift a flag up a flagpole.

Reversing the direction of a force can be useful. For example, a flagpole pulley changes a downward force to an upward force. When you pull down on one end of the pulley rope, it turns the wheel at the top of the flagpole. The turning wheel causes the rope to change direction and pull up the flag.

Like any simple machine, a pulley helps you do work. However, a pulley needs parts that work together. It may not be useful if its parts do not match.

For example, if the rope of a pulley is wider than the rim of the pulley wheel, the rope might slip off the wheel when you pull on it. The pulley would not be able to do its job.

FOCUS CHECK What simple machine allows you to raise a flag without climbing the flagpole?

> When you pull down on one end of the rope of a pulley, the other end of the rope pulls the flag up the pole. ▶

upward force

downward force

Express Lab

Activity Card
Lift With a Ramp

377

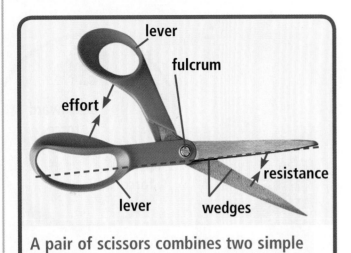

A pair of scissors combines two simple machines: wedges and levers.

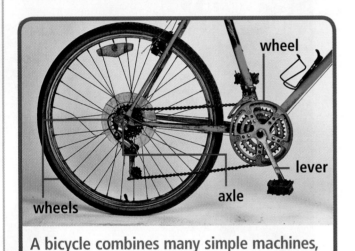

A bicycle combines many simple machines, including levers and wheels and axles.

A piano uses several different types of levers to make music.

Compound Machines

Many of the devices that you use every day are made of two or more simple machines. Such devices are called compound machines.

A pair of scissors is one example of a compound machine. The scissors are made of two levers with the fulcrum in the middle. The cutting blades of the scissors are wedges.

Another example is a bicycle. It uses pedals, which are levers, to apply force to the sprocket. The sprocket is a wheel and axle that uses gears to move the chain.

As the chain moves, it transfers force to a smaller sprocket attached to the axle of the rear wheel. So, the force applied to the pedal is converted through a combination of simple machines to make the back wheel turn.

A piano uses a variety of different types of levers to make the hammers strike the strings. The keys are first-class levers. Pushing down on a key causes the other end of the key to lift, pushing on a wooden post. The post pushes up into the end of the hammer, which is another first-class lever. The hammer strikes the string.

FOCUS CHECK What are compound machines?

Lesson Wrap-Up

Visual Summary

 A simple machine makes work easier by changing a force.

 An inclined plane is a slanted surface. A wedge and a screw are made up of inclined planes.

 A lever, a wheel and axle, and a pulley are other kinds of simple machines.

✔ Check for Understanding

LIFTING A PENNY
Design and build a compound machine to lift a penny from the floor to the top of your desk. You may use your hands to run the machine, but not to touch the penny.

✔ 0407.T/E.2

Review

❶ MAIN IDEA How do simple machines help people do work?

❷ VOCABULARY Write a sentence using the term *pulley*.

❸ READING SKILL: Problem-Solution Which type of simple machine would you use to pry open a can?

❹ CRITICAL THINKING: Synthesize Which three simple machines can be used to lift objects?

❺ INQUIRY SKILL: Use Numbers When you push down the short end of a certain lever, the long end moves twice as far. How far should you push down the long end to make the short end move 17 cm?

TCAP Prep

What simple machine is part of both a screw and a wedge?

A inclined plane
B pulley
C wheel and axle
D lever

SPI 0407.T/E.1

 Technology

Visit **www.eduplace.com/tnscp** to find out more about simple machines.

It's Great to Skate!

Roller skates have been around for nearly 250 years. For the first 100 years skates were made with wheels arranged in a single line. They were hard to control. Turning and stopping were almost impossible.

In 1760, Joseph Merlin, a London inventor, rolled into a party playing the violin and wearing boots with in-line wheels. Unable to control his speed or direction, he immediately crashed into a huge mirror.

In 1863, James Plimpton patented skates with two pairs of wheels. One pair was under the ball of the foot, and one pair was under the heel. These 4-wheel skates were much easier to control than the early in-line skates. The 4-wheel skate was the favorite model for the next 100 years.

In 1979, Scott and Brennan Olsen designed the first modern in-line skates. Plastic wheels and a toe brake made the modern skates easier to control than the old models. Today's in-line skates are faster, safer, and easier to control than ever before.

For safety, skaters should wear elbow and knee pads and a helmet.

➤ **GLE 0407.T/E.2** Recognize that new tools, technology and inventions are always being developed.

EXTEND

Today's high-tech in-line skates give skaters speed and flexibility. High-performance skates, like this one, are made from strong yet lightweight materials.

Ankle Cuff: The short ankle cuff allows the skater's foot to turn easily and quickly.

Padding: Inside the skate, pads provide support. A special liner keeps the foot cool and dry.

Laces, Strap, Buckles: Laces adjust quickly and easily. A Velcro strap holds the heel in place. An adjustable buckle keeps the foot stable.

Shell: The shell gives the foot support. Several openings, or vents, keep the skater's foot from overheating.

Wheels: The wheels shown here are made of lightweight material.

Note Book — Sharing Ideas

1. **READING CHECK** What did the first in-line skates look like?

2. **WRITE ABOUT IT** Write an ad convincing people to buy the ultra-modern fast skates that you make.

3. **TALK ABOUT IT** Discuss the design and special features you want in an ideal skate.

GLE 0407.11.1 Recognize that the position of an object can be described relative to other objects or a background. **Math GLE 0406.2.4** Understand and use the connections between fractions and decimals. **ELA GLE 0401.3.1** Write for a variety of purposes and to a variety of audiences.

Math How Force Affects Speed

A man and a boy take turns pushing a young girl sitting in a wagon. Then the boy pushes the man in the wagon. Each time, they measure the force of the push and the speed that the wagon moves after they stop pushing. The table shows the results.

	Force	Speed
	25 N	0.33 m/s
	50 N	0.67 m/s
	25 N	0.20 m/s

1. The range of a data set is the difference between the highest and lowest values. What is the range of the three speeds shown here?

2. Express each speed as a fraction. Use halves, thirds, fourths, or fifths.

3. When a wagon is pushed, what are two variables that affect the speed that it moves? Use data from the table to support your answer.

 **Narrative**

Write a short story in which something is in motion, then that motion changes. The moving object could be a baton, an ice skater, a bicycle, or an object of your choice. The story should identify the force that changes the motion.

Auto Mechanic

Hundreds of moving parts make an automobile run. Any of these parts could break, wear out, or stop working properly. Finding and fixing the faulty part is the job of an auto mechanic. In this career, you practice science inquiry every day!

What It Takes

- Training at a vocational or technical school
- On-the-job experience

Aeronautical Engineer

The first airplane flew for just a few seconds, and only a few feet off the ground. Today, airplanes fly higher, longer, and faster than ever before. Designing them is the job of aeronautical engineers.

These engineers may design helicopters, airliners, or military aircraft. Some of them design satellites and other devices for exploring space.

What It Takes

- For most jobs, a graduate degree in engineering
- Strong interest in math and physical science

Vocabulary

Complete each sentence with a term from the list.

1. An object's _____ is its location, or place.

2. The distance traveled in a unit of time is called _____.

3. The force of _____ pulls things toward Earth.

4. A simple machine made up of two inclined planes is a/an _____.

5. An object's change in position when compared to things around it is called _____.

6. The force that slows the motion between two surfaces that touch each other is called _____.

7. A push or a pull is a/an _____.

8. A simple machine made up of a slanted surface is a/an _____.

9. An object's _____ includes its speed and direction.

10. An inclined plane wrapped around a column is a/an _____.

force
★ friction
gravity
inclined plane
lever
motion
position
pulley
screw
★ simple machine
speed
velocity
wedge
wheel and axle

TCAP Inquiry Skills

11. **Compare** How are an inclined plane and a wedge alike? How are they different? **GLE 0407.Inq.4**

12. **Use Numbers** One bus travels 200 km in 4 hours. A second bus travels 300 km in 3 hours. What is the speed of each bus? **GLE 0407.11.3**

13. **Observe** Look about you to find three objects in motion. Describe the velocity of each object. **GLE 0407.Inq.4**

Map the Concept

Complete the statements below with words from the list.

distance   speed
direction   velocity

Motion Equations

_____ ÷ time = _____

speed + _____ = _____

GLE 0407.11.3

Critical Thinking

14. Evaluate Explain why a space shuttle orbiting Earth is affected by gravity but not by friction. **GLE 0407.11.2**

15. Analyze A hand-operated can opener has a cutting blade that pierces the lid. The can opener also has a handle that you turn to spin a smaller wheel, which pushes the cutting blade around the lid. Which two simple machines make up the can opener? **GLE 0407.Inq.3**

16. Synthesize In most motions, some of the mechanical energy goes through an energy transformation due to friction. Into what form of energy does friction transform the mechanical energy? (Hint: Quickly rub your hands together to observe friction.) **GLE 0407.11.2**

Check for Understanding

Identify Position

Look at things in your classroom like the bookshelves, the desks, and the chalkboard. Identify the position of these objects in relation to other objects. For example, where is your desk in relation to the teachers desk? Use the concepts from the chapter to describe their positions. **GLE 0407.11.1**

TCAP Prep

Write the letter of the best answer choice.

17 Raising or lowering the cab of an elevator is a job for a(n)

A wedge.
B pulley.
C lever.
D inclined plane. **SPI 0407.T/E.1**

18 An object may change its velocity because of

F gravity only.
G friction only.
H a machine only.
J any applied force. **SPI 0407.11.2**

19 In which of these places will gravity pull the least on a 10-kg box?

A on Earth's surface
B in an airplane above Earth's surface
C at the bottom of an Earth ocean
D on the surface of the Moon **SPI 0407.11.2**

20 Ted is pushing a toy box across a carpeted floor. What would make the box travel more slowly?

F adding toys
G removing toys
H replacing the carpet with smooth floor tiles
J adding wheels to the bottom of the box **SPI 0407.11.2**

9 Matter

Performance Indicator: SPI 0407.9.2 Determine the mass, volume, and temperature of a substance or object using proper units of measurement.

1 A student measures the mass of a bottle of water with its cap attached. She drinks all the water, then measures the mass of the empty bottle and the cap. The chart shows her results. What is the mass of the water she drank?

A 250 g

B 255 g

C 280 g

D 310 g

Part	Mass
Bottle, cap, and water	280 g
Empty bottle	25 g
Cap	5 g

12 Forces in Nature

Performance Indicator: SPI 0407.12.3 Determine the path of an electrical current in a simple circuit.

2 What is an electric current made up of?

F simple circuits

G watts

H magnets

J moving electric charges

3 Which type of circuit is shown below?

A simple circuit

B parallel circuit

C series circuit with a switch

D simple circuit with a switch

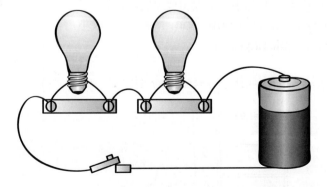

10 Energy

Performance Indicator: **SPI 0407.10.2 Determine which surfaces reflect, refract, or absorb light.**

4 The diagram shows white light passing through a prism, an example of

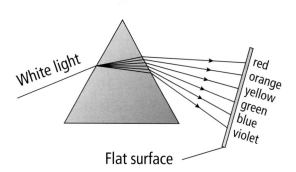

White light

red
orange
yellow
green
blue
violet

Flat surface

F refraction.
G absorption.
H reflection.
J destruction.

5 Green grass appears green because it

A reflects only green light.
B refracts green light.
C radiates green light.
D absorbs green light.

11 Motion

Performance Indicator: **SPI 0407.11.2 Identify factors that influence the motion of an object.**

6 What are two factors used to measure speed?

F direction and position
G distance and time
H distance and direction
J time and position

7 In what situation will the object accelerate more?

A small unbalanced force on a large mass
B large unbalanced force on a small mass
C small unbalanced force on a small mass
D large balanced forces on a small mass

Discover More

The cars of a roller coaster are pulled slowly up the first, and highest, hill. An electric motor does the work. An invisible change occurs as the cars climb the hill. The cars store energy. That energy shows up in another form as the cars go over the top of the hill.

When the cars of a roller coaster are pulled up a hill, they gain energy called **potential energy.**

When the cars reach the top of the hill, the force of gravity pulls them down the hill.

As the cars speed down the hill, the potential energy of the cars changes to **kinetic energy,** the energy of motion.

| PE | Potential Energy |
| KE | Kinetic Energy |

This pattern of changing energy continues throughout the ride. The higher the first hill is, the more potential energy the cars have at the top. This energy is used to move the cars along the entire ride. That is why the cars do not need any electrical energy after the first hill.

Go Digital Go to **www.eduplace.com/tnscp** to see how potential and kinetic energy affect your coaster.

Science and Math Toolbox

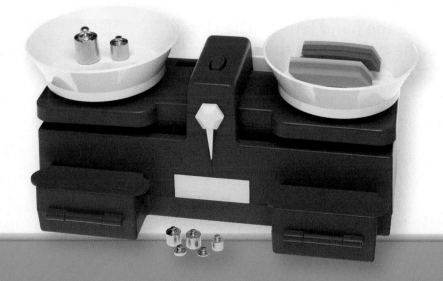

Using a Hand Lens

A hand lens is a tool that magnifies objects, or makes objects appear larger. This makes it possible for you to see details of an object that would be hard to see without the hand lens.

Look at a Coin or a Stamp

1. Place an object such as a coin or a stamp on a table or other flat surface.

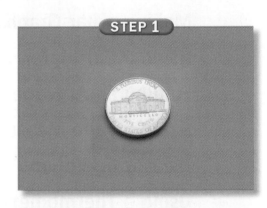
STEP 1

2. Hold the hand lens just above the object. As you look through the lens, slowly move the lens away from the object. Notice that the object appears to get larger and a little blurry.

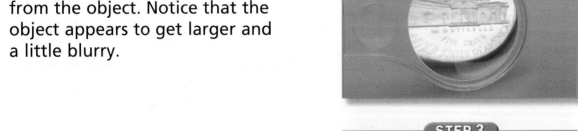
STEP 2

3. Move the hand lens a little closer to the object until the object is once again in sharp focus.

STEP 3

Making a Bar Graph

A bar graph helps you organize and compare data.

Make a Bar Graph of Animal Heights

Animals come in all different shapes and sizes. You can use the information in this table to make a bar graph of animal heights.

1. Draw the side and the bottom of the graph. Label the side of the graph as shown. The numbers will show the height of the animals in centimeters.

2. Label the bottom of the graph. Write the names of the animals at the bottom so that there is room to draw the bars.

3. Choose a title for your graph. Your title should describe the subject of the graph.

4. Draw bars to show the height of each animal. Some heights are between two numbers.

Heights of Animals

Animal	Height (cm)
Bear	240
Elephant	315
Cow	150
Giraffe	570
Camel	210
Horse	165

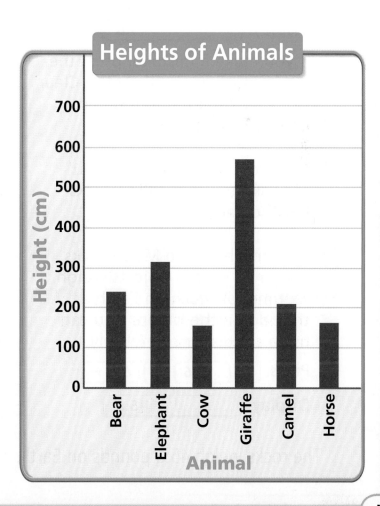

Heights of Animals

Using a Calculator

After you've made measurements, a calculator can help you analyze your data.

Add and Multiply Decimals

Suppose you're an astronaut. You may take 8 pounds of Moon rocks back to Earth. Can you take all the rocks in the table? Use a calculator to find out.

Weight of Moon Rocks	
Moon Rock	**Weight of Rock on Moon (lb)**
Rock 1	1.7
Rock 2	1.8
Rock 3	2.6
Rock 4	1.5

1. To add, press:

   [1] [.] [7] [+] [1] [.] [8] [+]
   [2] [.] [6] [+] [1] [.] [5] [=]

   Display: [7.6]

2. If you make a mistake, press the left arrow key and then the Clear key. Enter the number again. Then continue adding.

3. Your total is 7.6 pounds. You can take the four Moon rocks back to Earth.

4. How much do the Moon rocks weigh on Earth? Objects weigh six times as much on Earth as they do on the Moon. You can use a calculator to multiply.

   Press: [7] [.] [6] [×] [6] [=]

   Display: [45.6]

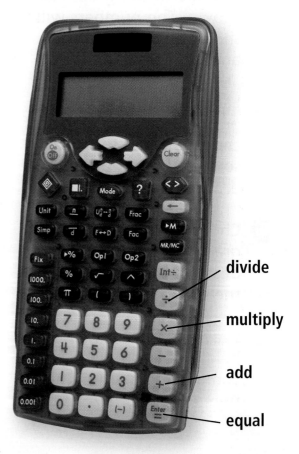

divide

multiply

add

equal

The rocks weigh 45.6 pounds on Earth.

Finding an Average

An average is a way to describe a group of numbers. For example, after you have made a series of measurements, you can find the average. This can help you analyze your data.

Add and Divide to Find the Average

The table shows the amount of rain that fell each month for the first six months of the year. What was the average rainfall per month?

1 Add the numbers in the list.

$$\left.\begin{array}{r} 102 \\ 75 \\ 46 \\ 126 \\ 51 \\ +\ 32 \\ \hline 432 \end{array}\right\} \text{6 addends}$$

2 Divide the sum (432) by the number of addends (6).

$$\begin{array}{r} 72 \\ 6\overline{)432} \\ -\ 42 \\ \hline 12 \\ -\ 12 \\ \hline 0 \end{array}$$

Rainfall

Month	Rain (mm)
January	102
February	75
March	46
April	126
May	51
June	32

The average rainfall per month for the first six months was 72 mm of rain.

Using a Tape Measure or Ruler

Tape measures and rulers are tools for measuring the length of objects and distances. Scientists most often use units such as meters, centimeters, and millimeters when making length measurements.

Use a Tape Measure

1. Measure the distance around a jar. Wrap the tape around the jar.

2. Find the line where the tape begins to wrap over itself.

3. Record the distance around the jar to the nearest centimeter.

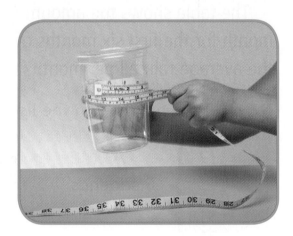

Use a Metric Ruler

1. Measure the length of your shoe. Place the ruler or the meterstick on the floor. Line up the end of the ruler with the heel of your shoe.

2. Notice where the other end of your shoe lines up with the ruler.

3. Look at the scale on the ruler. Record the length of your shoe to the nearest centimeter and to the nearest millimeter.

Measuring Volume

A beaker, a measuring cup, and a graduated cylinder are used to measure volume. Volume is the amount of space something takes up. Most of the containers that scientists use to measure volume have a scale marked in milliliters (mL).

Beaker
50 mL

Measuring cup
50 mL

Graduated cylinder
50 mL

Measure the Volume of a Liquid

1. Measure the volume of juice. Pour some juice into a measuring container.

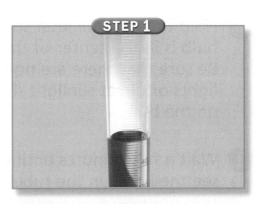

STEP 1

2. Move your head so that your eyes are level with the top of the juice. Read the scale line that is closest to the surface of the juice. If the surface of the juice is curved up on the sides, look at the lowest point of the curve.

STEP 2

3. Read the measurement on the scale. You can estimate the value between two lines on the scale.

Using a Thermometer

A thermometer is used to measure temperature. When the liquid in the tube of a thermometer gets warmer, it expands and moves farther up the tube. Different scales can be used to measure temperature, but scientists usually use the Celsius scale.

Measure the Temperature of a Liquid

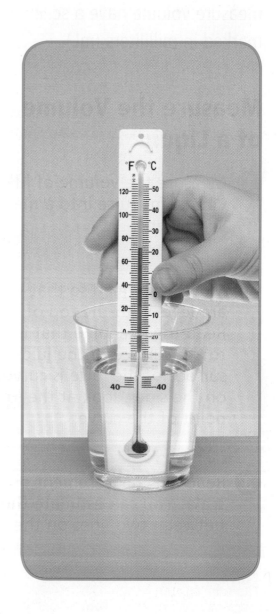

1. Half fill a cup with warm tap water.

2. Hold the thermometer so that the bulb is in the center of the liquid. Be sure that there are no bright lights or direct sunlight shining on the bulb.

3. Wait a few minutes until you see the liquid in the tube of the thermometer stop moving. Read the scale line that is closest to the top of the liquid in the tube. The thermometer shown reads 22°C (72°F).

Using a Balance

A balance is used to measure mass. Mass is the amount of matter in an object. To find the mass of an object, place it in the left pan of the balance. Place standard masses in the right pan.

Measure the Mass of a Ball

1 Check that the empty pans are balanced, or level with each other. When balanced, the pointer on the base should be at the middle mark. If it needs to be adjusted, move the slider on the back of the balance a little to the left or right.

2 Place a ball on the left pan. Then add standard masses, one at a time, to the right pan. When the pointer is at the middle mark again, each pan holds the same amount of matter and has the same mass.

3 Add the numbers marked on the masses in the pan. The total is the mass of the ball in grams.

Making a Chart to Organize Data

A chart can help you keep track of information. When you organize information, or data, it is easier to read, compare, or classify it.

Classifying Animals

Suppose you want to organize this data about animal characteristics. You could base the chart on the two characteristics listed—the number of wings and the number of legs.

1 Give the chart a title that describes the data in it.

2 Name categories, or groups, that describe the data you have collected.

3 Make sure the information is recorded correctly in each column.

Next, you could make another chart to show animal classification based on number of legs only.

My Data

Fleas have no wings. Fleas have six legs.

Snakes have no wings or legs.

A bee has four wings. It has six legs.

Spiders never have wings. They have eight legs.

A dog has no wings. It has four legs.

Birds have two wings and two legs.

A cow has no wings. It has four legs.

A butterfly has four wings. It has six legs.

Animals–Number of Wings and Legs

Animal	Number of Wings	Number of Legs
Flea	0	6
Snake	0	0
Bee	4	6
Spider	0	8
Dog	0	4
Bird	2	2
Butterfly	4	6

Reading a Circle Graph

A circle graph shows a whole divided into parts. You can use a circle graph to compare the parts to each other. You can also use it to compare the parts to the whole.

A Circle Graph of Fuel Use

This circle graph shows fuel use in the United States. The graph has 10 equal parts, or sections. Each section equals $\frac{1}{10}$ of the whole. One whole equals $\frac{10}{10}$.

Oil Of all the fuel used in the United States, 4 out of 10 parts, or $\frac{4}{10}$, is oil.

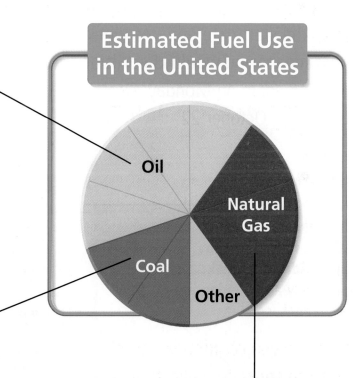

Estimated Fuel Use in the United States

Oil

Natural Gas

Coal

Other

Coal Of all the fuel used in the United States, 2 out of 10 parts, or $\frac{2}{10}$, is coal.

Natural Gas Of all the fuel used in the United States, 3 out of 10 parts, or $\frac{3}{10}$, is natural gas.

Measuring Elapsed Time

A calendar can help you find out how much time has passed, or elapsed, in days or weeks. A clock can help you see how much time has elapsed in hours and minutes. A clock with a second hand or a stopwatch can help you find out how many seconds have elapsed.

Using a Calendar to Find Elapsed Days

This is a calendar for the month of October. October has 31 days. Suppose it is October 22 and you begin an experiment. You need to check the experiment two days from the start date and one week from the start date. That means you would check it on Wednesday, October 24, and again on Monday, October 29. October 29 is 7 days after October 22.

October

Sunday	Monday	Tuesday	Wednesday	Thursday	Friday	Saturday
	1	2	3	4	5	6
7	8	9	10	11	12	13
14	15	16	17	18	19	20
21	22	23	24	25	26	27
28	29	30	31			

Days of the Week

Monday, Tuesday, Wednesday, Thursday, and Friday are weekdays. Saturday and Sunday are weekends.

Last Month

Last month ended on Sunday, September 30.

Next Month

Next month begins on Thursday, November 1.

Using a Clock or a Stopwatch to Find Elapsed Time

You need to time an experiment for 20 minutes.

It is 1:30 P.M.

Stop at 1:50 P.M.

You need to time an experiment for 15 seconds. You can use the second hand of a clock or watch.

Start the experiment when the second hand is on number 6.

Stop when 15 seconds have passed and the second hand is on the 9.

You can use a stopwatch to time 15 seconds.

Press the reset button on a stopwatch so that you see 0:00₀₀.

Press the start button. When you see 0:15₀₀, press the stop button.

Measurements

Volume

1 L of sports drink is a little more than 1 qt.

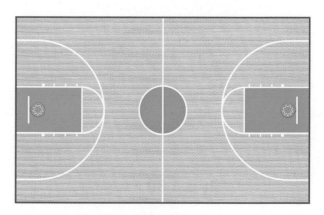

Area

A basketball court covers about 4,700 ft². It covers about 435 m².

Metric Measures

Temperature

- Ice melts at 0 degrees Celsius (°C)
- Water freezes at 0°C
- Water boils at 100°C

Length and Distance

- 1,000 meters (m) = 1 kilometer (km)
- 100 centimeters (cm) = 1 m
- 10 millimeters (mm) = 1 cm

Force

- 1 newton (N) =
  1 kilogram × 1 (meter/second)
  per second

Volume

- 1 cubic meter (m³) = 1 m × 1 m × 1 m
- 1 cubic centimeter (cm³) =
  1 cm × 1 cm × 1 cm
- 1 liter (L) = 1,000 milliliters (mL)
- 1 cm³ = 1 mL

Area

- 1 square kilometer (km²) =
  1 km × 1 km
- 1 hectare = 10,000 m²

Mass

- 1,000 grams (g) = 1 kilogram (kg)
- 1,000 milligrams (mg) = 1 g

Temperature

The temperature at an indoor basketball game might be 27°C, which is 80°F.

Length and Distance

A basketball rim is about 10 ft high, or a little more than 3 m from the floor.

Customary Measures

Temperature

- Ice melts at 32 degrees Fahrenheit (°F)
- Water freezes at 32°F
- Water boils at 212°F

Length and Distance

- 12 inches (in.) = 1 foot (ft)
- 3 ft = 1 yard (yd)
- 5,280 ft = 1 mile (mi)

Weight

- 16 ounces (oz) = 1 pound (lb)
- 2,000 pounds = 1 ton (T)

Volume of Fluids

- 8 fluid ounces (fl oz) = 1 cup (c)
- 2 c = 1 pint (pt)
- 2 pt = 1 quart (qt)
- 4 qt = 1 gallon (gal)

Metric and Customary Rates

km/h = kilometers per hour

m/s = meters per second

mph = miles per hour

Glossary

A

absorb (uhb SAWRB) to take in some of the light that strikes an object's surface (343)

★ **adaptation** (ad ap TAY shuhn) a physical feature or a behavior that helps an organism survive in its habitat (58)

adult (uh DUHLT) a fully-grown, mature organism (43)

air mass (air mas) a large body of air that has about the same temperature, air pressure, and moisture throughout (211)

air pressure (air PRESH uhr) the weight of air as it presses down on Earth's surface (194)

atmosphere (AT muh sfihr) the layers of air that surround Earth's surface (194)

axis (AK sihs) an imaginary line through the center of an object (123)

B

bay (bay) a body of water that is partly enclosed by land and has a wide opening (163)

C

camouflage (KAM uh flazh) the coloring, marking, or other physical appearance of an animal that helps it blend in with its surroundings (60)

carnivore (KAHR nuh vawr) an animal that eats only other animals (86)

★ **cell** (sehl) the basic unit that makes up all living things (18)

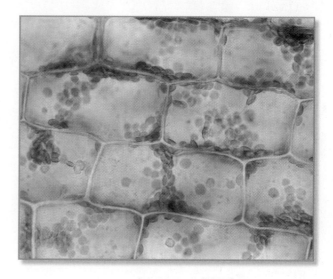

chlorophyll (KLAWR uh fihl) a green material in plants that traps energy from sunlight and gives leaves their green color (30)

climate (KYL muht) the average weather conditions in an area over a long period of time (220)

★ **condensation** (kahn dehn SAY shuhn) the change of the state of gas to a liquid (201)

conductors (kuhn DUHK tuhrz) materials that negatively charged particles can move through easily (289)

crescent moon (KREHS uhnt moon) the phase of the Moon when a thin part of the Moon's near side is sunlit (139)

D

delta (del TUH) a large mass of sediment deposited at the mouth of a river (164)

★ = Tennessee Academic Vocabulary

density (DEHN sih tee) the amount of matter in a given space, or a given volume (259)

deposition (dehp uh ZIHSH uhn) the dropping of sediment moved by water, wind, or ice (162)

egg (ehg) the first stage in the life cycle of most animals (42)

electric cell (ih LEHK trihk sehl) a device that turns chemical energy into electrical energy (242)

electric charges (ih LEHK trihk CHAHRJ ehs) tiny particles that carry units of electricity (282)

electric circuit (ih LEHK trihk SUR kith) the pathway that an electric current follows (290)

electric current (ih LEHK trihk KUR uhnt) a continuous flow of electric charges (288)

electromagnet (ih lehk troh MAG niht) a strong temporary magnet that uses electricity to produce magnetism (306)

embryo (EHM bree oh) a plant or animal in the earliest stages of development (35)

energy (EHN ur jee) the ability to cause change (268)

equator (ee KWAY tur) the imaginary line that circles Earth halfway between the North and South Poles (131)

★ **erosion** (ih ROH zhuhn) the movement of rock material from one place to another (158)

erratic (ih RAH tihk) a single large boulder moved by a glacier and deposited when the glacier melts (175)

★ **evaporation** (ih vap uh RAY shuhn) the change of state from a liquid to a gas (201)

extinct (ihk STIHNGKT) no longer living; when the last member of a species has died, the species is extinct (70)

food chain (food chayn) the path of food energy in an ecosystem as one living thing eats another (94)

food web (food wehb) two or more food chains that overlap (94)

force (fawrs) a push that moves an object away or a pull that moves an object nearer (364)

★ **friction** (FRIHK shuhn) a force that slows or stops motion between two surfaces that are touching (366)

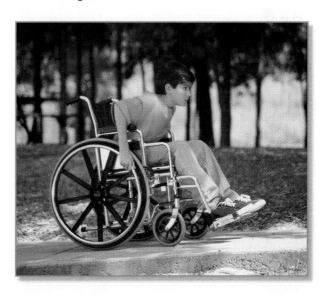

front (fruhnt) the place where two air masses meet (212)

full moon (ful moon) the phase of the Moon when all of the Moon's near side is sunlit (139)

★ = Tennessee Academic Vocabulary

generator (JEHN uh ray tuhr) a devise that uses magnetism to convert energy of motion into electrical energy (309)

germinate (JUHR muh nayt) the process in which a seed begins to grow into a new plant (35)

glacier (GLAY shur) a large mass of slow-moving ice that flows down a slope (158)

★ **gravity** (GRAV ih tee) the force that pulls bodies or objects toward other bodies or objects (368)

greenhouse effect (GREEN hows ih FEHKT) the process by which heat from the Sun builds up near Earth's surface and is trapped there by the atmosphere (196)

habitat (HAB ih tat) the place where an organism lives (58)

headland (HED land) a point of land, usually high, that extends out into the water (163)

herbivore (HUR buh vawr) an animal that eats only plants (86)

hibernate (HY bur nayt) to go into a deep sleep during which an animal uses very little energy and usually does not need to eat (62)

inclined plane (ihn KLYND playn) a simple machine made up of a slanted surface (374)

insulators (IHN suh lay tuhrz) materials that electric charges do not flow through easily (289)

larva (LAHR vuh) the wormlike form that hatches from an egg; the second stage of an organism that goes through complete metamorphosis (43)

lens (lenz) a piece of curved glass, plastic, or other material that refracts light (335)

lever (LEHV ur) a simple machine made up of a stiff bar that moves freely around a fixed point (376)

life cycle (lyf SY kuhl) a series of stages that occur during the lifetimes of all organisms (34)

life process (lyf PRAHS ehs) a function that an organism performs to stay alive and produce more of its own kind (16)

life span (lyf span) the length of time it takes for an individual organism to complete its life cycle (36)

★ = Tennessee Academic Vocabulary

light (lyt) a form of energy that travels in waves and can be seen when it interacts with matter (324)

magnet (MAG niht) an object that attracts certain metals, mainly iron (296)

magnetic poles (mag NEHT ihk pohlz) the two areas on a magnet with the greatest magnetic force (297)

mass (mas) the amount of matter in an object (252)

metamorphosis (meht uh MAWR fuh sihs) the process in which some organisms change form in different stages of their life cycles (43)

metric system (MEHT rihk SIHS tuhm) a system of measurement based on multiples of 10 (250)

migrate (MY grayt) to move to another region when seasons change and food supplies become scarce (90)

mimicry (MIHM ih kree) an adaptation that allows an animal to protect itself by looking like another kind of animal or like a plant (61)

moraine (muh RAYN) the long ridge formed by boulders, rocks, and soil carried and deposited by a glacier (175)

motion (MOH shuhn) a change in an object's position as compared to objects around it (356)

motor (MOH tur) a device that changes electrical energy into energy of motion (308)

new moon (NEW moon) the phase of the Moon when the Moon's near side appears totally dark (139)

niche (nihch) the role a plant or animal plays in its habitat (58)

nymph (nihmf) the second stage of an insect as it goes through incomplete metamorphosis (43)

omnivore (AHM nuh vawr) an animal that eats both plants and animals (86)

opaque (oh PAYK) an opaque material blocks light from passing through it (326)

organ (AWR guhn) a special part of an organism's body that performs a specific function (21)

organism (AWR guh nihz uhm) any living thing that can carry out life processes on its own (20)

organ system (AWR guhn SIHS tuhm) a group of organs that work together to carry out life processes (22)

★ **parallel circuit** (PAR uhlehl SUHR kiht) a circuit in which parts are connected so that the electric current passes along more than one pathway (291)

★ **phases of the Moon** (FAYZ ihz uhv thuh moon) changes in the amount of sunlight that reaches the side of the Moon that faces Earth as the Moon orbits Earth (140)

photosynthesis (foh toh SIHN thih sihs) the process plants use to make food (30)

physical change (FIHZ ih kuhl chaynj) a change in the size, shape, or state of matter that does not change it into a new kind of matter (266)

polar climate (POH lur KLY muht) places with polar climate have very cold temperatures throughout the year, and are located around the North Pole and the South Pole (221)

position (puh ZIHSH uhn) an object's location, or place (356)precipitation (prih sihp ih TAY shuhn) any form of water that falls from clouds to Earth's surface (202)

prism (prihzm) a piece of glass or other transparent material that separates white light into colors (342)

pulley (PUL ee) a simple machine made up of a rope fitted around the rim of a fixed wheel (377)

quarter moon (KWAHR tur moon) the phase of the Moon when half of the Moon's near side is sunlit (139)

reflect (rih FLEHKT) the method by which light waves bounce off the surface of most objects (334)

refract (rih FRAKT) the method by which light waves are bent by moving from one transparent material to another, such as from air to glass (335)

reproduce (ree pruh DOOS) to make more living things of the same kind (16)

revolve (rih VAHLV) To move in a path around another object (130)

★ = Tennessee Academic Vocabulary

river system (RIH vur sys tehm) the largest river and all the waterways that drain into it (164)

rotate (ROH tayt) to turn on an axis (123)

root (root) the part of a plant that takes in water and nutrients from the ground (26)

sand dune (SAND doon) a hill or pile of sand that was formed by the wind (178)

screw (skroo) a simple machine made up of an inclined plane wrapped around a column (375)

season (see SUHN) one of the four parts of the year—spring, summer, fall, and winter (131)

seed (SEED) an undeveloped plant sealed in a protective coating (27)

★ **series circuit** (seer EEZ SUHR kiht) a circuit in which parts are connected so that the electric current passes through each part, one after another, along a single pathway (291)

shadow (SHAD oh) an area where light does not strike (327)

★ **simple machine** (SIHM puhl muh SHEEN) a simple device that changes a force (374)

species (SPEE sheez) a group of living things that produces living things of the same kind (70)

speed (SPEED) a measure of the distance an object travels in a certain amount of time (358)

static electricity (STAT ihk ih lehk TRIHS ih tee) the build-up of electric charge on an object (284)

stem (STEM) the part of a plant that carries food, water, and nutrients to and from the roots and leaves (26)

temperate climate (TEHM pur iht KLY muht) places with temperate climate have warm, dry summers and cold, wet winters, and are located between the tropical zone and the polar zones (221)

tissue (TIHSH oo) a group of similar cells that work together, such as muscle tissue and stomach tissue (22)

translucent (trahns LOO suhnt) a translucent material allows some light to pass through it, but scatters the light in many directions (326)

transparent (trahns PAIR uhnt) a transparent material allows light to pass through it (326)

★ = Tennessee Academic Vocabulary

tropical climate (trap ih KUHL KLY muht) places with tropical climate are hot and rainy throughout the year, and are located directly north and south of the equator (221)

velocity (vuh LAHS ih tee) a measure of speed in a certain direction (360)

volume (VAHL yoom) the amount of space that matter takes up (253)

waning moon (WAY nihng moon) the phases of the Moon when a decreasing amoun of the Moon's near side is sunlit (139)

water cycle (WAH tur SY kuhl) the movement of water into the air as water vapor and back to Earth's surface as precipitation (202)

waxing moon (WAHK zihng moon) the phases of the Moon when an increasing amount of the Moon's near side is sunlit (139)

weather (WETH ur) the conditions of the atmosphere at a certain place and time (195)

weathering (WETH ur ihng) the slow wearing away of rock into smaller pieces, by ice, plant roots, moving water, wind, or chemicals (156)

wedge (wehj) a simple machine made up of two inclined planes (375)

weight (wayt) the measure of the pull of gravity on an object (254)

wheel and axle (hweel and AK suhl) a simple machine made up of two cylinders that turn on the same axis (376)

F

G

Index

Index

Credits

Photography

KEY: (b) bottom, (bg) background, (bl) bottom left, (br) bottom right, (c) center, (cl) center left, (cr) center right, (t) top, (tl) top left, (tr) top right.

TOC: iv ©Arco Images/Alamy; v ©Byron Jorjorian/Alamy; vi ©age fotostock/SuperStock; vii ©Tim Fitzharris/Minden Pictures/Getty Images; ix ©Ken Hackett/Alamy; xii–xiii ©Tony Sweet/Photodisc/Getty Images; xv ©Bob Pardue/Alamy; xvi–xvii ©Tennesse Valley Authority

Nature of Science: S1 Pete Atkinson/The Image Bank/Getty Images; S2 2004 Harbor Branch Oceanographic Institution; S3 Kenneth J. Sulak, Ph.D; S4 Nigel Hicks 2005/Alamy Ltd.; S5 HMCo./Ed Imaging; S6 Donald Nausbaum/Photographer's Choice/Getty Images; S7 HMCo./Ed Imaging; S9 HMCo./Ed Imaging; S10–S11 Alberto Behar, Ph.D/JPL/NASA; S11 ©Car Culture/Getty Images; S12 (br) HMCo./Bruton Stroube; S12–S13 (bkgd) Peter Mason/Getty Images; S14–S15 David Muench/Corbis; S15 HMCo./Ed Imaging;

Life Excursions: 2 (bg) blickwinkel/Alamy; 3 (tr) Courtesy of The Elephant Sanctuary; 3 (cr) Courtesy of The Elephant Sanctuary; 4 (bg) Gary Meszaros/Photo Researchers, Inc.; 5 (inset) Jerry Whaley/Alamy; 6 (bg) Jerry Whaley/age Fotostock; 6 (inset) Shaun Cunningham/Alamy; 7 (inset) JIM TUTEN/Animals Animals - Earth Scenes; 8 (inset) Lourens Smak/Alamy;

Unit A: 10–11 ©Byron Jorjorian/Alamy; 11 (tr) Claudia Kunin/Corbis; 11 (tc) David Noton Photography/Alamy; 11 (bc) Keith Brofsky/Getty Images; 11 (b) Jane SAPinsky/Superstock; 12–13 ©Naturfoto Honal/CORBIS; 14 (bl) Mattias Klum/National GeogrAPhic/Getty Images; 14–15 (bkgd) Freeman Patterson/Masterfile; 16 (bl) Gk Hart/Vikki Hart/Photodisc/Getty Images; 16 (b) J. David Andrews/Masterfile; 17 (tl) John Beedle/Alamy Images; 17 (tr) David Young-Wolff/Photo Researchers, Inc.; 17 (cl) M. T. Frazier/Photo Researchers; 17 (cr) Francois Gohier/Photo Researchers; 17 (br) Gail M. Shumwav/Bruce Coleman Inc.; 17 (bl) ©Dwight Kuhn; 18 ©Dwight Kuhn; 19 ©Dennis Kunkel; 20 (bl) ©Mehau Kulyk/Photo Researchers, Inc.; 20 (r) S Lowry/Univ Ulster/Stone/Getty Images; 21 (l) Kim Taylor/Bruce Coleman Inc.; 21 (r) ©Bill Curtsinger/NGS/Getty Images; 22 (tl) Peter Weber/PhotogrAPer'S Choice/Getty Images; 22 (cl) William B. Rhoten; 23 (t) Gk Hart/Vikki Hart/Photodisc/Getty Images; 23 (c) Kim Taylor/Bruce Coleman Inc.; 23 (b) Peter Weber/PhotogrAPer'S Choice/Getty Images; 24 (bl) ©Adam Jones/Photo Researchers, Inc.; 24–25 (bkgd) ©Martin Ruegner/Masterfile; 26 Gary Braasch/Corbis; 27 Peter Chadwick/DK Images; 28 (tl) ©Mark Boulton/Photo Researchers, Inc.; 28 (cl) A. Pasieka/Photo Researchers; 28 (bl) Richard Parker/Photo Researchers; 28 (bc) Michael Boys/Corbis; 28 (br) Michael P. Gadomski/Photo Researchers; 29 (t) R. A. Mittermeier/Bruce Coleman Inc.; 29 (bl) Photri; 29 (br) Steve Gorton/DK Images; 31 (t) Peter Chadwick/DK Images; 31 (c) Michael Boys/Corbis; 32 (bl) Dennis Flaherty/Photo Researchers; 32–33 (bkgd) Marc Moritsch/National Geographic Image Collection; 38 ©Jeff Miller/University of Wisconsin-Madison; 39 ©Austin Weeks/Courtesy of Fairfield Tropical Botanic Garden; 40 (bl) Tom Lazar/Earth Scenes/Animals Animals; 40–41 (bkgd) Peter Arnold, Inc./Alamy; 42 (tr) Joe Mcdonald/Bruce Coleman; 42 (c) ©Wendell Metzen/Bruce Coleman USA Inc.; 42 (b) ©Jerry Young/DK Images; 43 (t) Gilbert S. Grant/Photo Researchers; 43 (cl) Alan & Linda Detrick/Photo Researchers; 43 (cr) Bill Beatty/AG Pix; 43 (b) Kent Wood/Photo Researchers; 45 (t) ©Wendell Metzen/Bruce Coleman USA Inc.; 45 (c) Gilbert S. Grant/Photo Researchers; 47 Kim Taylor/Bruce Coleman Collection; 49 (tl) Jackson Smith/Alamy; 49 (br) Lwa-Dan Tardif/Corbis; 49 (bkgd) Phototone Abstracts; 51 ©Arco Images/Alamy; 52–53 ©Norbert Wu; 53 (t) David Cavagnaro/Peter Arnold, Inc.; 53 (c) Lloyd Cluff/Corbis; 53 (b) ©Photo Researchers, Inc.; 54 (b) Mauro Fermariello/Photo Researchers, Inc.; 54 (c) Danita Delimont/Alamy; 54 (t) ©John E. Fletcher/Getty Images; 54–55 (bkgd) Mickey Gibson/Animals Animals; 56 (bl) Anne DuPont, Delray Beach, Florida, USA; 56–57 (bkgd) Brandon D. Cole/Corbis; 58 ©Envision/Corbis; 59 (tl) Nigel J. Dennis; Gallo Images/Corbis; 59 (tr) ©Fletcher & Baylis/Photo Researchers, Inc.; 59 (bl) C.K. Lorenz/Photo Researchers, Inc.; 59 (br) John Eastcott/YVA Momatiuk/Photo Researchers; 60 (tr) ©Frank Lane Picture Agency/Corbis; 60 (bl) ©Leonard Lee Rue III/Photo Researchers, Inc.; 61 (cl) Benelux Press/Getty Images; 61 (c) Buddy Mays/Corbis; 61 (br) George Grail/National Gepgraphic/Getty Images; 62 (l) Stephen Dalton/Photo Researchers, Inc.; 62 (r) Bob and Clara Calhoun/Bruce Colemann; 63 Buddy Mays/Corbis; 64–65 ©Fred Bavendam; 65 (t) ©Doug Wechsler/Vireo; 65 (c) ©Michael & Patricia Fodgen/Minden Pictures; 65 (b) Constantino Petrinos/naturepl.com; 66 (bl) Keren Su/China Span/Alamy Images; 66–67 (bkgd) Japack company/Corbis; 68 Andrew Mounter/Taxi/Getty Images; 69 Lloyd Cluff/Corbis; 70 (inset) ©John E. Fletcher/Getty Images; 70 (b) ©RICHARD ALAN WOOD/Animals Animals - Earth Scenes; 71 (t) George D. Dodge/Bruce Coleman Inc.; 71 (c) Lloyd Cluff/Corbis; 71 (b) ©John E. Fletcher/Getty Images; 75 (br)Courtesy of Julia Kubanek; 75 (bkgd) ©Charles Stirling (Diving)/Alamy; 77 ©MICKEY GIBSON/Animals Animals - Earth Scenes; 78–79 ©Norbert Wu; 79 (tl) George Grall/National Geographic/Getty Images; 79 (br) Wim Van Egmond/Visual Unlimited/Getty Images; 80 (t) Jeremy Woodhouse/Pixelchrome.com; 80 (c) Konrad Wothe/Minden Pictures; 80 (b) S Lowry/Univ Ulster/Stone/Getty Images; 80–81 (bkgd) © Norbert Wu/Getty Images; 82 (bl) J.Borris/Zefa/Masterfile; 82–83 (bkgrd) J.Borris/Zefa/Masterfile; 84 (inset) Michael P. Gadomski/Photo Researchers; 84–85 © Frank Krahmer/zefa/Corbis; 85 (bl) Michiel Schaap/Foto Natura/Minden Pictures; 85 (r) ©Harry Taylor/DK Images; 86 (tl) ©Hal Horwitz/Corbis; 86 (tr) Paul Sterry/Worldwide Picture Library/Alamy; 87 (tl) Konrad Wothe/Minden Pictures; 87 (tr) Jeremy Woodhouse/Pixelchrome.com; 88 (t) hunzikerphoto.com/Alamy; 88 (t) (inset) Michiel Schaap/Foto Natura/Minden Pictures; 88 (c) John Cancalosi/Peter Arnold; 88 (b) Yva Momatiuk & John Eastcott/Photo Researchers; 89 (t) Michael P. Gadomski/Photo Researchers; 89 (c) Paul Sterry/Worldwide Picture Library/Alamy; 89 (b) hunzikerphoto.com/Alamy; 90–91 ©2004 Peter Batson/Image Quest Marine; 91 ©2004 Peter Batson/Image Quest Marine; 92 (bl) Mike Hill/Taxi/Getty Images; 92–93 (bkgd) ©Todd Gustafson/Panoramic Images; 94–95 (bkgd) Robert Marien/Corbis; 95 (tl) Mark Moffett/Minden Pictures; 95 (tc) ©TallisMan/Alamy; 95 (tr) Tom Vezo/Minden Pictures;; 95 (br) Joe McDonald/CORBIS; 96 (tcr) Stuart Westmorland/CORBIS; 96 (tr) Fred Hazelhoff/Minden Pictures; 96 (cl) David Tipling/GettyImages; 96 (bl) Flip Nicklin/Minden Pictures; 96 (bcr) Ken Lucas/Ardea; 96 (br) ©David Fleetham/Alamy; 96 (bkgd) ©Robert George Young/Masterfile; 97 (t) ©Todd Gustafson/Panoramic Images; 97 (pigeon) ©TallisMan/Alamy; 97 (c-tl) Mark Moffett/Minden Pictures; 97 (c-r) Darrell Gulin/Dembinsky Photo Associates; 97 (c-bl) Tom Vezo/Minden Pictures; 97 (b-tl) Stuart Westmorland/CORBIS; 97 (b-bl) © David Fleetham/Alamy; 97 (b-r) Ken Lucas/Ardea; 98–99 ©Jeff Greenberg/Index Stock Imagery; 100 ©Millard H. Sharp/Photo Researchers, Inc.; 101 © Michael Newman/PhotoEdit; 101 (b) ©A. Ramey/ Photo Edit; 103 ©Arthur Morris/CORBIS;

Earth Excursions: 108 (bg) David Massengill; 108 (inset) Visuals Unlimited/Corbis; 109 (inset) Bobby Boyd/National Weather Service; 110 (bg) wendy connett/Alamy; 110 (inset) AAGAMIA/Getty Images; 111 (inset) Sheri O'Neal/Houghton Mifflin Harcourt; 112 (bg) Byron Jorjorian; 113 (inset) Willard Clay Photography, Inc.; 114 (inset) Barrie Rokeach/Alamy;

Unit B: 116–117 P. Parvianinen/Photo Researchers, Inc.; 117 (tr) Frank Cezus/Photographer's Choice/Getty Images; 117 (cl) Royalty-Free/Corbis; 117 (cr) W.H. Muller/Masterfile; 118 (t) John Sanford/Photo Researchers, Inc.; 118–119 ©Tony Sweet/Photodisc/Getty Images; 120 ©Bob Krist/Corbis; 120–121 (bkgd) PhotoDisc; 122 (l) Joe Sohm/The Image Works; 122 (r) ML Sinibali/Corbis; 122 (b) ©Richard Cummins/SuperStock 126 NASA Johnson Space Center; 126–127 (bkgd) ©epa/Corbis; 127 (inset) ©Reuters/CORBIS; 128–129 (bkgd) ©ComStock; 132 George Wuerthner; 133 ©Gibson Stock Photography; 134 @David Young-Wolff/Photo Edit; 135 @David Young-Wolff/Photo Edit; 136–137 (bkgd) Lawrance Brennon/Masterfile; 138 PhotoDisc; 141 John Sanford/Photo Researchers, Inc.; 142 (b) ©Roger Ressmeyer/Corbis; 142 (t) ©David Nunuk/Photo Researchers, Inc.; 143 (b) John Sanford/Photo Researchers, Inc.; 143 (t) Kevin Kelley/The Image Bank/Getty Images; 147 (bkgrd) ©Eurelios/Photo Researchers, Inc.; 147 (inset) ©Harry Y. McSween Jr.; 150–151 ©Tim Fitzharris/Minden Pictures/Getty Images; 151 (tr) ©RICH REID/Animals Animals - Earth Scenes; 151 (cl) Payne Anderson/Index Stock Imagery/Photolibrary; 151 (br) Ulf Wallin/The Image Bank/Getty Images; 152 (t) Science Source Nature Source People/Photo Researchers, Inc.; 152 (c) G. R. Roberts/Photo Researchers, Inc.; 152–153 George Ranalli/Photo Researchers, Inc.; 154–155 (bkgd) ©Bob Stefko/Getty Images; 156 Gary Hayes; 157 (tl) ©blickwinkel/Alamy; 157 (tr) ©Mike Dobel/Masterfile; 158 (tl) Jim Steinberg/Photo Researchers, Inc.; 158 (b) ©Jon Arnold Images/SuperStock; 159 (t) ©blickwinkel/Alamy; 159 (c) ©Mike Dobel/Masterfile; 159 (b) James Steinberg/Photo Researchers, Inc.; 160–161